I0797628

About the authors
HAZEL BLOMKAMP & PHILLIPA TURNBULL

HAZEL BLOMKAMP has taught embroidery and beadwork in South Africa for over 30 years. She is the author of *Crewel Twists, Crewel Intentions, Crewel Creatures, Hand-Stitched Crazy Patchwork, Crewel Animal Portraits,* two stitch guide books – *Needle Lace Techniques* and *Needle Weaving Techniques* – and has collaborated on *Freestyle Embroidered Mandalas* with Di van Niekerk and Monique Day-Wilde. She is a regular contributor to local and overseas publications, and runs a busy website from home, providing embroidery supplies and kits globally. Travelling extensively both around South Africa and abroad to teach and promote her work, Hazel is regularly invited to teach at international conventions. Her teaching has taken her to Australia, New Zealand, Western and Eastern Europe, North America and Asia.

Visit Hazel's website www.hazelblomkamp.com to see more of her work.

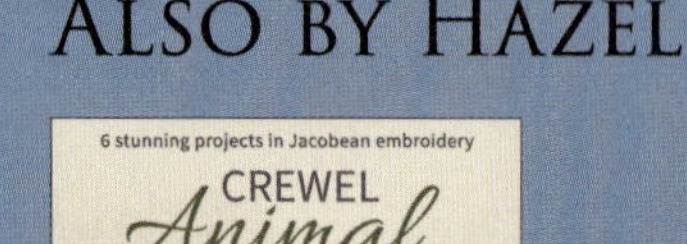

978-1-80092-130-6

PHILLIPA TURNBULL is an expert on British crewelwork, and an experienced embroidery designer, tutor and lecturer who has been teaching crewelwork with a passion for 30 years. Along with her daughter, Laura Turnbull, she is joint owner of The Crewel Work Company and Lady Anne's Needlework Retreats, which sell exquisite crewel embroidery kits, offer online courses and organize luxury embroidery retreats both in the UK and abroad. Phillipa researches private and public collections in castles, country houses and museums, and shares her studies with historic needlework enthusiasts worldwide from her home in the English Lake District.

See more of Phillipa's work at: www.crewelwork.com and @crewelworkco on Instagram.

CREWELWORK
THEN AND NOW

First published in 2026
Search Press Limited
Wellwood, North Farm Road,
Tunbridge Wells, Kent TN2 3DR

1 2 3 4 5 6 7 8 9 10

Image on page 12: *The Progress of the Soul: The Entrance*, Phoebe Anna Traquair. Provided with thanks from the National Galleries of Scotland. Bequest of the artist 1936. Images on page 13 by Phillipa Turnbull. All other photographs by Mark Davison at Search Press Studios

ISBN: 978-1-80092-288-4
ebook ISBN: 978-1-80093-279-1

Editor: Carrie Baker
Managing Editor: Becky Robbins
Head of Design: Marrianne Miall
Publishing Director: Samantha Warrington

Bookmarked Hub
Extra copies of the charts are available to download free from the Bookmarked Hub. Search for this book by title or ISBN: the files can be found under 'Book Extras'. Membership of the Bookmarked online community is free: www.bookmarkedhub.com

Publishers' notes

For errata, please visit our website (www.searchpress.com) or the Bookmarked Hub (www.bookmarkedhub.com).

GPSR information can be found at www.searchpress.com

Printed in China, AP092025

Dedication

We dedicate this book to friendship and family, and to all current and future embroiderers who might be inspired by the fun we enjoyed while creating this book. If you love the fanciful nature of crewelwork, be it traditional or modern, we hope this book will give you hours of pleasure.

Acknowledgements

To all our past, present and future fellow crewelwork tutors, designers, students, conservators and curators in castles and museums, a huge thank you. To family, students and kit testers, for all your support and encouragement.

Thank you to Phillipa's kit testers Clare Banham, Kristen Godwin, Stephanie Heron and Danise Hetland; The Crewel Work Company home team Laura Turnbull, Georgina Pilsbury and Frankie Pilsbury, Lisa Johnstone, Karen Brownrigg and Priti Ballinamore who kept the wheels turning while I was in my own paradise designing and stitching.

Thank you also to Carrie Baker, who had the hard task of assimilating the work of two authors into a well-balanced book.

CREWELWORK
THEN AND NOW

Exploring traditional designs and contemporary stitching

HAZEL BLOMKAMP & PHILLIPA TURNBULL

SEARCH PRESS

CONTENTS

Introduction 6

HISTORICALLY INSPIRED CREWELWORK

by Phillipa Turnbull 8

The history of traditional crewelwork 10

Greedy Squirrel 16

Phoebe's Vineyard 26

CONTEMPORARY CREWELWORK

by Hazel Blomkamp 38

The evolution of crewelwork 40

Summer Jewels 44

Tiny the Tabby 62

THEN & NOW: A CREWELWORK COMPARISON
by Hazel Blomkamp & Phillipa Turnbull 82

Traditional Eagle 88

Contemporary Eagle 100

Traditional Blue Bird 114

Contemporary Blue Bird 124

Tools and materials 138
Stitch directory 144
Index 216

INTRODUCTION

This book is an exploration of crewelwork, comparing the historic and modern methods of interpretation over eight projects. It is an exploration of this art in its broadest sense.

With Hazel in South Africa and Phillipa in England, part of the charm of this book is that it developed from opposite ends of the world: a collaboration made possible by modern methods of communication. With an enthusiasm for the fanciful flora and fauna which are traditionally depicted in crewelwork, we each have different styles of designing, stitching and teaching our projects.

Those who count hand embroidery as a passion, or at the very least a hobby, tend to fall into two categories. First are those who are interested in the history of a particular style of embroidery and who want to recreate what has gone before. As far as this book is concerned, these are the stitchers that have studied crewelwork from centuries past, who have more than likely visited museums and stately homes where examples of the style can be found in all its glory; and who have, no doubt, accumulated books on the subject. These are the crewelwork purists who will work with crewel wool and enjoy recreating the stitches that were used in earlier centuries.

Second are those who appreciate the style of the designs, who love the fanciful shapes of the motifs, be they animals, birds, flowers or leaves. Far from wanting to recreate what has gone before, they see those motifs as empty canvases which can lend themselves to endless creativity. They will use a wide variety of threads, from cotton through silk to metallics, will use beads and will widen their stitch repertoire to include techniques from other styles of embroidery, and even other sorts of needlework.

The projects in this book are divided into three sections and cater to both categories of stitchers. The first section is for those who are passionate about historic crewelwork, where Phillipa has created interpretations of two designs: Phoebe's Vineyard is from the Scottish Arts and Crafts era, the late nineteenth and early twentieth centuries, which is held at The National Museum of Scotland; Greedy Squirrel from an early twentieth-century bed pelmet.

In the second section of the book, Hazel has worked up two designs that may best be described as contemporary or creative crewelwork. Using traditional motifs, she has designed two projects worked with cotton threads and beads. Stitched on cotton, they use traditional stitches along with bead embroidery techniques, needle lace techniques which have been modified for use as embroidery stitches, that and loom weaving patterns that have been similarly modified for use as needle-weaving patterns.

The third section of the book compares two identical historic designs: a pair of mid-twentieth century embroidered pillowcases, which were acquired from the daughter of the original embroiderer, a Lake District farmer's wife near Phillipa's home. The Eagle and Blue Bird designs were stitched by Phillipa and Hazel, using both traditional and modern methods and materials. Working some 6,000 miles apart and on different continents, the designs in this section were stitched independently; sharing only the design outlines before embarking on these projects – there was no discussion or sharing of photographs during the stitching process. It is safe to say that we enjoyed the process enormously, and having intended to provide only one design, we ended up stitching two!

In addition to the projects with stitching instructions and handy hints, you will find useful information about tools and materials at the back of the book, and, most importantly, our comprehensive stitch directory detailing every stitch used throughout the projects in the book – over 80 in total! In some instances, there are slight differences in the execution of stitches depending on the yarn used and how closely the stitch follows traditional methods, which are noted where necessary.

It has been a fascinating journey for us and we hope that you will share our interest in the comparisons, and enjoy the results.

HISTORICALLY INSPIRED

CREWELWORK

Embroidery is an age-old craft that allows individuals to create stunning works of art using needle and thread. The earliest known examples of crewelwork can be traced back to long before the most famous crewel artefact, the Bayeux Tapestry, an embroidered cloth nearly 70m (around 76yd) long, which depicts the events leading up to the Norman conquest of England. Recent research has also identified wool embroidery on linen cloth in Ancient Egyptian tombs.

Throughout history, crewelwork has been a favoured embroidery technique. From the unknown designs in the past, through the Jacobean era of the late seventeenth century, to the delicate motifs of the Arts and Crafts movement, crewelwork has stood the test of time and continues to capture the imagination of interior designers and the hearts of embroidery enthusiasts around the world. It allows for endless creativity and offers a sense of connection to the rich heritage of needlework; one that I hope you too can take pleasure in when stitching with woollen threads on linen twill.

By
Phillipa Turnbull

The history of TRADITIONAL CREWELWORK

Crewelwork (sometimes written as crewel work) is a type of traditional surface embroidery, using finely spun two-ply worsted woollen threads on a ground fabric of linen twill. It has a rich history that stretches back over many thousands of years. The origins of crewelwork are somewhat obscure, but wherever there were sheep to provide woollen thread and flax to make linen cloth, or these materials were available by trading with other cultures, there was the opportunity for crewelwork to evolve.

The term 'crewel' itself is believed to be derived from the Anglo-Saxon word *cleow*, meaning a ball of thread, but crewel can also mean the long 'staples', the highly valued part of a sheep's fleece which hang from the underside of the thigh area and can produce the longest spun thread. The Italian word for crewelwork is *ricamo*; in Dutch it is *orduurwerk* or *borduursel*; in French, the language of the European Court, it is *broderie* and in Russian it is *rabota ekipazha*.

From the burial cloths in Ancient Egypt circa sixth century BC, to the Arts and Crafts designs of May Morris, crewelwork has survived despite changes in fashion, in its use, and through the disruption of trade routes and the limited availability of materials.

Designs were heavily influenced by the trade of decorative artefacts, and by the exotic flora and fauna encountered on printed cotton Palampores (screen-printed cotton bedcoverings with Indian 'Tree of Life' designs), a home furnishing which became affordable and popular through Britain's increased trade by sea through the East India Company and by land through trade routes such as the Silk Roads.

In traditional crewelwork, the woven twill linen ground fabric is an essential part of the design. Therefore, unlike many other forms of embroidery, there is no need to stitch the background and fill the entire cloth with stitches, so it is relatively quick and always interesting to produce.

Top: the original 1940s eagle design pillowcase
Lower: the original 1940s blue bird design pillowcase.

The eagle and blue bird designs were embroidered onto pillowcases during World War II when, due to wartime rationing, materials were in short supply. The enthusiastic embroiderer used items from her laundry cupboard to replace her usual ground material of Jacobean linen twill.

The first panel from the set of embroideries *The Progress of the Soul* by Phoebe Anna Traquair. The human soul is represented by a 'perfect' young man dressed in an animal skin, full of hope and optimism, in harmony with nature. The figure was based on the character of Denys L'Auxerrois from *Imaginary Portraits* by the English critic and writer Walter Pater. The set, *The Victory*, was made around 1893–1902. My interpretation of the work (page 26) takes elements from all four panels and the scenes which unfold in this powerful work: the birds in song, in flight, at rest and as observers; the vines; and the weather patterns.

The seventeenth and eighteenth centuries marked a golden age of crewelwork in the British Isles, when crewelwork was used to create household items such as bed hangings, curtains and clothing, reflecting the wealth, status and knowledge of the owner. A huge variety of stitches were used to create intricate and textured designs, often depicting exotic flora and fauna, as well as royal figures copied from printed pamphlets and used as patterns.

Crewelwork has enjoyed moments of high fashion when it was profitable for studios to create furnishings for the wealthy, and at other times the home embroiderer – the 'amateur' – carried the evolution of crewelwork to the next phase of designs and stitches. The overlap of skill between when a designer/draughtsperson draws the design onto cloth, and when the embroiderer adds their stitches and colours, is where the magic has happened throughout history.

The popularity of crewelwork continued into the eighteenth century, with the technique spreading beyond England to other parts of Europe and to the American colonies, where relatives sent materials and drawn designs to loved ones who had left their birth countries. The designs became more refined, and the range of stitches expanded, allowing for greater creativity and intricacy in the patterns. Emigration from the British Isles to America, Canada, Australia, New Zealand and beyond led to new designs and new uses as the New World emerged.

Despite its decline in popularity during the Industrial Revolution, mass-produced textiles became more readily available, crewelwork experienced a revival in the late nineteenth and early twentieth centuries. This resurgence was largely due to the Arts and Crafts Movement, which emphasized traditional craftsmanship and the beauty of handmade objects. Artists and designers such as William Morris and his daughter May Morris encouraged the use of natural materials and traditional techniques, leading to a renewed interest in wool embroidery.

The enduring appeal of crewelwork lies in its ability to connect us with the past while allowing for personal expression and creativity. Whether adorning a piece of clothing or a decorative pillow, crewel embroidery remains a testament to the skill and artistry of those who practise it, preserving a tradition that has been cherished for centuries.

In the modern era, crewelwork continues to be appreciated for its rich textures and intricate designs. Crewelwork has evolved to incorporate contemporary themes and materials, while still honouring its historic roots.

The original pelmet shown above and left shows the squirrel, an animal often kept as a pet, or used for its fur on clothing or in paint brushes. The red squirrel was associated with high intelligence and having forethought, as it gathered its food to store for later use. From a bed or curtain pelmet made over 100 years before, but never completed, the original squirrel has it's very own slightly fierce charm! In my replica (page 16) I have broadened the range of colours and stitches for added interest.

Today, as in past centuries, crewel embroidery is practised by hobbyists and professionals alike, with workshops and courses available to those interested in learning this timeless art form.

The name 'Jacobean' derives from the very short reign of James II of England and VI of Scotland, who ruled in the late seventeenth century, but the styles referred to are more usually from the time of William III and Mary II, who ruled at the end of the seventeenth century and into the early eighteenth century, when new trading routes opened and exotic designs with newly accessible dyes in a range of bright colours became the most fashionable home decoration. It is clear that the skills of the weavers, spinners, embroiderers, the designers, the master broderers and the apprentices were highly valued before industrialization made textiles more affordable. Now we are in an era where we honour the past and hope to learn, and carry these forward in our future.

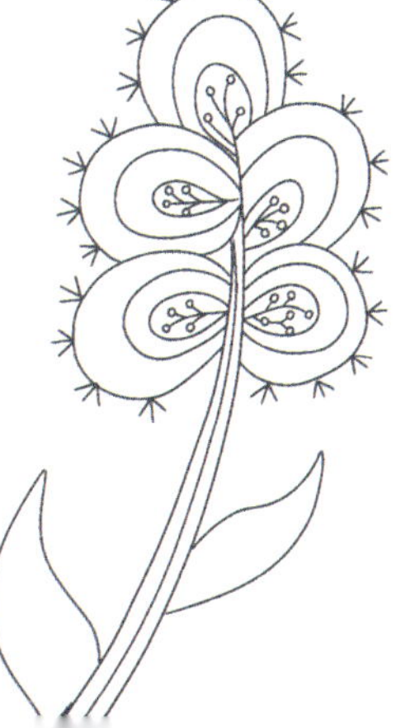

General project instructions

The general instructions below apply to the following projects: Greedy Squirrel (page 16), Phoebe's Vineyard (page 26), Traditional Eagle (page 88) and Traditional Blue Bird (page 114). Please read through the project instructions before you beginning stitching your designs.

- Assemble the frame so that the top left of the design area is in the frame with a margin between the design and the edge of the frame of approximately 1.25cm (½in).
- Make sure that the linen is tight in the frame and makes a hollow sound when tapped with a finger. If it is loose then the wools will not glide through the fabric.
- All threads in these designs are Appleton's two-ply crewel wool.
- Use thread lengths of between 30–38cm (12–15in long).
- Use a size 2 crewel needle for single thread; for double thread use a size 1 crewel needle.
- Secure your thread in a place where the anchoring stitch will be covered later by the progress of your embroidery.
- Securing your thread: for a single thread, leave a waste knot on the surface of the linen, then make three small straight 'seeding' stitches to anchor your thread. Remove the knot when each length of thread has been used.

  For double thread, use the larger size 1 needle and the folded method to secure your thread. Take a 61–76cm (24–30in) length of thread, fold it in half, then thread the folded end through the needle, drawing the thread through until the loop is at the opposite end of the thread to the needle. Leave the loop on the surface of the linen, then catch the needle through the loop to secure the thread. A neater trick is to then take your needle and thread over the end of the loop and back down the same hole.
- All of the general stitches and techniques are in the stitch directory (page 144).
- A general rule is to begin the design by stitching the background elements before the foreground. As a right-hander I began each design in the top left corner, but where you begin is personal choice.
- Use a sharp HB pencil to mark any guidelines for the long and short stitch.
- Rather than trace out the laid and couched work, measure carefully and add dots at the edge of each area where the laid thread ends on the actual drawn out linen, using the weave in the twill to count the gaps between the first layer of laid work. This should mean that you do not need to trace the lines onto the fabric.
- Cover any stitched areas of your embroidery with a linen napkin or handkerchief so that the wool does not become felted by your hand as you continue with the rest of the design.
- If using a hoop, always block your work once the stitching is complete to remove creases and hoop marks. Blocking is not necessary if you use a slate frame.

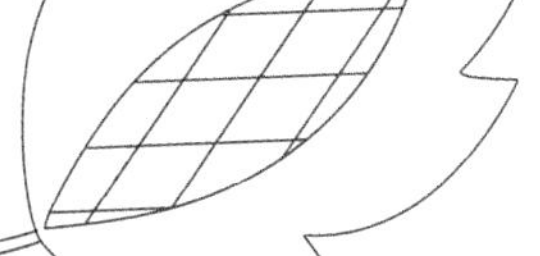

Using the charts

You will find the chart for each project printed on a loose sheet folded inside the pocket at the back of the book.

Before you begin stitching, transfer the outline from the chart onto your background fabric. See page 143 for more details on how to do this.

Note: the charts for the traditional and contemporary projects are presented in slightly different formats. When using the charts for the traditional projects, it is important to note the following:

- The charts should be used in conjunction with the instructions for each project.
- The numbers shown on each chart refer to the wool colour used in each area, along with abbreviations of the stitches used. See the 'You will need' page preceding each design for more information on the wool colours and stitch abbreviations.

The charts are also available to download from the Bookmarked Hub. Search for this book by title or ISBN: the files can be found under 'Book Extras'. Membership of the Bookmarked online community is free: www.bookmarkedhub.com

1 GREEDY SQUIRREL

This little squirrel is typical of the native red squirrel that was common throughout Britain in earlier centuries, but is now a rare survivor as the larger grey squirrels have invaded our land. Sixteenth and seventeenth-century paintings, tapestries and early eighteenth-century crewelwork often show these precious creatures eating in a forest or as a child's favourite pet.

This design begins with relatively easy stitches and then progresses to build your skills and confidence, before the final challenge of creating the bushy tail and the smoothly blended stitches over its curved body.

Dimensions: 24 x 35cm (9½ x 13¾in)

YOU WILL NEED

Chart

Greedy Squirrel chart

Fabric

41 x 50cm (16 x 20in) piece of Jacobean linen twill

Embroidery frame

Embroidery hoop, 20cm (8in) or 25.5cm (10in)

Floor or seat frame, or a slate frame if you prefer

Two pairs of 40cm (16in) stretcher bars, assembled into a frame

Needles

Crewel needles, sizes 46.5 (size 2) and 48.5 (size 1)

Beading needle

Threads

Black cotton thread

Appleton's crewel wool

One skein each of the following:

Greens
241
242
243
245
291
294
332
642
644

Blues
152
155
156
324
746
925

Pinks/reds
207
208
223
713

Browns
479
762
904

Yellows
312
691
694
696

Beads

4mm (⅛in) black glass bead

Stitch abbreviations (see chart)

L&S	Long and short as 'soft shading'
FK	French knot
CS	Crewel stem stitch
Bl	Block shading
P	Pistil stitch
S	Satin stitch
B	Backstitch
F	Fan stitch
Fe	Fern stitch
Se	Seeding stitch
CF	Closed fly stitch
St	Straight stitch
C	Coral stitch
L&C	Laid and couched work (trellis)

Wherever you see (D) on the stitch chart, use double thread, otherwise use single thread.

Stitching instructions

Begin in the top left corner of the design.

Moth

1. Crewel stem around the moth's wings in a single thread. Begin by securing your thread in the moth's body, then bring your needle up at the top left corner of the rear wing and outline this wing using small crewel stem stitches. Outline the upper left-hand wing in the same way. Then work the lower two wings in the same order, the background wing before the foreground wing.
2. Use tiny backstitches in a single thread to create the moth's antennae and the legs. Then decorate the wings with tiny irregularly directed seeding stitches.
3. Finally, complete the moth with raised satin stitch in a double thread over the whole length of the body, followed by bands of individually spaced straight stitches in the opposite direction, across the body, in a single thread.

Flowers below the moth

4 Next, begin the bud. Use long and short stitch to create your first stitch across to the tip of the pointed bud, and stitch one half of the bud at a time. Use a double thread for the first colour. Then, in a single thread in the second colour, take your stitches in the opposite direction, again making one half of the bud before the remaining half. The third colour is worked in the same direction. Use slightly fewer stitches with each colour as you work down the shape.

5 Stitch the two leaves in the same way, then make a scattering of pistil stitches for the stamens in a single thread. Use a double thread and, starting from the top, make the stem in coral stitch in a double thread, from the flower bud all the way to the base of the design.

6 Now begin the second flowerhead (which crosses the first) by creating its flowerhead using the same stitches as the first, but in the deeper blues. Then work the leaves, this time using French knots in a double thread.

7 Begin at the tip of a leaf, and stitch along over the upper line of the leaf. Begin again at the tip and continue around the lower perimeter of the leaf. Next, work in lines in ever-decreasing lengths, in subtle colour changes, until the lines become random knots in the final colour, which fill the centre of the leaf.

8 As before, use coral stitch for the flower stem, and long and short stitch for the taller leaf on the curve of the stem.

Note: depending on the size of your frame, you could now complete this plant, or move up to the upper area and stitch the large leaf above the squirrel.

9 Complete this plant by working closed fly stitch in a double thread on the leaves at the very bottom of the plant. As you did with the moth's wings, begin with the background leaf and work forwards; begin with the left-hand leaf, then work the remaining two in turn.

Large leaf above squirrel

10 Use laid and couched work (use variation 6, see page 159).

11 Take a single thread in the base colour, and measure how long the thread needs to be so that you can make every stitch across one direction of lines. If you begin in the centre of the leaf, then work each side in turn (as you did with the satin and long and short stitches) you will find it easier to maintain a consistent angle. Re-thread before you begin the second and each subsequent layer of laid work and couching.

12 Working from the tip of this leaf, use stem stitch around the perimeter. Add decorative fan stitches, and make a pleasingly integrated leaf by taking the straight stitch in the centre of the 'fan' over the inside edge of the crewel stem outline.

13 Beginning inside this leaf at the tip of the upper line, use crewel stem in a double thread down each line on the main trunk, all the way to the base. Use a double thread to add French knots in between the last two lines on the trunk.

14 Stitch the small seed pod in the upper centre of the design, and then the three leaves below, all of which branch from this main stem. Use the same order of stitches as before.

Large seed pod, top right

15 Next, stitch the large, stylized seed pod. The outer areas of this seed pod are worked in two rows of block shading. This stitch uses slightly encroaching satin stitches all in similar length, worked in rows.

16 First, bring your needle up through the line under the highest point of the outer border, then either draw with pencil, or add three straight stitches, at the 'shoulders' or the area to be stitched in this colour. This will help to keep your angle true to the curved shape. Now stitch one half of the area before returning to the highest point and completing the second half in the same way. (See page 147 for more on block shading.)

17 Next, come up at the base of the second row, repeat the direction of this stitch but this time take your needle into the line of stitches above. Complete this plant and the remaining leaves on this stem all the way down to the hummocks below.

18 Work the small plant on the far right-hand side of the design (pictured to the left), and the two curved fronds alongside the stems (pictured opposite).

Hummocks/hillocks

19 Work in long and short stitch to complete the hummocks along the base of the design. Begin with the central hillock, followed by the far right-hand hillock. Leave the remaining hillock until the squirrel is completed to ensure that you have an area to begin and end your squirrel stitches securely.

Spiked plant

20 Use fern stitch in a double thread to stitch the plant directly in front of the squirrel. As with many other stitches in this design, begin each line of stitching at the top of the printed line, and stitch each line in turn.

Squirrel

21 Now for the grand finale! Stitch this little person with confidence and he will repay you by making a characterful central feature. Begin by stitching a few spikey long stitches around the perimeter of his tail – these will form the angles to guide you as you use the next rows of long and short stitch fur. Then follow this with layer upon layer of long and short stitches, worked from his body outwards and down over the previous layer of stitches.

22 Next, stitch the paws using heavily worked satin stitches in double thread, starting at the back of the design and working the paw in the foreground last.

23 Then, work his neck and chest in a double thread using long and short stitch, as well as satin stitch where space is limited, adding these in the direction of his fur.

24 Stitch the background ear in satin stitch with a single thread, backmost leg with satin stitch in double thread, then his foreground ear using satin stitch in a single thread.

25 Use as many stitches as you can to create texture and depth, and continue by stitching the top of the head with long and short stitch.

26 The hazelnut is worked stem stitch, starting on the outside and working in an ever-decreasing circle.

27 Long and short stitch the back of the head, down to the shoulder area using double thread, then single throughout the remaining areas.

28 Create his foreground paw and his foreground leg in satin stitch, again in a in double thread.

29 Add a small circle of crewel stem stitches around the eye area then, using black cotton thread and a beading needle, attach a bead for the eye. Add small straight stitches over the top of the previously worked areas to create the nose, mouth and claws.

30 Finally, use long and short stitch over the remaining hummock underneath the squirrel.

2 PHOEBE'S VINEYARD

This design was inspired by the birds in the four panels in Phoebe Anna Traquair's (1852–1936) mesmerizing set of four embroidery panels, *The Progress of the Soul,* 1893–1901 (see page 12 for a photograph), which once graced the stairwell of her Edinburgh home, but are now on public display in the National Museum of Scotland. Phoebe's creative use of traditional stitches, the influence of ancient cultures, illuminated manuscripts and stained glass, as well as her other artwork including colourful enamelled jewellery and enormous painted murals, modernized embroidery at this time. Her work is vivid, energetic and her use of primary colours as the story concludes in the final panel, and her strong symbolism, is a stark contrast to the sparse designs produced by other designers of the time, such as the equally talented but more minimalistic embroidery tutor Jessie Newbery (1864–1948).

On the left side of the design, the swallows – the musicians of nature – are silent in their sadness, but as the soul progresses these same birds swoop and sing once more, while the trio of doves watch and listen with wonder.

Dimensions: 35 x 48cm (14 x 19in)

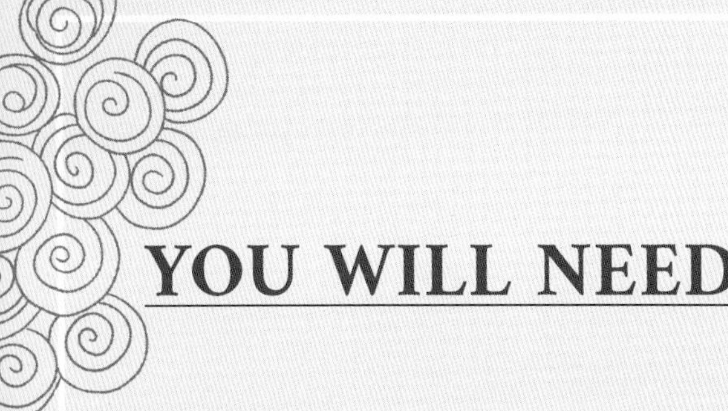

YOU WILL NEED

Chart
Phoebe's Vineyard chart

Fabric
55 x 68cm (22 x 27in) piece of Jacobean linen twill

Embroidery frame
Embroidery hoop, 20cm (8in) or 25.5cm (10in)

Floor or seat frame, or a slate frame larger than the width of the linen

Needles
Crewel needles, sizes 46.5 (size 2) and 48.5 (size 1)

Beading needle

Beads
Seven 2mm (1⁄16in) and three 4mm (1⁄8in) black glass beads

Stitch abbreviations (see chart)

CF	Closed fly stitch
CS	Crewel stem stitch
FK	French knots
L	Leaf stitch
L&C	Laid and couched work
L&S	Long and short as soft shading
RS	Raised satin stitch
S	Satin stitch

Wherever you see (D) on the stitch chart, use double thread, otherwise use single thread.

Threads
Black cotton thread

Appleton's crewel wool

One skein each of the following:

Blues	Greens	Reds
158	242	202
159	243	204
565	244	206
566	251	225
567	255	504
743	293	864
744	294	866
921	331	**Yellows**
924	351	312
927	402	313
928	641	692
Purples	642	693
605	643	695
607	**Browns**	696
	903	
	904	
	972	

Two skeins each of the following:

Blues	Yellows
155	311
156	691
328	
Greens	
354	
402	
644	

Three skeins of the following:

Greens

252

253

Stitching instructions

Leaves

Begin in the top left-hand corner of the design with laid and couched work on the leaves in the upper areas. In this design there are four variations of this stitch; they all begin with a base layer, in a single thread, 'laid' diagonally across the entire area, and then use a new thread in the same colour in the opposite direction. The 'couch' stitch secures each square and is worked in a variety of stitches.

Top left-hand leaves

1 Use the base layer of laid work as usual, then couch with a short straight stitch over each junction where the laid lines cross. When making these couching stitches, rather than following each diagonally laid thread, follow a vertical path over each junction, dissecting each square in half. This will keep your squares neatly in place. Next add a French knot in double thread at the tip of each straight stitch. When creating the French knot, come up 2mm (1⁄16in) away from the tip of the straight stitch and go down in the same hole as the top of the straight couching stitch.

2 Next, move to the right and work the small leaf in the background at the top of the trunk in simple laid work. Couch this leaf with crosses. Work one half of each cross at a time, completing the whole leaf in one direction before stitching the final layer.

3 The largest leaf in this top left-hand corner is worked in a more complex version of laid and couched work. Use the same base layer, then add couching using two parallel lines of stitching, each couch stitch jumping over two of the original base laid lines of thread. Work each line of couching in turn so that the tension on each stitch is the same. Finally, couch to secure the laid work, in one direction at a time, and create small crosses over the previous layer of couching, within the centre of alternate squares.

4 You can now continue to work this area by stitching first the veins in double thread, and then the undulating borders around these first three laid and couched leaves, in a single thread. If you prefer, you can move to the top right-hand side of the whole design and make the fourth version of laid and couched work in the top right leaf.

Top right-hand leaf

5 This leaf is simply worked with the base layer followed by couching, then fly stitches which come up on one side corner then go down in the other side corner. At the base of each 'V' shaped stitch, couch down each junction of laid stitches. Add a pattern of French knots in double thread.

6 Crewel stem stitch the leaf veins in double thread and the outline and stem in single thread on this remaining laid and couched leaf.

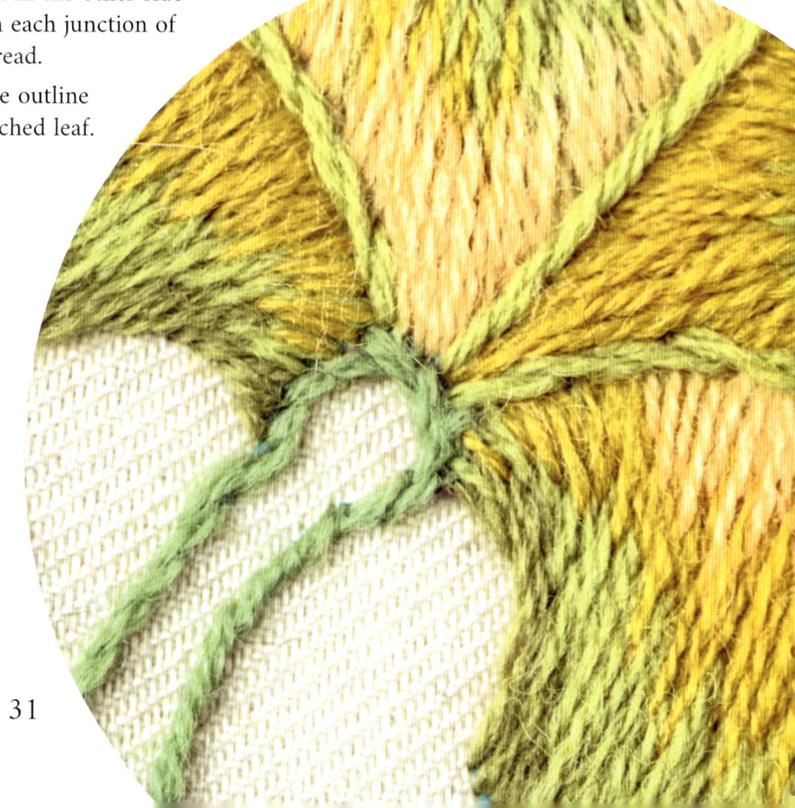

Rainbow

7 Create the rainbow behind the five perching birds. Beginning at the top line, work bands of colour in split stitch with double thread. Work in lines of stitches of each colour in turn, continuing under the branch and the tail feathers.

8 Next, add the swirls of grapes, using crewel stem stitch in double thread, beginning at the perimeter of each swirl and working inwards. As with the leaves, stitch the background grapes before the foreground grapes to give a sense of perspective.

9 While you are in this area, you can begin adding a frame in crewel stem stitch, an outer border of the whole design, using a double thread.

Birds on the branch

10 Add the first three birds perching on the branch. Begin with the left-hand bird with long and short stitch on the chest area. Bring your needle up in the centre of the chest, then stitch downwards with the first colour. With the second colour, come up through the first layer of colour, reversing the direction so that you stitch down onto the top of the branch.

11 Next add heavily worked satin stitch for the back and wings, then repeat stitch this area, so that the back becomes a slightly raised feature. When stitching the top of the head, take your needle down into the line of holes made by the lower end of the back and wing satin stitches.

12 Add the tail feathers, swapping colours and angling on each feather, in densely stitched double-threaded satin stitch.

13 Before you finish stitching the bird's face, embroider the branches. Beginning at the top of each branch, work lines of split stitch in double thread. Make long, loose stiches, altering the angle of each line slightly as you progress down each branch and trunk. Use crewel stem stitch to border each side of the branch, keeping the loops of this stitch overlapping the main part of the branch so that the needle comes up cleanly without disturbing the previously worked stitches. Later, after you have worked the subsequent leaves and stems, use up the remaining thread in your needle to add a few extra stitches in brown, yellow or green to the branch.

14 Go back to the birds and add the chin and beak, taking the beak stitches to a sharp point, down over the top of the branch. All the perching and the swooping birds are stitched in this order and sit gently over the leaves and stems behind them.

15 As you work down the design, stitch all the water swirls and rainbows in the same way, taking care always to work from background to foreground where they overlap with another feature.

Largest leaf

16 Begin the largest leaf in the lower left-hand corner. This is quite a daunting challenge, but you could work a small patch of each colour before you complete each colour in turn, and then you will see that the way each colour splits the last one makes it much easier in practice! The first colour, the outer area, is your main challenge: work the leaves in long and short stitch, all with a double thread for the first (outer) colour, and a single thread for each of the inner colours. Use extra layers of inner colours as needed to negotiate the corners and to fill the shapes, referring to the pictures as you complete each colour. Work each colour in turn and keep going!

17 Stitch the veins and then the stems of the leaf using a double thread and crewel stem stitch. All the remaining leaves are stitched in this way.

Birds

18 Now move to the right-hand side of the design and, starting at the top, stitch the main branch, remaining birds which are in flight, and the leaves and swirls. The wings and tail feathers of the birds in flight (swallows) are worked in closed fly stitch in double thread, with each stitch beginning at the tip of the tail or wing.

19 The wing and tail feathers on the three turtle doves (on the far right-hand side) are worked in leaf stitch from each feather tip towards the body. The three doves are also stitched in long and short stitch on the head, neck and chest.

20 Use satin stitch in double thread to make each of the grapes in the lower right corner. Begin, as always, with the background grapes and end with the foreground grapes. Vary the grapes by using raised satin stitch on some, and completing others with only one layer of stitching.

Eyes

21 Complete all of the swallows and turtle doves using black cotton thread to secure a small seed bead for an eye on each of the birds. Use 2mm (1/16in) beads for the small swallows, and 4mm (1/8in) beads for larger turtle doves.

CONTEMPORARY CREWELWORK

The designs in this section use traditional crewel motifs that have been woven together to create fresh ideas.

Summer Jewels (pages 44–61) is a spray of flowers and leaves that are typical of the motifs found in crewelwork. Their shapes and colours have been inspired not only by crewelwork but also the motifs found in textiles, on wallpapers and even on bone china. Tiny the Tabby (pages 62–81) includes the face of a cat that is markedly different from the animals that were depicted in traditional crewelwork designs. Instead, it has been worked from a photograph of a much-loved family cat called Tiny.

Worked with cotton threads and glass beads on cotton or cotton/linen blend fabrics, the techniques used include a range of traditional crewelwork stitches along with stitches more commonly used in different styles of embroidery. You will find bead embroidery stitches, many of them modified from African beading techniques. There are also needle lace techniques modified for use as embroidery stitches, and loom weaving patterns that have been modified for needle weaving.

The evolution of CREWELWORK

If, like me, you were born of parents with a European heritage, and grew up in the 'colonies', you likely spent your childhood in a home surrounded by the sort of art and design that is typical of Europe. It was to be found in the upholstery fabrics of the furniture you sat on, in the curtains that adorned your windows, and on the plates which you ate from. It was also to be found in the paintings and trinkets that were displayed in your childhood home, your grandparents' homes, and in the homes of the friends that you visited and played with.

The dominant culture of where you lived – in my case, Central Africa – was influential, but the culture of your heritage played an equally important role in what appreciation you had for art and music. You might say that this was the best of both worlds. There is a saying that goes 'a little education is a bad thing'. In a lot of respects that is true but equally it can be the opposite: in having only a rudimentary knowledge of the crewelwork style, it left me free to tread my own path.

When I started to dabble with embroidery as a young adult, I was attracted to the shapes, the motifs, the overall designs that grew out of this centuries-old embroidery style. I knew very little of the history or, indeed, the materials used, and having little knowledge of what one was 'supposed' to do, this meant that the path was open for me to do what I wanted with what I had in front of me – to develop my own style in a way that was typical of my rather unrestrained creativity.

Along with this freedom, what I did with these designs was restricted by the availability of materials. Along with linen twill, crewel wool is not readily available in Africa and, besides, the hot environment in which we live is not suited to the use of wool. The very thought of it makes one itch! Add the fact that wool tends to swell in high humidity, leaving it difficult to work with, this meant that the obvious choice of thread was cotton. Readily available, easy to work with and, importantly – in a dusty African environment and living in homes filled with a lot of large, slobbery dogs – also colourfast and washable.

I used cotton threads on whatever cotton or linen fabric was easily available. I was not alone in this, as many of the hand-embroidery stitchers around me were doing much the same thing, garnering a lot of criticism from the purists.

Once you have started following an independent path, it logically involves not only using different materials, but also stitches and techniques that are not traditionally associated with crewelwork. This has meant that my repertoire of stitches has more than doubled, allowing me to look at a traditional crewel motif and see it as an empty canvas waiting to be filled with whatever I like, to be as creative and imaginative as I want to be. In the process, along with many others who have done the same, this has brought about an evolution in crewelwork to the extent that perhaps, it should be given a different name. I have chosen to call it 'creative crewelwork', feeling that it best describes the results of this evolution.

It is worth noting that, while my contribution to this evolution has happened in Africa, there are similar evolutions that have taken place as far apart as Eastern Europe and the Antipodes. Each with their own style and colour palette, artists have created designs that, like mine, may look traditional but are decidedly not.

Apart from different use of colour, the designs have evolved to make use of modern materials, materials often more suited to the environment of the designer. Most of all, with the world having opened up in the past 30 years or so with the arrival of the internet, they have evolved to make use of a wider range of techniques, giving the stitcher room for endless innovation and wild creativity. The result is a true meeting of cultures, which has brought about the evolution of so much art over the centuries.

General project instructions

The general instructions below apply to the following projects: Summer Jewels (page 44), Tiny the Tabby (page 62), Contemporary Eagle (page 100) and Contemporary Blue Bird (page 124). Please read through the project instructions before you beginning stitching your designs.

- Stretch the fabric print over the frame.
- Summer Jewels and Tiny the Tabby were worked using two pairs of Edmunds stretcher bars, assembled into a rectangular frame.
- Attach the fabric to the side of the bars with a staple gun or thumb tacks.
- The size of the stretcher bars is listed in the You Will Need list at the beginning of each project.
- Make sure that the fabric is taut. This will improve the quality of your work.
- If you are unsure of any of the stitches or techniques, practise on a scrap piece of fabric before working on your project.
- Assume that threads are stranded cotton unless otherwise described.
- Assume that you should work with two strands of cotton, using a size 8 embroidery needle, unless otherwise advised.
- If advised to use a single strand, use a size 10 embroidery needle.
- For all bead embroidery stitches, work with a single strand of stranded cotton, doubled over and threaded onto a size 11 Sharps quilting needle.
- Work with single strands of perle thread using a size 7 embroidery needle for perle #12 and a size 8 embroidery needle for perle #16.
- Use a size 26 tapestry needle for the needle lace detached buttonhole stitches and for the weaving weft stitches.
- All the stitches and techniques used the projects are in the stitch directory in this book (page 144).
- Most elements of the design are outlined, usually with outline stitch and sometimes with whipped backstitch.
- The outlining is noted in context, but you should only do it when you have completed all surrounding embroidery.

Using the charts

You will find the chart for each project printed on a loose sheet and folded inside the pocket at the back of the book.

Before you begin stitching, transfer the outline from the chart onto your background fabric. See page 143 for more details on how to do this.

Note: the charts for the traditional and contemporary projects are presented in slightly different formats. When using the charts for the contemporary projects, it is important to note the following:

- The charts should be used in conjunction with the instructions for each project.
- The numbers shown on each chart refer to the numbered instructions in each project: locate the chart number for each section and find the specific guidelines for that number in the project instructions.

The charts are also available to download from the Bookmarked Hub. Search for this book by title or ISBN: the files can be found under 'Book Extras'. Membership of the Bookmarked online community is free: www.bookmarkedhub.com

Summer Jewels page 45

Tiny the Tabby page 63

Contemporary Eagle page 101

Contemporary Blue Bird page 125

3 SUMMER JEWELS

Using traditional crewelwork flowers and fruit as a starting point, the elements in this design have been redrawn to include many additional shapes within each motif, thereby providing an extensive canvas on which to work. The motifs are filled with a variety of stitches and techniques. Some are traditional crewelwork stitches, while others have been borrowed from other genres. In addition, needlework techniques such as needle lace and loom weaving have been modified for inclusion in the stitching of the project.

Dimensions: 30 x 34cm (12 x 13¼in)

YOU WILL NEED

Chart

Summer Jewels chart

Fabric

60 x 60cm (24 x 24in) lightweight (290gsm) cotton twill in ecru

60 x 60cm (24 x 24in) cotton voile backing fabric in off-white

Embroidery frame

Two pairs of 43cm (17in) Edmunds stretcher bars

Needles

Embroidery needles, sizes 7, 8 and 10

Sharps quilting needle, size 11

Tapestry needle, size 26

Threads

DMC stranded cotton

One skein each of the following:

28 Medium light eggplant
29 Eggplant
777 Deep red
3031 Very dark mocha brown
3831 Dark raspberry
3832 Medium raspberry
3833 Light raspberry
3854 Medium autumn gold
3862 Dark mocha beige
3863 Medium mocha beige
3864 Light mocha beige

Two skeins each of the following:

3011 Dark khaki green
3012 Medium khaki green
3013 Light khaki green

Presencia Finca perle cotton size #12

5g (¼oz) of each of the following:

1915 Dark cranberry
2699 Medium lavender
3000 Ecru
7720 Light autumn gold

Presencia Finca perle cotton size #16

5g (¼oz) of:

4799 Ultra-light avocado green

Beads and crystals

Miyuki beads

4g of 15°, 196 24kt Yellow gold lined opal

2g of 15°, 356 Purple lined amethyst AB

4g of 15°, 459 Metallic olive

Preciosa Viva 12 flat-back crystals

Six pieces of 20ss Olivine AB

Stitching instructions

Use the chart for Summer Jewels in conjunction with these stitching instructions. The numbers on the chart refer to the numbered instructions below.

Large flower 1 (right-hand side)

1 Fill the centre of the petals in trellis with cross stitch couching, using a single strand of cotton.

Work a vertical and horizontal trellis over the centre of the petal, placing the long, straight stitches 3mm (⅛in) apart. Use a single strand of 28.

Using 29 for the darker crosses and 28 for the lighter ones, work a cross stitch over each intersection of the trellis.

2 Working with single strands of thread, fill the outside borders of each petal with rows and part-rows of chain stitch.

Starting at the base of the border, work chain stitch on the inside line of the border, adjacent to the inside of the petal, using 3012.

With a single strand of the same thread, work chain stitch over the top of each curve in the border.

With a single strand of 3013, work chain stitch on the outside lines of the border.

With a single strand of the same, lighter thread, fill in the remaining space in the border around the petals with part lines of chain stitch.

With a single strand of 3011, work outline stitch on both sides of the chain stitch border.

Centre of the flower

3 Fill the golden background with needle weaving texture no. 5 (see page 213).

Using Finca perle #12 7720, work the golden colour 1 warp stitch from the left to the right side of the shape.

Using Finca perle #12 3000, weave the ecru colour 2 weft stitches from the bottom to the top of the shape.

4 Curving around the top of the woven area are five flowers. Each one is worked in the same way:

Pad the flower with outline stitch.

Using a single strand of cotton that is the same colour as the padding work buttonhole stitch flowers over the padding.

Work the flower centre with 3833. Moving out to the side, use 3832 for the next flower on either side of the centre flower. The remaining flowers on each side are worked with 3831.

Outline each flower with outline stitch using a single strand of 777.

Using a doubled-over strand of 3854, stitch nine beads 15° 196 into the centre of each flower.

5 To create the twisted floral tendril within the centre of the flower, and having covered the lines with needle weaving, use the lines on the chart as your guide.

Make the twisted thread with a 2m (2¼yd) length of two strands of thread, 3011, double it over, knotting the raw ends together, so that you are twisting the equivalent of four strands.

Couch the twisted thread into place so that you create the impression of a three-part twisted branch.

Work small, detached chain leaves that radiate from the twisted branches using two strands of 3013.

Using a doubled-over single strand of thread colour 29 and beads 15° 356, work a four-bead picot at the tip of each twisted branch.

6 Moving out to the sides of the flower, the instructions below apply to both sides the one being worked as a mirror image of the other.

Starting with the brown petal, fill the centre with long and short stitch shading using single strands of thread. Working from the base of the petal, use 3862, shading through 3863 to 3864 at the tip.

Using a single strand of 3862, work trellis couching over the long and short stitch shading, placing the stitches diagonally.

Starting at the base of the border, work chain stitch on the inside line using a single strand of 3862.

Work chain stitch on the outside line of the border using a single strand of 3864.

Fill in the remaining space in the border with chain stitch using a single strand of 3863.

With a single strand of 3031, work outline stitch on both sides of the chain stitch border.

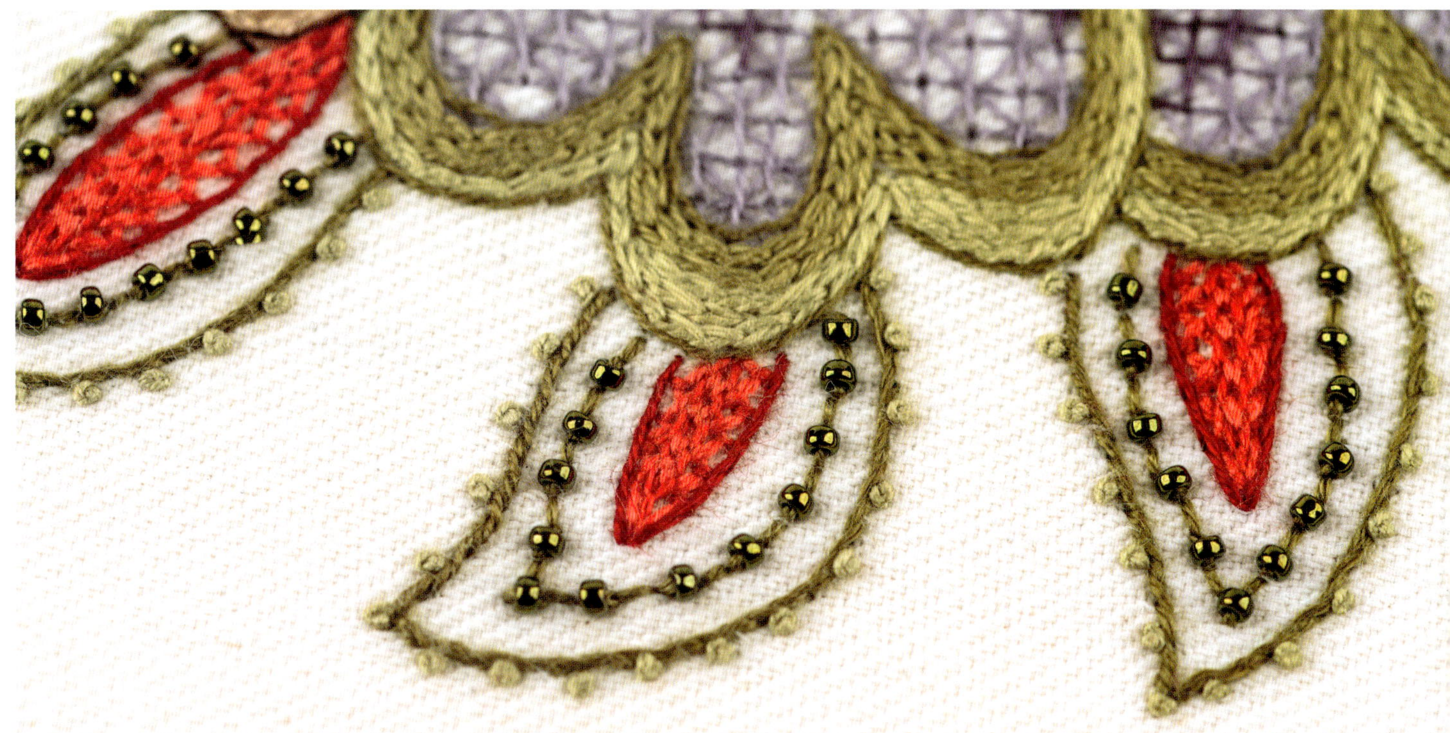

7 Moving further outwards, fill the three segments within the adjacent leaf with chain stitch–backstitch combination.

Work the chain stitch with 28 and the backstitch with 29.

Fill each of the three segments with lines of the stitch combination that start on the longest outside line of the segment, complete the segment with shorter lines.

Fill the border of the leaf with chain stitch using 3012 for the inside and 3013 for the outside halves of the border.

Outline both edges with outline stitch using a single strand of 3011.

8 The seven petals that radiate out of the top of the flower are worked in the same way.

Fill the centre of the petal with interlaced chain stitch. Use 3831 to work the reverse chain stitch and the straight stitches on each side. Interlace the chain stitch with 3832. Outline the shape with outline stitch using a single strand of 777.

Work the single line within the shape with beaded backstitch. Use 3011 and beads 15° 459.

Using 3011, work whipped backstitch on the perimeter lines of the shape. With the same thread, work single wrap French knots at intervals, adjacent to the whipped backstitch.

9 Moving down the flower, fill the red area on each side with long and short stitch shading.

Starting at the base and working with single strands of thread use 3831 shading through 3832 and 3833 to 3832 at the tip.

Using a single strand of 777, work basic trellis couching over the shading.

With two strands of the same thread, work heavy chain stitch on the inner outline of the shaded area.

With the same thread, add a French knot to each of the small dots that curve under the green curlicue. Work the knot closest to the petal with three wraps, working outwards to two wraps with the last knot being worked with a single wrap.

When you have completed the small leaves described in step 12, return to this area and work the outer outline with outline stitch using a single strand of 777.

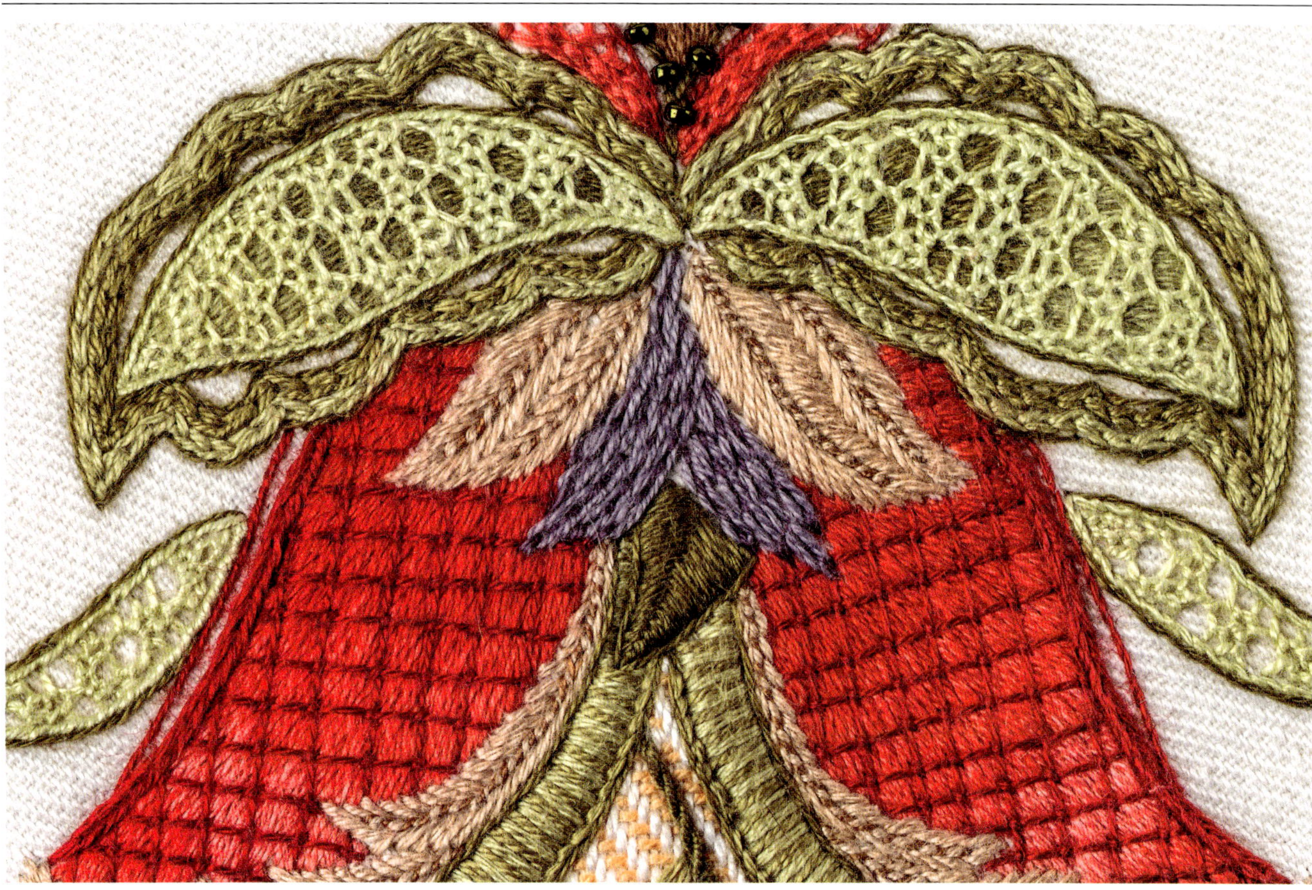

10 Starting at the tip of each shape, use two strands of 3864 for the fly stitch and a single strand of 3862 for the whipping.

11 Fill the green shapes with padded and striped blanket stitch.

Pad the shape with two strands of 3013.

Use 3012 to work the blanket stitch and 3013 to work the straight stitch stripes.

With a single strand of 3011, work outline stitch to define both edges of the padded shape.

12 The small leaves radiating away from the shaded areas on each side are filled with needle lace stitch no. 9 (see page 208).

Familiarise yourself with stitch no. 9, then fill both small leaves, using Finca perle #16, 4799.

Note: everyone's stitching tension is different, and while the photos show how the stitch placement worked out for me, it may be slightly different when you work it. This shouldn't matter if you have familiarized yourself with the pattern for stitch no. 9, as this will enable you to adjust it according: you fit as many stitches as will sit comfortably in any loop.

Outline the entire leaf with backstitch. When you reach the tip, work an additional horizontal backstitch across that tip. You will use this stitch to anchor the first row of detached buttonhole stitch.

As the shape widens, increase the number of stitches at the beginning and ends of rows.

Around halfway down, the shape will narrow and you decrease by leaving out stitches.

Reduce the number of stitches down to just one at the bottom of the shape, attaching it with a detached buttonhole stitch in the point at the base.

When the needle lace is complete, whip the backstitch on both sides.

Returning to the last instruction in step 9, work the second, outer outline of that section with a single strand of 777.

Outline the needle lace leaf with outline stitch worked adjacent to the whipped backstitch. Use a single strand of 3011.

13 Moving to the leaves and petals in the middle of the flower, start with the green leaf in the centre. Using 3011, pad the leaf with horizontal satin stitch.

Using a single strand of the same thread, work raised herringbone stitch over the padding.

With a single strand of the same thread, work outline stitch around the visible edges of the leaf.

14 Working downwards, fill the two purple leaves with the chain stitch backstitch combination following the instructions in step 7.

15 The fronds below that are filled with whipped fly stitch, following the instructions in step 10.

16 The leaves of the calyx are filled with needle lace stitch no. 9 using Finca perle #16 4799. The guidelines set out in step 12 apply to these leaves, and once again your pattern may vary from the pictures, depending on your stitching tension.

When you have completed the needle lace, whip the backstitch with the same thread.

Fill the scalloped edge with rows of chain stitch using two strands of thread. Start with the curves adjacent to the needle lace using 3012. Using 3013, work chain stitch on the outer edge. If there is any space between the two lines of chain stitch, fill those with part rows of chain stitching using 3013.

With a single strand of 3011, work outline stitch adjacent to the chain stitch on both top and bottom of the scallops.

With the same thread, work outline stitch adjacent to the whipped backstitch that goes around the needle lace centre.

17 Moving downwards to the small calyx leaves, follow the instructions in step 8.

Fill the centre of each leaf with interlaced chain stitch.

When you have completed the embroidery described in step 18, work a line of beaded backstitch on the outline of each leaf.

18 Moving to the bottom of the calyx, each curve is worked in the same way.

Using two strands of thread, pad the curves with outline stitch padding.

Using single strands of thread, work from the bottom widest curve up to the to the smallest space adjacent to the flower. Work close buttonhole stitch perpendicular to the padding.

The purl of the buttonhole stitch should be on the lower edge and when you are working the second and third curves, cover the raw edges of the buttonhole stitch worked previously.

Starting from the bottom, use 3864 for the bottom curve, 3863 in the middle and 3862 closest to the flower.

Outline the outside, bottom edge with outline stitch worked with a single strand of 3031.

Large flower 2 (top left-hand side)

19 Start with the middle of the calyx. Fill the space with long and short stitch shading using single strands of thread.

Start at the base with 3011, shading through 3012 to 3013 into the tips.

Thereafter, work backstitch around the shape using perle #16, 4799.

Turn your work around so that, while working from the base to the tips, you are working towards yourself.

Fill the area with needle lace stitch no. 8 (see page 207), until you reach the point where the shape splits into 3 separate areas.

When you reach the point where you need to divide each row into three separate parts, continue working the pattern separately in each tip of the shape.

Whip the backstitch lines that define the shape and thereafter, work outline stitch adjacent to the outside of the whipped backstitch with a single strand of 3011.

20 The pairs of leaves on each side of the calyx are worked in the same way. Fill the curved shape in the centre of each leaf with long and short stitch shading using single strands of thread, starting at the base with 3011, shading through 3012 to 3013 at the tip.

With a single strand of 3011, work diagonal basic trellis couching over the shading.

With the same thread, outline the visible edges of the shape with outline stitch.

Work basic interlaced chain stitch on the line the lies outside the shaded area. Use 3012 for the chain stitch and interlace with 3013.

Using a doubled-over strand of 3011 and beads 15° 459, work beaded backstitch on the curved line just below the tip of the shape.

Using two strands of 3011, work whipped backstitch on the visible outline of the leaf.

With two strands of 3013, work single-wrap French knots at regular intervals adjacent to the outside edge of the pair of leaves.

21 Referring to step 18, fill the curved shape above the needle lace centre of the calyx with padded buttonhole stitch.

Use two strands of 3863 for the outline stitch padding and a single strand of the same thread for the buttonhole stitch.

Work outline stitch on the outside of the purl of the buttonhole stitch, using a single strand of 3031.

22 Fill each oval with burden stitch, working the horizontal stitches that form the basis of the stitch with 3832.

Thereafter, starting at one end of the shape, work two rows with 3831.

Changing to 3832, work a single row in the smaller shapes and two rows in the larger ovals.

Changing to 3833, work two rows in the smaller shapes and three rows in the larger ovals.

Work to the other end of the shape with 3832 and 3831, working as many rows of each colour as necessary, depending on the size of the oval.

With a single strand of 777, work whipped backstitch around each shape.

23 Work beaded backstitch on the visible outlines of each segment using 3011 and beads 15° 459.

24 Moving up, work the oval shapes in the second row of segments highlighted in the image above.

Using 29, pad each oval shape with vertical outline stitch padding.

With a single strand of the same thread, work horizontal satin stitch over the padding.

Using perle #12 2699, work backstitch around the shape on the edge of the satin stitch. Work the stitches in pairs so that they are level with one another (see page xxx).

With the same thread, work the interlacing through the backstitches.

With two strands of 29, work a single wrap French knot at the intersections of the backstitches.

Work beaded backstitch on the visible outlines of each segment using 3011 and beads 15° 459.

25 Both buds on the side are worked in the same way.

Using 3831, pad the bud with horizontal outline stitch.

With a single strand of the same thread, work buttonhole stitch perpendicular to the padding.

Work the pair of calyx leaves with whipped fly stitch using 3013 whipped with a single strand of 3011.

Using 3854, stitch beads 15° 196 into the space that remains below the bud and between the calyx leaves.

26 The three larger shapes towards the top of the flower are worked in the same way.

Fill the centre of each of the ovals with needle weaving texture no. 5.

Using Finca perle #12 7720, work the golden colour 1 warp stitch from the left to the right side of the shape.

Use Finca perle #12 3000 to weave the ecru colour 2 weft stitches from bottom to top.

To create the twisted floral tendril within the centre of the flower, use the lines on the chart as your guide.

Referring back to step 5, work the twisted couching with 3011.

The small, detached chain leaves that radiate from the twisted branches are worked using two strands of 3013.

Using thread 29 and beads 15° 356, work a 4-bead picot at the tip of each twisted branch.

27 The borders on each side of the needle weaving are filled with layered buttonhole stitch.

Starting on the inside, closest to the needle weaving, work the first row with two strands of 3864.

Thereafter, work rows with 3863 and 3862.

The outside row is worked adjacent to the purl of the previous row using two strands of 3031.

With a single strand of 3031, outline the bottom edge of the border by working outline stitch in the ditch adjacent to the needle weaving.

28 Worked the padded buttonhole stitch flower at the tip of each shape following the directions in step 4.

The flower in the middle is worked with 3833. The flowers on each side are worked with 3832.

The groups of tiny leaves are worked with whipped fly stitch, using 3013 for the lighter and 3012 for the darker leaves. Whip both with a single strand of 3011.

Work the small, darker leaves following the guidelines for satin stitch leaves using a single strand of 3011.

29 The buds that are between the oval shapes are worked following the guidelines set out in step 26.

Large fruit (lower left-hand side)

30 Fill the red semi-circles with padded buttonhole stitch.

Using two strands of thread for the padding and a single strand for the buttonhole stitch, work the two at the top with 3831.

Moving downwards, the middle and bottom rows are worked in the same way. Use 3831 for the semi-circles on each side and 3832 for the semi-circle in the middle.

31 Moving down, the green leaves that face into the red semi-circles are filled with long and short stitch shading. Using single strands, start at the base of the leaf with 3011, shading through 3012 to 3013 at the tip.

Using a single strand of 3011, work basic trellis couching over the shading.

When you have completed any surrounding embroidery, outline the visible edges with outline stitch using 3011.

32 Moving down into the centre of the fruit, fill the space with needle weaving texture no. 5.

Using Finca perle #12 7720, work the golden colour 1 warp stitch from the left to the right side of the shape.

Use Finca perle #12 3000 to weave the ecru colour 2 weft stitches from the bottom to top.

33 To create the twisted floral tendril within the centre, use the lines on the chart as your guide.

Referring to step 5, work the twisted couching with 3011.

The small, detached chain leaves that radiate from the twisted branches using two strands of 3013.

Using thread 29 and beads 15° 356, work a 4-bead picot at the tip of each twisted branch.

34 Moving down towards the base of the fruit, the leaves wrap around the centre. Start with the leaf on the left.

Fill the left side of the leaf with long and short stitch shading.

Using single strands, start at the base of the leaf with 3011, shading through 3012 to 3013 at the tip.

Using perle #16 4799, work needle lace stitch no. 9 (see page 208) over the shading.

Unlike previous needle lace, do not outline the area with backstitch. Start, instead, with a single horizontal backstitch worked across the tip.

The guidelines set out in step 12 apply to this space too.

When you have completed the shading described in step 35 below, outline this half of the leaf by working beaded backstitch on the perimeter lines on both sides. Use thread 3011 and beads 15° 459.

35 Fill the right-hand side of this leaf with diagonal long and short stitch shading.

Working with single strands, start closest to the vein using 3831. Shade through 3832 to 3833 on the edge.

Work basic trellis couching over the shading using a single strand of 777.

With two strands of the same thread, work heavy chain stitch on the visible outline on the right of the shape.

36 Moving to the leaf on the right, this is filled with needle lace no. 10 (see page 209) worked with perle #16 4799.

Work backstitch around the entire leaf with a horizontal backstitch across the tip of the leaf.

Fill the leaf with needle lace stitch no. 10, starting at the tip and working down to the base.

Whip the backstitch that defines the shape and outline the visible edges with outline stitch using 3011.

Moving outwards, the sections described below are worked on both sides of the fruit.

37 Moving to the petal behind the leaf described in step 37, fill the centre with shaded trellis with cross stitch couching.

Work the trellis with a single strand of 29 placing the stitches 2mm (1/16in) apart.

Using 28, work single strand cross stitch over each intersection of the trellis stitches.

Fill the border of the leaf with rows of chain stitch using single strands of thread using 3012 on the inside and 3013 on the outer edges.

Outline the visible edges of the leaf and the inside edge of the border with outline stitch using a single strand of 3011.

38 Following the instructions in step 6, fill the next brown leaf in the same way using 3862, 3863 and 3864, outlined in 3031.

39 Fill the leaves with whipped fly stitch using two strands of thread using 3011, 3012 and 3013, as dictated by the colour image. All are whipped with a single strand of 3011.

40 Starting with the bottom half of each leaf, use perle #16 4799.

Work backstitch from base to tip on the lower, outside perimeter line, with a stitch across the tip.

As you have done in steps 12, 16 and 34, fill the space with needle lace stitch no. 9, using the horizontal backstitch across the tip to anchor the first detached buttonhole stitch.

When filled, whip the backstitch on the bottom line of the shape and work outline stitch adjacent to the outside of the whipped backstitch.

41 Fill the top of each leaf with interlaced chain stitch variation.

Use two strands of 3831 for the reverse chain stitch and the small straight stitches on each side.

Work the interlacing with two strands of 3832.

Outline both sides of the top section with beaded backstitch using thread 3011 and beads 15° 459.

42 Working on the leaves below the fruit, start with the leaf on the right.

Fill the green shape that curves over the top of the leaf with padded and striped blanket stitch.

Pad the shape with 3013, work the blanket stitch with 3012, and the straight stitch stripes with 3013.

With a single strand of 3011, work outline stitch to define the outer edge of the blanket stitch.

43 Fill the bottom of the leaf with interlaced chain stitch variation following the guidelines in step 41.

44 Fill the outer leaf segment with chain stitch backstitch combination following the guidelines in step 7.

45 The green leaf below is filled with long and short stitch shading using single strands of thread.

Start at the base with 3011, shading through 3012 to 3013 at the tips.

With a single strand of 3011, work basic trellis couching over the shading.

With the same thread, outline the visible edges with outline stitch.

46 Work the two small fronds with whipped fly stitch using two strands of 3864 whipped with one strand of 3862.

47 Moving to the left of the fruit, fill the top leaf following the directions in steps 42 and 43.

48 Fill the two purple leaves with chain stitch backstitch combination, following the directions in step 7.

49 Moving downwards and to the far left, fill the leaf with long and short stitch shading overlaid with needle lace stitch no. 9, as you have done in steps 12, 16 and 34.

Work the shading from the base of the leaf with 3011, shading through 3012 to 3013 at the tip.

Use perle #16 4799, to work the backstitch and the needle lace and whip the backstitch with the same thread.

With a single strand of 3011, work outline stitch adjacent to the outside edge of the whipped backstitch.

50 Moving to the right, fill the segment that curves around the frond with padded and striped blanket stitch, following the instructions in step 42. When you have completed the frond described in step 51 below, work outline stitch at the base of the striped blanket stitch using a single strand of 3011.

51 Work the frond following the guidelines in step 46.

52 Moving to the base of the fruit, and using two strands of 3831, pad the bud with horizontal outline stitch.

With a single strand of the same thread, work buttonhole stitch perpendicular to the padding with the purl of the stitch facing outwards.

Work the pair of calyx leaves with raised herringbone stitch using a single strand of 3011.

Using thread 3854, stitch beads 15° 196 into the space that remains.

Work outline stitch outside the padded buttonhole stitch using a single strand of 777.

53 Work the small section of branch with two lines of chain stitch. Using two strands of thread, use 3862 for the (lower) inside of the curve and 3864 above it on the outside of the curve.

With a single strand of thread, outline both sides of the branch with outline stitch using 3031.

54 The main branch is worked with three lines of chain stitch. Using two strands of thread throughout, use 3862 for the (darker) inside of the curve.

Work the (lighter) outside of the curve with 3864 and fill the space in between with chain stitch using 3863.

With a single strand of thread, outline both sides of the branch with outline stitch using 3031.

Leaf

55 Work the leaf at the very base of the branch.

Starting with the bottom half of the leaf, using perle #16 4799, fill the space with needle lace stitch no. 9 as you have done in steps 12, 16 and 34.

Whip the backstitch on the bottom line of the shape and outline that with outline stitch using 3011.

56 Using thread 3011 and beads 15° 459, work beaded backstitch on the three veins that curve inside the leaf.

With two strands of 3011, work whipped backstitch up the vein above the curved beaded backstitch and around the upper edge of the leaf.

Using two strands of 3013, work single-wrap French knots adjacent to the outside of the leaf, placing them at regular intervals.

Small flowers

57 Work the small flowers with double needle weaving.

When working the purple flower, use perle #12 3000 to work the warp stitches and perle #12 2699 for the weft stitches. Outline the petals with whipped backstitch using two strands of 29.

When working the red flower, use perle #12 1915 to work the warp stitches and perle #12 3000 for the weft stitches. Outline the petals with whipped backstitch using two strands of 777.

Following the directions for caged crystals, stitch a 20ss Olivine AB flat-back crystal into the circle at the base of the petals of each flower, using a single strand of 3011.

Using thread 3854, create a bead circle of 15 beads 15° 196 around the caged crystals.

Fine stems

58 When the small flowers are complete, work the stems and tendrils.

The stem that comes out of the main branch and goes into the base of the purple flower is worked with beaded backstitch using a doubled-over strand of 3011 and beads 15° 459.

The stem that comes out of the main branch above that starts with beaded backstitch using the same thread and beads.

Referring to the photos for placement and to the instructions for beaded backstitch picot lines (page 200), add picots to the line when the stem begins to curve into a tendril.

Work two beaded backstitches after each picot and finish the tendril with a bead and a backstitch.

The stem of the red flower is whipped backstitch worked with two strands of 3031.

The small branch further up the stem is worked in the same way.

59 Move along to the checked red flower that comes out of this small branch.

Fill each petal individually with needle weaving pattern checks and stripes no. 1.

With the warp stitches being worked vertically and the weft stitches horizontally in each petal, use perle #12 1915 for colour 1, and perle #12 3000 for colour 2.

Outline each of the petals with whipped backstitch using two strands of 777.

Following the instructions in step 57, place a caged 20ss Olivine AB flat-back crystal, surrounded with a circle of 15° 196 beads in the middle of the flower.

Work the stem of the flower with whipped backstitch using two strands of 3031.

60 Moving up the project, work the two parts of the branch.

Work the shorter branch that attaches to the flower following the instructions in step 53.

Thereafter, work the remainder of the main branch following the instructions in step 54.

Leaves

61 Work the leaves that come out of the stem on each side following the instructions in step 55.

Smaller flowers

62 Move up the main branch to the checked purple flower that comes out of the right of the branch. It is worked in the same way as the red flower described in step 59.

Use perle #12 1915 for colour 1, and perle #12 3000 for colour 2 to work the needle weaving checks and stripes no. 1 pattern.

Outline each of the petals with whipped backstitch using two strands of 29.

Following the instructions in step 57, place a caged 20ss Olivine AB flat-back crystal, surrounded with a circle of 15° 196 beads in the middle of the flower.

Work the stem of the flower with whipped backstitch using two strands of 3031.

63 The smaller three-petal flowers and stems are worked in needle weaving and beaded backstitch, following the instructions in steps 57 and 58.

4 TINY THE TABBY

A random freestyle embroidery technique, used to fill most of the kitten's face, provides texture and interest. The traditional crewelwork flowers and leaf motifs are filled with a variety of crewelwork stitches, in addition to needlework techniques that have been modified for use as embroidery stitches. These include needle lace, loom weaving patterns and bead embroidery stitches. The use of stranded cotton in place of the more traditionally used crewel wool means that it is possible to provide fine detail in this design.

Dimensions: 37 x 28cm (14½ x 11in)

YOU WILL NEED

Chart

Tiny the Tabby chart

Fabric

60 x 60cm (24 x 24in) 200gsm cotton–linen blend in natural, with a thread count of approximately 32 threads per inch

60 x 60cm (24 x 24in) cotton voile backing fabric in off-white

Embroidery frame

One pair each 43cm (17in) and 35cm (14in) Edmunds stretcher bars

Needles

Embroidery needles, sizes 8 and 10

Sharps quilting needle, size 11

Tapestry needle, size 26

Chenille needles, size 18 and 22

Threads

DMC stranded cotton

One skein each of the following:

–	Ecru
154	Dark grape
209	Dark lavender
210	Medium lavender
211	Light lavender
320	Medium pistachio green
367	Dark pistachio green
368	Light pistachio green
369	Very light pistachio green
437	Light tan
604	Light cranberry
646	Dark beaver grey
758	Very light terra cotta
926	Medium grey green
927	Light grey green
934	Black avocado green
963	Ultra very light dusty rose
967	Light peach
3021	Very dark brown grey
3032	Medium mocha brown
3051	Dark green grey
3052	Medium green grey
3053	Green grey
3371	Black brown
3687	Mauve
3688	Medium mauve
3689	Light mauve
3778	Light terra cotta
3781	Dark mocha brown
3782	Light mocha brown
3824	Light apricot

DMC stranded cotton, colour variations

4065	Morning meadow
4145	Sand dune
4150	Desert sand
4170	Whispering wind

DMC Special Dentelles cotton size #80

5g (¼oz) of each of the following:

–	Ecru
210	Medium lavender
368	Light pistachio green
553	Medium violet
605	Very light cranberry
3688	Medium mauve

Beads and crystals

Miyuki beads

2g of 15°, 645 Tawny pink silver lined alabaster

2g of 15°, 459 Metallic olive

2g of 11°, 577 Butter cream gold lined alabaster

2g of 8°, 645 Tawny pink silver lined alabaster

2g of 5°, 131 Crystal

Preciosa Viva 12 flat-back crystals

Two pieces of 20ss Smoke topaz

Stitching instructions

Use the chart for Tiny the Tabby in conjunction with these stitching instructions. The numbers on the chart refer to the numbered instructions below.

The face

1 Fill the various areas of the cat's face that are marked with 1 on the chart with random freestyle embroidery, using single strands of thread throughout. Referring to the guidelines for random freestyle embroidery (see page 193), use the following stitches:

- 3-petal lazy daisy bud
- 9-petal lazy daisy flowers
- Buttonhole buds
- Buttonhole stitch flowers (half)
- Eye stitch variation
- Sheaf stitch
- Single weaving filler stitch

The main objective is to create an interesting texture: the variety of stitches you use provide this texture and should be seen less as individual stitches and more as just a part of that texture.

Work small stitches, leaving very little space between them. Add French knots to fill spaces that are too small to be filled with any of the other stitches. Work these as you go along, using the same thread.

When you have worked the random freestyle stitching in an area, create additional shading.

The illustration to the right sets out the main and supplementary colours to use in the areas defined by both the solid and the dotted lines. Use the supplementary colour to work additional French knots that create the subtle shading.

Referring to the colour images, and without overfilling the areas, work as many knots as you can to create the shading and to fill spaces.

When the shading needs to change, transition by tailing off the knots of one colour, interspersing them with knots of the new colour, eventually working only with the new colour.

The spots on the cheeks which accommodate the whiskers are worked with groups of French knots. Using single strands, work the top two rows with 3021. The bottom row on each side is worked with 646.

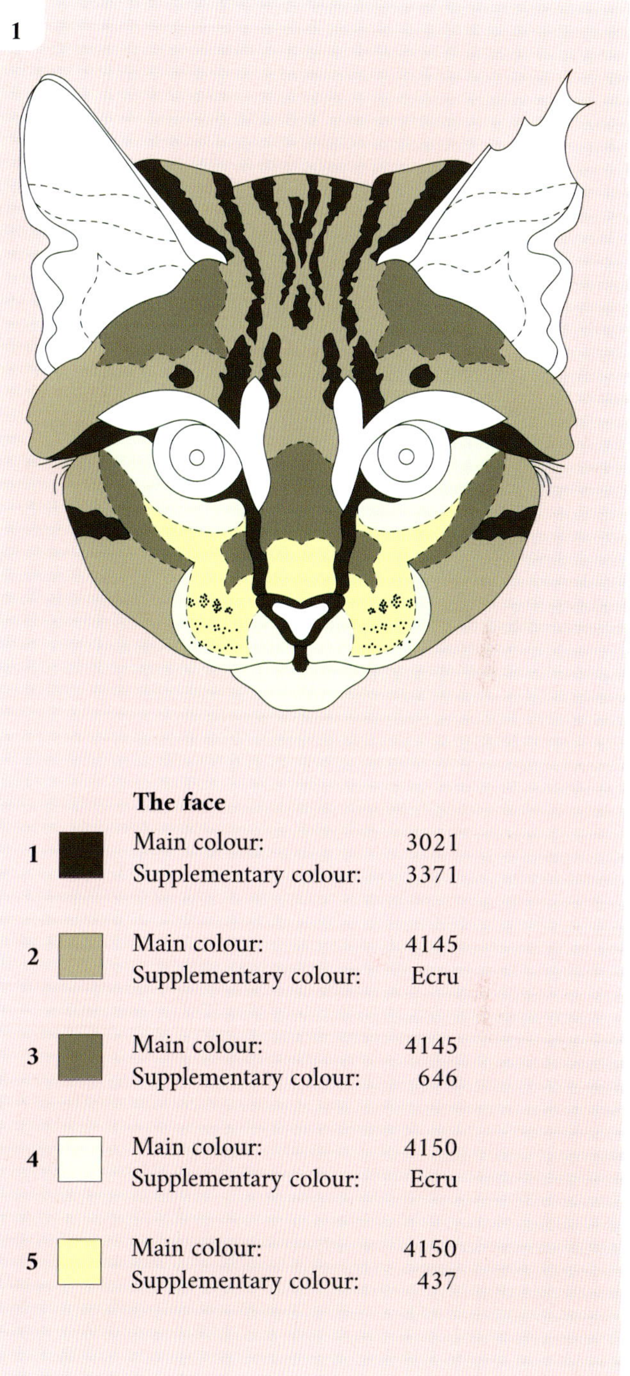

The ears

2 Fill the inside of the cat's ears with random freestyle embroidery, using single strands of thread.

Using the illustration to the right to guide you, work in the same way as you did for the face, with only a slight difference in the shading.

3 When the inside of each ear is complete, work the sides of the ears marked with padded satin stitch using 3782.

Use two strands for the padding and a single strand for the perpendicular satin stitch that is worked over the padding.

Outline the outside edge with whipped backstitch using a single strand of 3781.

The inside edge will be outlined when you have completed the tufting described in step 4 below.

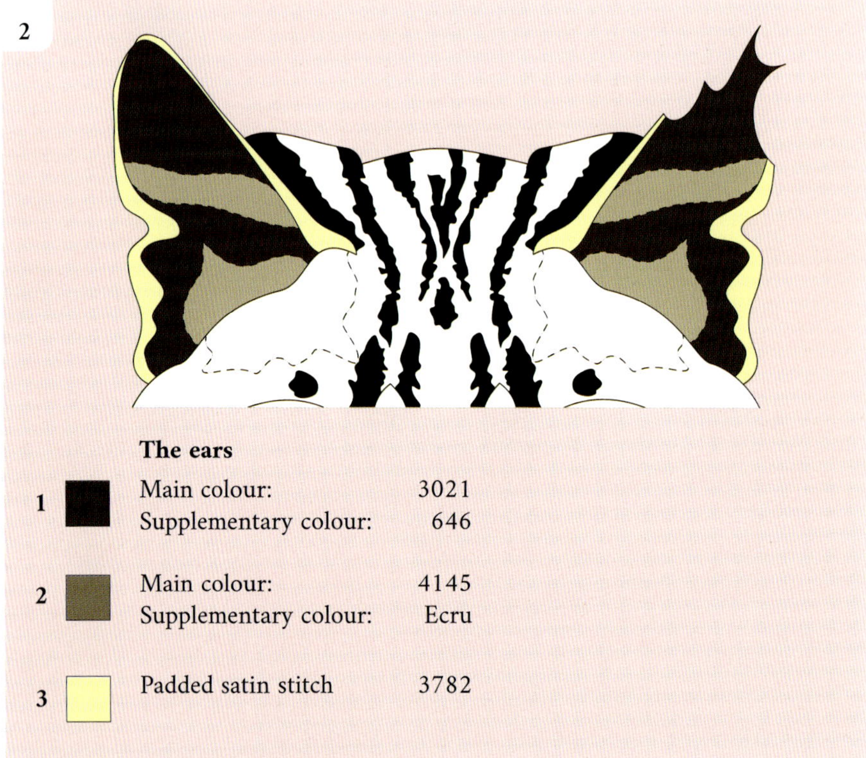

4 Create the longer hairs that lie along the base and on the inside edge of each ear with scruffy tufting using ecru (see page 189).

Start on the outer reaches at the base of the ear, working between the random freestyle embroidery in the main part of the head and at the bottom of the ear. Continue working inwards and, when you reach the corner of the ear, head upwards between the random freestyle embroidery and the padded satin stitch that forms the inner edge of the ear.

Before cutting the loops of the tufting, work the outlines as described below.

Using a single strand of 3781 and starting at the top of the outside edge of the ear, work whipped backstitch on the outside edge of the padded satin stitch on the side of the ear.

When you reach the bottom, using the same thread, work outline stitch in the ditch between the inside of the satin stitch padding and the random freestyle stitching of the inner ear.

Continue down the other side of the ear, working outline stitch on the inside of the padded satin stitch. When you reach the tufting, work between that and the satin stitch taking the opportunity to mask the backstitches that secure the loops with the outline stitch. Stop working outline stitch when you have reached the base of the padded satin stitch.

Starting at the top of the ear again and working on the outside of the padded satin stitch that forms the edge of the inner side of the ear, work whipped backstitch to outline that edge. When you get to the bottom of the padded satin stitch, continue around the base of the ear.

Working between the face and the base of the ear, outline that area of the face using the whipped backstitch to mask the backstitches that secure the loops of the tufting.

Continue outlining the face, all the way around the side, down to the bottom and back around the side of the face.

When you reach the ear on the other side, continue working the whipped backstitch to mask the backstitches of the tufting at the base of that ear, and finally, up the side of the padded satin stitch that is outside the ear and faces the middle of the face.

As you did for the other ear, work the outline stitch and the whipped backstitch that outlines the edges of that ear, using the same thread and the same stitches as described above.

To complete the outlines and using the same thread, work whipped backstitch around each cheek and also, the bottom of the chin.

With the same thread, complete the small hairs that are level with the eyes on the outside of the face with short lines of outline stitch.

The eyes

5 Start in the centre of each eye.

Following the directions for caged crystals (see page 203), stitch a 20ss smoke topaz flat-back crystal over the dark circle in the centre of each eye. Use a single strand of 3021.

Fill the circle on the outside of the centre with a spiral of outline stitch using two strands of 3021. Stitch a circle of outline stitch to outline that circle using a single strand of 3371.

Moving out to the large circle, work a spiral of outline stitch using two strands of 3032. Outline the bottom of the eye with whipped backstitch using two strands of 3371. You will outline the top edge when you have completed the twisted long and short stitch covered in step 6.

The nose

6 Starting on the side of the nose, fill the eyebrows with twisted long and short stitch.

Twist two identical sets of variegated thread.

Because the threads are variegated, you will want to be working with sections of the thread that have the same colours in each part. Starting with a 2m (2¼yd) length of the six strands of 4145, pull out single strands and twist them separately, following the guidelines in the stitch directory (see page 189).

This will give you six lengths of twisted thread that are about 50cm (20in) long and each one will have the same mix of colours.

Separate these lengths, keeping them in two piles of three twisted threads each.

In the same way, starting with a 2m (2¼yd) length of the six strands of 4150, pull out single strands and twist them separately. Add three piles of twisted lighter threads to the two existing piles of darker variegated and twisted threads.

Following the guidelines in the embroidery stitch directory (see page 190) and starting at the base on the side of the nose, fill the area that comprises the 'eyebrows', starting with the lighter twisted thread for about two rows.

When you are approximately level with the caged crystals in the eye, change thread to use the darker 4145 twisted thread.

As you get close to the 'fork' in the brow, angle your stitches so that you will be able to continue the long and short stitching in both directions – up and to the side.

Complete the vertical space that goes up the middle of the face with the darker twisted thread, 4145.

Come back to the eyebrow that is above the eye, using the darker thread 4145 until you are adjacent to the far edge of the eyeball.

Complete the eyebrow by changing to the lighter twisted thread, 4150.

With two strands of 3371, outline the top of the eyeball by working whipped backstitch between the eye and the eyebrow using the colour image opposite to guide you.

7 Pad the nose with horizontal satin stitches using two strands of 758.

Using single strands of thread 3778 shading to 758, work vertical long and short stitch perpendicular to the padding.

The whiskers are worked at the end of the project, see step 43.

Leaf, top right

Moving to the top of the design, work on the leaf above the cat's head.

8 Referring to the chart, the areas marked 8 are filled with two-tone vermicelli couching (see page 192).

Work the first stage with two strands of 3053, couched into swirls with a single strand of the same thread.

Work the second stage with single strands of 3052, couched with a single strand of the same thread.

There are veins in the sections at the tip and the base of the leaf. Work each part of each vein with whipped backstitch using two strands of 3051.

Outline the five sections of vermicelli couching with whipped backstitch using 3051.

Thereafter, work outline stitch adjacent to the outside of the whipped backstitch using a single strand of 934.

With the same thread, work outline stitch adjacent to the lines of the vein. In each instance, work the stitches on the inside of the curve.

9 The areas marked 9 in the same leaf are filled with long and short stitch shading worked with single strands of thread.

When filling the middle shape, start a little way above the tip of the vein with 3052, working diagonal long and short stitches down both sides, going into the line that defines the vein.

Thereafter, shade into the darker colour with 3053.

At the tip of the shape, work into the lighter green with 926, shading up to 927 at the tip.

The two remaining shapes are worked with 3052 shading through 3053 and 926 to 927 at the tip.

Outline the outer edge of the shaded areas with outline stitch using a single strand of 934.

10 Using a single strand of variegated 4065, fill the shape marked 10 with eye stitch filler following the guidelines in the stitch guide (see page 178).

Outline both sides of the filled area with whipped backstitch using 3051.

Thereafter, work outline stitch adjacent to the outside of the whipped backstitch using a single strand of 934.

11 Moving down to the middle area of the leaf, fill the areas marked 11 with trellis with cross stitch couching (see page 187).

The stitches of the trellis should be placed 2mm (1/16in) apart and, to assist you, it is wise to draw a grid over both sections using a heat-erasable pen.

Both the trellis and the cross stitches are worked with a single strand of 4065.

Outline both sections of the leaf with whipped backstitch using two strands of 3051.

Thereafter, work outline stitch adjacent to the outside of the whipped backstitch using a single strand of 934.

12 When you have completed all sections of the leaf, work the vein.

Using two strands of 3051, work heavy chain stitch (see page 180) on each of the lines that make up the vein.

Work outline stitch adjacent to the outside of the heavy chain stitch using a single strand of 934.

With a doubled-over strand of 934 on a bead embroidery needle and starting at the tip, work single wrap French knots at evenly spaced intervals between the lines of heavy chain stitch.

When the space becomes wider, transition into stitching single beads 15° 459 at evenly spaced intervals between the lines.

As you move down the vein, start at the tip of each side vein as you come to it, starting with single wrap French knots at the tips and transitioning into adding single beads.

Flower, middle right

13 Fill the middle section of the flower with needle weaving checks and stripes no. 9, using DMC Special Dentelles 553 for colour 1 and ecru for colour 2.

Referring to the guidelines on needle weaving (page 215), you will note that the warp stitches are worked in groups of six stitches per colour.

When working the warp stitches for this shape, start in the middle with the two middle stitches of a group of six colour 1 (purple) warp stitches worked vertically down the middle of the shape, followed by a pair of purple stitches on either side.

Thereafter, work out to each side with groups of six stitches in colour 2 (ecru) followed by as many stitches as you can fit into the shape with the colour 1 (purple) thread.

To work the weft stitches, start at the tip working with colour 1 (purple), weaving over the two middle weft stitches for two rows.

The pattern requires that you work two identical weft stitches in a colour: going over and under the same pair of warp stitches.

Thereafter, you work two weft stitches in the other colour, going over and under the opposite pairs of stitches.

Continue working the pattern, changing the colour after working each pair of weft stitches and making sure that where you have gone under a pair in the one colour, you go over that pair when working the two rows required in the opposite colour.

Continue to the bottom until you have filled the shape.

14 The curlicues on each side of the woven area are worked in the same way. Working with single strands of thread, fill each curlicue with long and short stitch shading using 209 at the base, shading through 210 to 211.

Using Special Dentelles 210, work backstitch on the visible outside edges of the curlicue, including a horizontal backstitch across the tip.

Familiarize yourself with needle lace stitch no. 7 (page 206) and then work each curlicue from tip to base. The left-hand side is worked as a mirror image of the right-hand side.

Using Special Dentelles 210, work a single detached buttonhole stitch into the horizontal backstitch at the tip of the shape. This is the equivalent of the first row.

Following the guidelines of the stitch no. 7 pattern, increase as the shape widens.

Decrease the length of the rows as you work towards the bottom, ending off at the base of the shape.

Whip the backstitches on the visible edges of the curlicues and, using a single strand of 154, work outline stitch adjacent to the outside edge of the whipped backstitch on both sides.

With the same thread, outline both sides of the weaving described in step 13 with outline stitch.

15 The three-pointed petals either side are filled with two-tone vermicelli couching using 4170 throughout.

Outline the visible edges of each petal with whipped backstitch using a single strand of 963.

With a single strand of 604, work outline stitch adjacent to the outside of the whipped backstitch.

16 The flowers on the tips of the stems that radiate from the petal on the right are worked as buttonhole stitch flowers.

Referring to the guidelines in the stitch directory (page 173) and working with single strands of thread, use 210 for the flower on the top left. Use 211 for the flower on the right and 209 for the remaining flower at the bottom.

Before completing each flower, stitch a bead 11° 577 into the middle.

Using a single strand of 3051, create the stems with outline stitch.

Work all of the leaves with diagonal satin stitches that face into the vein on both sides.

Using single strands of thread, work the two leaves adjacent to the stems with 3051.

The leaves that radiate from the flowers are worked with a mix of 3051, 3052 and 3053.

17 Moving down the flower, work the petal on the left-hand side.

Using a single strand of 3052, work whipped backstitch on the visible lines of the semi-circles that run down the middle of the inside of the petal.

Using a doubled-over strand of 3688 on a bead embroidery needle, stitch a bead 8° 645, held down with bead 15° 645 into the first semi-circle at the top of the line of beads that go down the middle of the inner petal.

Stitch a covered bead 5° 131 into the next five semi-circles.

Use a single strand of 3688 to cover beads 1, 3 and 5. Use a single strand of 3689 to cover beads 2 and 4.

Finish by working a size 15° 645 into the middle of all the covered beads.

Stitch a bead 8° 645, held down with bead 15° 645 into the remaining semi-circles at the bottom of the petal.

Using a single strand of 4170, fill the remaining space in the inside petal with eye stitch filler, working the eye stitches to accommodate the space available and filling in with French knots where necessary.

18 Moving to the outside of the petal, work the scallop shapes that form the outside edge of the petal.

Working each scallop individually, create the background with vertical satin stitch using a single strand of 3688.

Thereafter, using Special Dentelles 3688, work backstitch around the outside edge of the shape.

Work needle lace stitch no. 7 over the vertical satin stitch.

Start on the right-hand side of the shape, working a single detached buttonhole stitch into the backstitches around the top of the shape. Step down on the left.

Work from left to right, working a group of two detached buttonhole stitches in the loops between the single stitches in the previous row. Step down on the right.

Moving from right to left, work a single detached buttonhole stitch in between two stitches that make up each group in the previous row. Step down on the left.

Continue working the pattern down to the bottom of the shape, increasing the number of stitches in each row by working into the loops at the beginning and the end of each row.

When you reach the bottom of the shape, attach the needle lace by coming up through the fabric, on the line, directly below a loop that you need to go through.

Depending on which row of the pattern you need to do, work a single or a group of two detached buttonhole stitches into that loop.

Go back into the fabric on the line, coming up again below the next loop that needs to be attached.

Before moving onto the next scallop, whip the backstitch that anchors the needle lace.

When you work the backstitch for the tip that is at the bottom of the petal, work a horizontal backstitch across the tip. This is the equivalent of the first row.

Following the guidelines of the stitch no. 7 pattern (page 206), increase as the shape widens.

Work on either side of the split, attaching the lace at the bottom. Whip the backstitch that anchors the needle lace.

19 Fill the space between the scallops and the inner petal with raised stem stitch using 3052 (see page 185).

Work each side separately, making rows shorter or longer as necessary, according to the shape, and gliding them together where they join.

Using a single strand of 3051, work outline stitch adjacent to the raised stem stitch on both sides.

With two strands of the same thread, work French knots at regularly spaced intervals between the outside edge of the raised stem stitch and the base of the needle lace scallops.

20 Following the instructions in step 16, work the small flower branch radiating from the left of the petal. Work the small flower with a single strand of 209. Stitch a bead 11° 577 into the middle of the flower.

21 The middle petal is worked in the same way as the side petal described in steps 17–20. Some of the thread colours used are different and these are set out below.

Use a single strand of 3053 work the whipped backstitch on the visible lines of the semi-circles that run down the middle of the inside of the petal, as described in step 17.

The thread-covered large beads that lie within those semi-circles, are placed from the top downwards. Use 3688 to cover beads 1, 3 and 5, with 3689 being used for beads 2 and 4.

Stitch beads 8° 645, held down with bead 15° 645 into the last three semi-circles at the bottom of the line of beads that go down the middle of the inner petal. Use a doubled-over strand of 3688.

The eye stitch filler that completes the inner petal is worked with the same thread, 4170.

The scallops described in step 18 are worked with lighter shades of thread. Use stranded cotton 3689 to work the satin stitch. Use Special Dentelles 605 to work the needle lace along with the backstitch and whipped backstitch that are part of that technique.

The outline stitch that outlines each scallop is worked with the same thread, 3687.

The raised stem stitch, its outline and the French knots described in step 19 are worked with the same threads.

As described in step 20, work the small branch that radiates from the petal in the same way but use a single strand of 210 to work the buttonhole flower, still stitching a bead 11° 577 into the centre.

22 Moving to the right, the petal is worked in the same way as the side petal described in steps 17–20, using the same threads and beads.

As described in step 20, work the small branch that radiates from the petal in the same way using a single strand of 210 to work the buttonhole flower, still stitching a bead 11° 577 into the centre.

23 The green leaf on the right of the petal is worked with vermicelli couching, whipped backstitch and outline stitch following the instructions set out in step 8. Use the same threads.

Flower, bottom right

Moving down, work on the flower on the bottom right-hand side of the project.

24 Starting with the petals, fill each petal with long and short stitch shading using single strands of thread.

Working from the base, use 3824, shading through 967 to 963 at the tip of each petal.

With a single strand of 4170, work diagonal basic trellis couching (see page 187) over the shading. Work the couching stitch at the intersections with a single strand of 604.

Using two strands of 604, outline each petal with whipped backstitch.

With a single strand of 3687, work a fine outline stitch adjacent to the outside edge of the whipped backstitch.

25 Fill the larger of the two areas in the middle of the flower with needle weaving checks and stripes no. 1 (see page 214) using Special Dentelles thread 368 for colour 1 and ecru for colour 2.

Outline the visible, outside edge of the weaving with whipped backstitch using a single strand of 367.

26 Fill the smaller shape with padded satin stitch using 369.

Work horizontal padding with two strands of thread and the satin stitch with a single strand, placing it perpendicular to the padding.

Outline the outside visible edge with whipped backstitch using a single strand of 367.

27 Moving to the base of the flower, fill the green outside leaves with long and short stitch shading.

Start at the base with 320, shading through 368 to 369 at the tip of each leaf.

With a single strand of 320 and using the photo below to guide you, work basic trellis couching over the bottom, darker half of the leaf.

Outline each leaf with outline stitch using a single strand of 367.

28 Moving inwards, work lines of knotted interlaced chain stitch (see page 176) on the lines of each side petal.

Using two strands of thread throughout, work the reverse chain stitch and small straight stitches on each side with 3824. Work single straight stitches between the lines of reverse chain stitch so that when working the interlacing, you will weave through each of those stitches twice – once for each side.

Use 963 for the interlacing and 604 for the French knots within the loops of the reverse chain stitch.

Using two strands of 604, outline each petal with whipped backstitch.

With a single strand of 3687, work a fine outline stitch adjacent to the outside edge of the whipped backstitch.

29 To complete the flower, work the circle in the centre along with the stem and small flowers.

Fill the circle with vertical long and short stitch using a single strand of 368.

Using Special Dentelles 368, work backstitch around the circle and thereafter, using the same thread, work needle lace stitch no. 7 over the long and short stitch filling.

To complete the circle, whip the backstitch with the same thread.

Thereafter, using a single strand of 367, work intermittent French knots around the circle, adjacent to the outside edge of the whipped backstitch.

30 Moving to the stem, work a line of heavy chain stitch between the lines of the stem using two strands of 320.

Using a single strand of 367, work outline stitch adjacent to each side of the heavy chain stitch.

Following the instructions in step 16, work the small flower branches that come out of the sides of the stem. Using the same green threads as set out, work the small flowers with single strands of 209. Stitch beads 11° 577 into the middle of the flowers.

Leaf, bottom middle

31 Moving to the left of the flower, below the cat's face, work the second large leaf in the project. Follow the instructions in steps 8–12 to stitch the leaf.

Flower, bottom left

32 The two semi-circles that depict the calyx at the bottom of the flower are filled with double weaving using Special Dentelles 3688 for both the warp and weft stitches. Outline each semi-circle with whipped backstitch using the same thread.

Create the stalk below the smaller semi-circle by working a bullion knot on each of the lines of the stalk. Use two strands of 3781.

Further outline each semi-circle with outline stitch worked adjacent to the outside of the whipped backstitch. Use a single strand of 3687.

33 The four petals that come out of the side of the flower on each side are worked in the same way. The instructions below refer to the petals on the right of the flower.

Starting with the purple curlicue in the petal, fill the shape with long and short stitch shading using single strands of thread. Start at the base of the shape with 209, shading through 210 to 211 at the tip.

Using Special Dentelles 210, work backstitch around the shaded area, placing an additional horizontal backstitch across the tip to accommodate the first row of needle lace described below.

With reference to the guidelines for needle lace stitch no. 7 (see page 206), work from the tip of the shape.

When you get to the bottom, and referring to the photo on the facing page, attach the loops with detached buttonhole stitches that come out of and go into the fabric.

Whip the backstitch that anchors the needle lace using the same thread.

Using a single strand of 154, work outline stitch adjacent to the outside edge of the whipped backstitch.

34 Moving to the pink scallop shapes within the petals, fill each one with double weaving.

Working with Special Dentelles thread, use 3688 for colour 1, the weft stitches and 605 for colour 2, the warp stitches.

With a single strand of 3687, outline each scallop with outline stitch.

35 Using a single strand of 4170, fill the empty space within the inner petal with eye stitch filler, adjusting the shape of each eye stitch to accommodate the available space.

In the narrow areas, work French knots. Place some of those knots in bunches and others on their own so that the overall effect is not too symmetrical.

36 Moving to the outside of each petal shape, work the bottom outline with heavy chain stitch using two strands of 320. With a single strand of 367, work outline stitch adjacent to the outside edge of the heavy chain stitch.

To work the top edge, start by working padded satin stitch between the two lines that define this wide border using 369. Work the outline stitch padding horizontally with vertical satin stitch perpendicular to the padding and fanning it slightly as you work around the shape.

Using a strand of Special Dentelles 368, work lines of backstitch adjacent to the top and bottom edges of the satin stitch.

With the same thread and following the guidelines in the needle lace stitch directory (page 205), work needle lace bars over the satin stitch.

When you have completed the line of bars, whip the lines of backstitch at top and bottom.

When you have completed the surrounding embroidery, use a single strand of 367 to work outline stitch adjacent to the outside of the whipped backstitch.

37 Following the instructions in steps 33–36, work the petals on the left side of the flower.

38 The leaf radiating from the flower is filled with vermicelli couching following the instructions in step 8.

39 Moving to the centre of the flower, start by filling the top section with buttonhole flowers.

Start at the top of the shape, working downwards to the point at the base, using single strands of thread. For each tiny flower, start on the perimeter line and work into the centre.

Working with single strands of thread, use 209 for the darkest flowers, 210 for the medium shades and 211 for the lightest flowers.

Stitch a single bead 11° 577 into the centre of each flower.

When you have completed the surrounding embroidery, outline the top of the shape with outline stitch worked adjacent to the purl edges of the top row of buttonhole flowers. Use a single strand of 154.

40 Moving downwards within the centre of the flower to the ovate shapes at the base and following the guidelines in step 34, work double weaving in the scallop shapes, outlining each one and filling the remaining empty space with eye stitch filler.

Work whipped backstitch on the inner outlines of the ovate shapes on both sides.

With two strands of 320, work heavy chain stitch on the continuous double lines that curve around the outside of the ovate shapes.

With a single strand of 367, work intermittent French knots at evenly spaced intervals between the lines of heavy chain stitch.

When you have completed all of the surrounding embroidery and using a single strand of 367, work outline stitch adjacent to the outside of both lines of heavy chain stitch.

41 Moving to the tip of the flower, fill each of the three petals with long and short stitch shading, overworked with basic trellis couching and outlined. Follow the guidelines set out in step 24.

42 Moving inwards, work the green leaves that lie within the two outside petals.

Using single strands of thread, fill each leaf with long and short stitch shading. Start at the base with 320, shading through 368 to 369 at the tip of each leaf.

With a single strand of 320, and using the photo on the facing page to guide you, work basic trellis couching over the bottom, darker half of the leaf, moving up slightly towards the inside edge of each leaf.

Outline the inside edge of each leaf with whipped backstitch using a single strand of 367.

On the outside edge of each leaf is a double line. Work the line closest to the body of the leaf with heavy chain stitch using two strands of 320.

Work the outside line with whipped backstitch, all the way up to the tip, using a single strand of 367.

With the same thread, work intermittent French knots at evenly spaced intervals between the two outlines.

43 Finally, work the whiskers of the cat to complete the project.

Using two strands of ecru stranded cotton in each instance, twist two 2m (2¼yd) lengths of thread (see page 189). As you twist the threads, try to keep a count of how many twists you are doing so that all of the lengths will have a similar look.

Couch the twisted thread into place using a single strand of ecru thread (see page 190).

Work backwards and forwards, travelling between the whiskers at the back of the work where you can but ending off if the space between whiskers is too far apart.

When you stitched the leaf over which the whiskers are placed, you will have covered up many of the lines that depict the whiskers. Use the embroidery chart to guide you in the placement of the twisted couching.

THEN & NOW

A CREWELWORK COMPARISON

The motivation behind this book was to compare traditional crewelwork with modern, updated versions of this ancient art. In this chapter, we explore two designs, an eagle and a blue bird, each stitched two ways to take a look at the fascinating ways in which crewelwork has evolved across the centuries.

The traditional designs, worked in crewel wool, are near replicas of beautiful crewelwork pillows, as seen on page 11.

A world away, without reference to the originals and on another continent, Hazel has interpreted the designs using cotton threads and glass beads on cotton fabric.

By

Hazel Blomkamp
& Phillipa Turnbull

Eagle

Then

Worked with crewel wool on linen twill, this eagle is an example of crewelwork using traditional materials and techniques. The four main stitches typically used in traditional crewelwork are laid and couched work, which covers the areas quickly and with little wool; densely worked long and short stitch; French knots; and crewel stem stitch. The heavy linen twill supports the repeated passage of needle and thread, with the needle often taken through the same holes to create a three-dimensional effect at the edge of a feature.

Now

Worked with cotton thread and glass beads on cotton twill, this eagle is an updated version that uses not only traditional stitches but also modified needlework techniques that add extra interest. The use of brighter cottons updates the colour palette to suit modern décor schemes.

Blue Bird

Then

Worked with crewel wool on linen twill, this blue bird is an example of crewelwork using traditional materials and techniques.

Now

Like the Eagle, the Bluebird has been worked with cotton thread and glass beads on cotton twill, providing an updated version that uses both traditional stitches and modified needlework techniques. Using similar colours, it has been worked to pair with the Eagle so that stitchers could work up a pair of matching designs.

5 Traditional Eagle

The origin of this design is the heraldic eagles that can be found throughout world history. In Europe, the eagle was used as the emblem of the Roman Empire from the time of consul Gaius Marius around 102BC, but it also has religious connections. In the Holy Catholic Church, in early medieval iconography, the eagle emblem represented Saint John the Evangelist.

As a result, the eagle has long been popular in heraldry and on coats of arms, where the head usually faces right. Unusually, this eagle turns to its left, the 'sinister' side, which could be deliberate, or it could be the switch often made when transferring a design in reverse onto the fabric.

Dimensions: 33 x 40.5cm (13 x 16in)

YOU WILL NEED

Chart

Traditional Eagle chart

Fabric

53 x 61cm (21 x 24in) of Jacobean linen twill

Embroidery frame

20cm (8in) or 25cm (10in) embroidery hoop on a floor or seat frame, or a slate frame larger than the width of the linen

Needles

Crewel needles, sizes 46.5 (size 2) and 48.5 (size 1)

Beading needle

Threads

Black cotton thread

Appleton's crewel wool

One skein each of the following:

Reds	Yellows	Blues
202	311	156
221	312	643
223	313	746
224	471	921
714	696	925
753	Greens	Purples
754	244	603
755	253	604
756	293	605
Greys	544	606
962	647	
971		
972		
973		
974		

Two skeins each of the following:

Red	Greens
947	242
	255
	355

Beads

4mm (⅛in) black glass bead

Stitch abbreviations (see chart)

C	Coral stitch
CF	Closed fly stitch
CS	Crewel stem stitch
FK	French knots
L	Leaf stitch
L&C	Laid and couched work
L&S	Long and short as 'soft shading'
P	Pistil stitch
S	Satin stitch
WSW	Woven spider's web

Wherever you see (D) on the stitch chart, use double thread, otherwise use single thread.

Stitching instructions

Large pink flower, top left

Begin in the top left-hand corner of the design. Note carefully where the stitch chart indicates using single, double, or double then single thread.

1 Begin with laid and couched work on the leaves behind the flower in the top left-hand corner of the design.

   Use the flower petal or the outline of the leaves to secure each end of your threads, or, for a single thread, use a waste knot, as described on page 14.

   Create the inner area of each leaf using a base layer of laid and couched work (use variation 2, see page 155).

2 Add French knots in double thread on the top left-hand leaf's laid and couched work. Secure each end of your double threads with the looped method, as described on page 14. Add a French knot in the centre of each square of one leaf, then complete the second leaf as shown on the stitch chart.

3 Add crewel stem stitch in a single thread around the perimeter of both leaves, then, starting with the upper line, work lines of crewel stem stitch down the stem of the pink flower.

Now use laid and couched work (variation 2 with French knots added, see pages 155 and 153) and crewel stem stitch on the third pointed leaf in this area.

4 Working all the colours of each petal in turn, stitch the upper left petals, then the petals in the background, in long and short stitch.

5 Pistil stitch over these upper petals, then complete the lower petals in long and short stitch, and again, complete all the colours on each petal in turn.

6 Beginning at the upper half circle, work rows of French knots in double thread.

7 Using the same order and long and short stitch, embroider the petals then the stem of the smaller pink flower at the top of the design.

8 Complete this flowerhead by adding closed fly stitch in double thread for the sepals. Tension your wool thread gently so that the leaf sits on top of the previously worked petals.

9 Now stitch the three oak leaves in long and short stitch (see page 164). The oak leaf below the first flower you stitched is worked in two layers of colour, the remaining two oak leaves are worked in three colours.

10 Complete each oak leaf by adding crewel stem stitch veins, then continue to complete each area of crewel stem stitch in this corner until you reach the bird's wing.

11 Next add the final detail in this area and make the coiling tendrils in coral stitch in double thread. This gorgeous stitch adds texture and interest.

A coral stitch tendril.

Left: a coral stitch tendril winding around the stem.

12 Now move to the top right corner of the design and stitch the green vine leaf in long and short stitch using three colours (see page 161) and adapting the vine leaf shape in the stitch directory (see page 165).

13 Complete the leaf with two rows of stem-stitched veins, and then the right side of the wider stem below.

14 Work in coral stitch on the tendril winding around the stem.

15 Add French knots in double thread to create the grapes. Begin on the perimeter and work in ever-decreasing circles until each grape is full.

16 Use laid and couched work on the three leaves in this area. Begin with a basic grid of lines, and add couching before decorating with added French knots where shown on the chart.

17 Next add crewel stem stitch around the perimeter of these three leaves, to the stems and branches, and all the way to the bird's wing.

18 Move to the lower left-hand area and create the purple seed pod in laid work couched, using pistil stitch in single thread as your couching thread. As before, add crewel stem stitch on the stem, then complete the outer area of this seed pod with long and short stitch.

19 Stitch the smaller leaf in this area with long and short stitch.

20 Now create the larger leaf in laid and couch work with trellis stitch (use variation 4, see page 157).

21 Complete all the crewel stem stitch in this area, all the way to the main branch.

22 Next use whipped spider's web for the centre of the small pink flower. Stitch the flower centre first, before the surrounding petals, so that your needle does not become entangled while whipping through the spokes of the spider's web. Leave the edges of the spokes unwhipped.

23 Long and short stitch the petals on this small pink flower. Begin with the top left-hand flower that is slightly behind the other petals, then work the petal over the stem and the petal on the right-hand side, before stitching the remaining foreground petals. Surround the whipped spider's web with French knots.

Above: laid work with pistil stitch couching on the top leaf, and a form of laid and couched work often referred to as 'trellis couching' on the lower leaf.

Main branch

24 Create the main branch behind the tail feathers. Starting at the lowest edge, make lines of crewel stem stitch in double thread.

Wing, left-hand side

25 Begin at the outer tip of the lowest feather on the left-hand wing. Use leaf stitch in single thread along this lowest feather, then stitch each of the seven feathers in turn, slightly overlapping the feathers where one crosses over the edge of its predecessor.

26 Repeat this order from the lowest to the highest up the next row of feathers, the pink row, again in leaf stitch.

27 Complete this wing using heavily worked long and short stitch, firstly in densely worked double thread, overlapping the top of the pink feathers just completed, then secondly, in sparsely worked long and half-length long and short single thread stitches, creating a raised edge to this wing.

Tail feathers

28 Now move to the end of the tail. Use long and short stitch in single thread for the three forked feathers. Take care when making the first layer of stitches at the tip of each shape, then angle the next layer of stitches so that a very small alteration of angle occurs with each layer of colour. Use two layers of the same colour if the angle appears too steep or if your stitches look too long in the curved areas.

29 The next four layers of tail feathers are worked in the same way: firstly, satin stitch the curved bands of pale grey at the lower end of each of these tail feathers. Stitch densely, especially when stitching down into the top of the end of tail areas, and remember to keep your needle at a right angle to the surface of the linen. Continue in a single thread, with two layers of long and short densely stitched at the lower end and the sides of each feather. Use the images to check on the angle of these stitches or alternatively, before you begin, draw on your fabric in sharp HB pencil as a guide.

Claws

30 Starting with the background toes, create the claws and then the legs in densely stitched satin stitches in a double thread. Add extra stitches until the legs look raised above the linen.

31 Add the toes in satin stitch in a single thread with all stitches going down into the same hole at the end of each claw.

32 Continue by stitching up the belly, the back and the neck. Always begin with the outer area of each feather.

33 Stitch the remaining wing using the same methods as the first.

Head

34 The head decoration is stitched in leaf stitch with a single thread.

35 Sew the beak in satin stitch. Take care to keep the edges tidy, and the beak pointed!

36 Now create the eye with a satin-stitched disc of navy blue, followed by the glass bead. Take care to angle the bead to create the expression you desire before stitching it firmly in place using black cotton.

Leaves, lower right-hand side

37 Lastly, create the two remaining leaves in long and short and crewel stem stitches as before.

6 CONTEMPORARY EAGLE

Using the identical outline of the Traditional Eagle project (pages 88–99), this Contemporary Eagle has been worked with stranded and perle cottons instead of crewel wool. It incorporates bead embroidery along with stitches and techniques not usually associated with crewelwork. These include needle lace techniques and loom weaving patterns modified for use as embroidery stitches.

Dimensions: 31 x 25cm (12¼ x 9¾in)

YOU WILL NEED

Chart

Contemporary Eagle chart

Fabric

45 x 45cm (18 x 18in) seeded cotton canvas (200gsm) in off-white, with a thread count of approximately 32 threads per inch

45 x 45cm (18 x 18in) cotton voile backing fabric in off-white

45 x 45cm (18 x 18in) 100gsm polyester wadding (batting), optional

Embroidery frame

One pair each of 35cm (14in) and 30cm (12in) Edmunds stretcher bars

Needles

Embroidery needles, sizes 8 and 10

Betweens quilting needle, size 10

Sharps quilting needle, size 11

Tapestry needle, size 26

Threads

DMC stranded cotton

One skein each of the following:

150 Ultra very dark dusty rose
154 Very dark grape
561 Very dark jade
563 Light jade
564 Very light jade
610 Dark drab brown
611 Drab brown
612 Light drab brown
613 Very light drab brown
676 Light old gold
677 Very light old gold
796 Dark royal blue
797 Royal blue
798 Dark Delft blue
799 Medium Delft blue
961 Dark dusty rose
962 Medium dusty rose
3716 Medium light dusty rose
3781 Dark mocha brown
3834 Dark grape
3835 Medium grape
3836 Light grape
3850 Dark bright green
3865 Winter white

Presencia Finca perle cotton size #12

5g (¼oz) of each of the following:

3301 Baby blue
3312 Medium baby blue
3319 Dark baby blue
3405 Royal blue

Presencia Finca perle cotton size #16

5g (¼oz) of each of the following:

3000 Ecru
4350 Emerald green
4379 Light Nile green
8060 Very light brown

Beads

Miyuki beads

2g of 15°, 17F matte silver lined, blue-green

2g of 15°, 4248 Duracoat silver lined, dark lilac

2g of 15° 4266 Duracoat silver lined, hibiscus

One bead of 15°, 458 metallic brown, iris

One bead of 8°, 2035 matte metallic, khaki iris

Stitching instructions

Use the chart for the Contemporary Eagle in conjunction with these stitching instructions. The numbers on the chart refer to the numbered instructions below.

Main branch

1 The main body of the branch is filled with rows of chain stitch using two strands of thread.

Using 610, work a line of chain stitch up the outside line of the branch, returning down the outside line on the other side. Working towards the centre and using the same thread, work an additional two rows of chain stitch on each side.

Fill the remaining space in the middle of the branch, working rows of chain stitch backwards and forwards using 611. You will probably work three rows in the lighter colour to fill the space.

Work outline stitch adjacent to the outside edges of the chain stitch on both sides using a single strand of 3781.

2 Fill the small area that forms the base of the branch with freestyle flower embroidery (see page 197).

When you have completed the freestyle flower embroidery, work whipped backstitch on the outline of the circular shape using two strands of 3781.

3 Moving to the leaves below the branch, start with the leaf on the left.

Using perle #16 8060, work backstitch on the outline of the leaf including a horizontal backstitch across the tip.

Familiarize yourself with needle lace stitch no. 10 (page 209) and then work the leaf with reference to the picture on the left.

As the shape widens, increase the number of stitches at the beginning and ends of rows.

A little way into the second or third set of triangles you will encounter the vein of the leaf.

Allow a gap for the vein; without losing the pattern sequence, go into the fabric on one side of the vein, coming up on the other side. Then continue working the pattern to the end of the row.

Work each row thereafter, leaving the necessary space in the middle for the vein and making sure that you don't lose the pattern sequence.

Around halfway down, the shape will narrow, and you decrease by leaving out detached buttonhole stitches at the beginning and ends of rows.

Step 3 continued overleaf

Reduce the number of stitches as you work down, attaching the bottom of each row, as you need to, by working detached buttonhole stitches that come out from under the backstitch. Go through the loop you need to, and go back into the fabric tucking the needle under the backstitch.

When you have completed the needle lace filler and using the same perle #16 thread, number 8060, whip the backstitches on both sides of the leaf.

With a single strand of 610, work outline stitch adjacent to the outside edge of the whipped backstitch, on both sides.

Fill the vein with rows of chain stitch using two strands of 611. Work up the one side, return to the bottom of the vein and work up the other side, finishing that row when you meet up with the first row.

With a single strand of 3781, work outline stitch adjacent to the outside edge of the vein on both sides.

4 The green leaf is filled with diagonal long and short stitch shading using single strands of cotton.

Use 563 closest to the vein, shading out to 564 on the edge of the leaf.

With a single strand of thread 561, work basic trellis couching (see page 187) over the shading.

With the same thread, work outline stitch around the perimeter of the leaf.

Fill the vein with chain stitch, outlined with outline stitch following the directions in step 3 above.

5 Complete the rest of the main branch following the instructions in step 1.

There will be less space to fill on this side of the branch, and when you are working on the area on the left of the claws and between the wing feathers, you are unlikely to work any of the lighter rows.

Tail feathers

6 Moving to the bird and working from the bottom, start with the blue tail feathers.

Using two strands of 798 and beads 15° 17F, work beaded wheatear stitch from the tip of each feather to the base. Attach the beads with 3850.

With a single strand of 797, outline each side of each feather with whipped backstitch.

With a single strand of 3850, work single wrap French knots adjacent to the outside of the whipped backstitch at the tip of each spoke of the wheatear stitch.

7 Moving up the tail of the bird, fill each of the paddle-shaped feathers in the same way.

The main area of each feather is filled with needle weaving texture no. 5 (see page 213). Work the warp stitches over the shortest side, using perle #16 3000. Work the weft stitches with perle #16 4379.

The wider part of the border around each feather is filled with padded satin stitch. Using two strands of 3835, pad the shape with horizontal outline stitch padding following the shape of the curve. Use a single strand of 3835 to work vertical satin stitch perpendicular to and over the padding.

Using two strands of 3835, outline the woven area with whipped backstitch. Start at the base of each paddle-shaped feather, working the line below the padded satin stitch as you work around to the other side, finishing when you meet up with the feather below it.

With a single strand of 154, work outline stitch adjacent to the outside of the whipped backstitch, working between the outline and the padded satin stitch as you work around to the other side.

With the same thread, work outline stitch around the outer edge of the padded satin stitch, joining up with the outline of the whipped backstitch on each end.

With a doubled-over strand of 154 and beads 15° 4248, work a line of beaded backstitch on the vein of each feather. Having covered the line with needle weaving, use the chart to guide you.

8 Following the guidelines for beaded fly stitch on page 201, work the small pink feathers on the left of the tail.

Use two strands of 962 and beads 15° 4266.

Using a single strand of 150, work single-wrap French knots at the tip, and thereafter on the perimeter line on both sides between the legs of the fly stitch.

Wings

9 Fill the small feathers marked 9D (dark) and 9L (light) on the chart, with needle weaving texture no. 5 (see page 213).

Working over the shortest side, work the warp stitches with perle # 16 3000.

Thereafter work the weft stitches with perle #16 4379 for the top, lighter row, and 4350 for the bottom, darker row.

Outline each feather with whipped backstitch using two strands of 3835.

Work outline stitch adjacent to the outside of the whipped backstitch using a single strand of 154.

With a doubled-over strand of 154 and beads 15° 4248, work a line of beaded backstitch on the vein of each feather. Having covered the line with needle weaving, use the chart to guide you.

10 The feathers further down the wing are filled with interlaced and beaded chain stitch (see page 204).

Using two strands of thread, work the reverse chain and side straight stitches with 962 and the interlacing on both sides with 3716.

With a doubled-over single strand of 961, stitch a bead 15° 4266 into the middle of each reverse chain stitch loop.

Outline each feather with whipped backstitch using two strands of 961 and, with a single strand of 150, work outline stitch adjacent to the outside of the whipped backstitch.

Following the instructions here and in step 9, and using the picture above to guide the colour choice of the small woven feathers, work the left wing in the same way.

Body

11 Fill each segment of the body with double weaving.

Work the warp stitches of each segment vertically from base to tip. The weft stitches are worked horizontally at right angles to the warp stitches.

As marked on the chart, work the dark segments using perle #12 3405 for the warp and 3319 for the weft.

Use perle #12 3319 for the warp stitches and 3312 for the weft stitches when working the medium-shade segments.

Use perle #12 3312 for the warp stitches and 3301 for the weft stitches when working the lightest segments.

Outline each segment with split backstitch using two strands of 796, only outlining those adjacent to the wings when you have filled the top part of the wings described in step 12.

12 Go back and complete the wings, before moving on to the head. Fill the top segment of each wing with freestyle flower embroidery (see page 197).

Outline the visible edge of each segment with whipped backstitch using perle #16 4350.

With a single strand of 561, work outline stitch adjacent to the outside of the whipped backstitch.

Head

13 Moving up to the bird's head, fill each section of the beak with long and short stitch shading.

Use a single strand of 612 for the top half of the beak and 611 for the bottom section.

With a single strand of 611, work basic trellis couching over the shading of the top half.

Outline each section of the beak with outline stitch using a single strand of 610.

14 Moving to the back of the head, work the plumage feathers following the directions set out in step 8.

Working with two strands of thread, use 961 for the fly stitch of the top feather, 962 for the middle feather and 3716 for the bottom feather.

Use beads 15° 4266 for all the feathers and work all the French knots with a single strand of 150.

15 Other than the eye, fill the head with two-tone vermicelli couching (see page 192).

Work the first series of swirls with two strands of 564 couched down with a single strand of the same thread.

Work the second series with a single strand of 3850 couched down with a single strand of the same thread.

With a single strand of 610, work whipped backstitch on the circle that defines the eye.

With a doubled-over strand of the same thread, attach a bead 8° 2035 with a bead 15° 458 in the centre of the eye, following the guidelines for attaching a bead with a bead (see page 199).

Outline the top and bottom of the head with whipped backstitch using two strands of 3850.

With a single strand each of 564 and 561 threaded on the same needle, work loose French knots at the back of the head. Allow the loose knots to encroach on the head on the right of the plumage feathers and the top segments of the body.

Legs and feet

16 The legs and feet of the bird are worked with split backstitch.

Starting on the outside edge of the leg where it abuts the bird's body using two strands of 612, work a continuous line all the way around the leg and the three parts of the feet, finishing up on the other side of the outside line where the leg joins the body again.

Work a second line of split backstitch using the same thread.

Using 613, fill in the centre of the leg and foot with lines and part lines of split backstitch.

Using a single strand of 3781, outline the legs and feet with outline stitch.

Each claw if made up of two bullion knots that start in the same hole and finish in the same hole. Use a single strand of 612.

Leaves and stem (top right-hand side)

17 Starting with the group of three leaves, the top leaf and its stem are worked following the instructions set out in step 3, using the same threads.

18 The leaf and stem below that are worked following the instructions set out in step 4.

Instead of the green, use single strands of 612 and 613 for the long and short stitch shading, with 611 being used for the trellis couching and outline of the leaf.

19 The bottom leaf and its stem are worked following the instructions set out in step 3.

Instead of the golden colour, use perle #16 4379 for the needle lace stitching and a single strand of 561 for the outline stitch around the perimeter of the leaf.

20 Fill the trefoil-shaped leaf at the top of the stem with needle weaving texture no. 2 (see page 211).

Work vertical warp stitches with perle #16 4350, leaving gaps where the vein goes up the middle of the leaf.

Work the horizontal weft stitches with perle #16 3000, taking the vein of the leaf into account and leaving the space necessary.

Outline the outside edge of the leaf with whipped backstitch using perle #16 4350.

With a single strand of 561, work outline stitch adjacent to the outside of the whipped backstitch.

Fill the vein with rows of chain stitch using two strands of 611.

With a single strand of 3781, work outline stitch on both sides of the vein.

21 Fill each circle of the bunch of grapes with Rhodes stitch (see page 185), using two strands of 3836.

Using single strands of thread, work three chain stitch circles around the filled circle.

Starting adjacent to the filled circle, work a circle with 3834. Thereafter, work a circle with 3835 followed by a third circle worked with 3836.

Using a single strand of 154, work outline stitch adjacent to each outside chain stitch circle.

22 Fill the main branch that curves in towards the grapes with rows of chain stitch using two strands of 611.

With a single strand of 3781, work outline stitch adjacent to the outside edge of the branch on both sides.

Using two strands of 3835, work the tendril that curves around the branch with Portuguese knotted stem stitch.

With a single strand of 154, work outline stitch on the inside of the curve, adjacent to the tendril.

Leaves and stem (top centre)

23 Start by working the vein that goes into the leaf with chain stitch, following the instructions for the vein in the leaf described in step 20, using the same threads.

24 Work the tendril with Portuguese knotted stem stitch following the directions set out for the tendril in step 22, using 3836 and working the additional outline stitch with a single strand of 154.

25 Outline the oak leaf with whipped backstitch using perle #16 4350.

Using a single strand of 561, work outline stitch adjacent to the outside of the whipped backstitch. Fill the oak leaf with freestyle flower embroidery (see pages 197–198).

26 Moving further left, fill the oak leaf and its stem following the instructions in steps 23 and 25.

27 Moving upwards, work the stem of the pink flower following the instructions in step 20.

28 Fill the petals of the pink flower with woven trellis couching following the guidelines on page 188.

Starting with the petal at the back and working with two strands throughout, use 961 for shade no. 1, 150 for shade no. 2 and 962 for shades 3 and 4.

Outline the petal with whipped backstitch using two strands of 961. With a single strand of 150, work outline stitch adjacent to the outside edge of the whipped backstitch.

Moving to the front petal of the flower and working with two strands throughout, use 962 for shade no. 1, 961 for shade no. 2 and 3716 for shades 3 and 4.

Outline the petal with whipped backstitch using two strands of 961. With a single strand of 150, work outline stitch adjacent to the outside edge of the whipped backstitch.

29 Fill each of the calyx leaves with long and short stitch shading.

Working with single strands of thread, start at the base of the leaf with 563, shading to 564 at the tip of each leaf.

With a single strand of 561, work basic trellis couching over the shading and, with the same thread, work outline stitch around each leaf.

Flowers, leaves and stem (top left-hand side)

30 Start by working the main flower in this section.

Fill each of the three purple petals with long and short stitch shading using single strands of thread, using 3834 and shading through 3835 to 3836 at the tip. Outline each petal with outline stitch using a single strand of 154.

Fill the semi-circle that forms the centre of the flower with striped up and down buttonhole stitch.

Use 3836 for the up and down buttonhole stitch and 3835 for the straight stitch that makes the stripe.

31 Moving down the flower to the leaves of the calyx, each one is filled with needle weaving texture no. 2.

Starting with the outside leaves on each side of the flower, work vertical warp stitches with perle #16 4350.

Work the horizontal weft stitches with perle #16 3000.

Work the inside leaves in the same way using perle #16 4379 for the vertical warp stitches and perle #16 3000 for the horizontal weft stitches.

Outline the visible outside edge of each leaf with whipped backstitch using perle #16 4350.

With a single strand of 561, work outline stitch adjacent to the outside of the whipped backstitch.

32 The green leaf that comes out of the top of the flower is filled with needle lace stitch no. 8 (see page 207).

Using perle #16 4379, work backstitch on the visible outlines of the leaf. Work a horizontal backstitch across the tip.

Familiarize yourself with needle lace stitch no. 8 and work the stitch to fill the leaf. As the shape widens, increase the number of stitches at the beginning and ends of rows.

When you reach the base of the leaf, shorten the rows as you work down, attaching the loops of the detached buttonhole stitches where it is appropriate to do so, eventually finishing off by attaching the last single loop at the bottom.

Using the same thread, whip the backstitch that forms the visible edges of the leaf.

With a single strand of 561, work outline stitch adjacent to the outside edge of the whipped backstitch.

33 Fill the leaf to the left with diagonal long and short stitch using single strands of thread.

Start with 611 on the right, shading through 612 to 613 on the left edge.

Using a single strand of 610, work basic trellis couching over the shading, and outline the visible edges of the leaf with outline stitch with the same thread.

34 Moving below the flower, work the leaf that comes out of the right of the branch.

Using perle #16 8060, follow the directions in step 32 to fill the leaf. When you reach the base of the leaf, shorten the rows as you work down, attaching the loops of the detached buttonhole stitches where it is appropriate to do so, eventually finishing off by attaching the last single loop at the bottom.

Using the same thread, whip the backstitch that forms the visible edges of the leaf.

With a single strand of 610, work outline stitch adjacent to the outside edge of the whipped backstitch.

35 Using two strands of 610, work the branch with rows of chain stitch, as you have done throughout this project. Outline each side of the branch with outline stitch using a single strand of 3781.

36 Moving to the left of the branch, fill the oak leaf and the stem with its tendril following the instructions in steps 23–25.

Flower, leaves and stem (bottom left-hand side)

37 Moving down the left of the design, fill the centre of the brown leaf.

Using perle #16 8060, work backstitch on the outline of the centre of the leaf and thereafter work needle lace stitch no. 10 (see page 209).

When you reach the base of the leaf, shorten the rows as you work down, attaching the loops of the detached buttonhole stitches where it is appropriate to do so, eventually finishing off by attaching the last single loop at the bottom.

Using the same thread, whip the backstitch that forms the visible edges of the leaf.

When you have worked the shading in the outer edge of the leaf, work outline stitch adjacent to the whipped backstitch using a single strand of 610.

38 Fill the outer edge of the leaf with long and short stitch shading overlaid with basic trellis couching and outlined with outline stitch.

Using single strands throughout, work the shading from the inside, using 611 and shading through 612 to 613 at the edge.

Using a single strand of 610, work basic trellis couching (page 187) over the shading and work outline stitch on the outside edge of the leaf with the same thread.

39 Using two strands of 610, work the branch with rows of chain stitch, as you have done throughout this project. Outline each side of the branch with outline stitch using a single strand of 3781.

40 Following the directions set out in step 4, fill the green leaf with diagonal long and short stitch shading overlaid with basic trellis couching and outlined with outline stitch. Work the vein and branch with outlined rows of chain stitch.

41 Moving down to the bottom left of the design, fill the main body of the leaf and its stem, which widens into the branch that attaches to the main branch, following the instructions in steps 23 and 25 above.

42 The tip of the leaf is filled with needle weaving texture no. 2 (see page 211).

Work vertical warp stitches, down the length of the space, with perle #16 4350.

Work the horizontal weft stitches with perle #16 3000.

Outline the needle weaving with whipped backstitch using perle #16 4350.

With a single strand of 561, work outline stitch adjacent to the outside of the whipped backstitch.

43 Fill the centre of the flower with Rhodes stitch using two strands of 3836.

Fill each of the purple petals with long and short stitch shading using single strands of thread.

Start at the base of each petal with 3834, shading through 3835 to 3836 at the tip.

When you have completed the branch, outline each petal with outline stitch using a single strand of 154.

With a single strand of 3834, work a chain stitch circle, stitching in the ditch between the Rhodes stitch centre and the petals. Outline the outside edge of the circle with outline stitch using a single strand of 154.

44 Using two strands of 610, work the branch with rows of chain stitch, as you have done throughout this project. Work each side of the branch with outline stitch using a single strand of 3781.

Finishing

This design, along with the Contemporary Blue Bird on page 124, have been made into a pair of small pillows. To provide extra weight, both projects were backed with lightweight wadding (batting) and an additional layer of cotton voile (see page 138). When your embroidery is complete, remove it from the frame, place the wadding and an extra piece of cotton voile behind the embroidery. Place the pieces together over the embroidery frame, making sure that you have no creases in any of the fabrics and that it is tightly stretched. Work quilting stitches through all the layers of fabric.

7 TRADITIONAL BLUE BIRD

This version of the Blue Bird design is a near replica of a beautiful crewelwork pillow which I acquired many years ago from the daughter of the original embroiderer. This English farmer's wife developed her skills throughout World War II, starting her collection with beautiful fabrics and chosen colours and, towards the end of her life, creating this pair of very beautiful birds (the Eagle from page 100 and the Blue Bird) onto evenweave linen pillow cases from her linen cupboard after she ran out of linen twill material.

Follow the stitch chart, relax and enjoy!

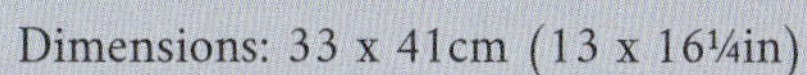

Dimensions: 33 x 41cm (13 x 16¼in)

YOU WILL NEED

Chart

Traditional Blue Bird chart

Fabric

53 x 61cm (21 x 24in) of Jacobean linen twill

Embroidery frame

20cm (8in) or 25cm (10in) hands-free embroidery hoop, on a floor or seat frame, or a slate frame wider than the width of the linen

Needles

Crewel needles, sizes 46.5 (size 2) and 48.5 (size 1)

Beading needle

Stitch abbreviations (see chart)

B	Buttonhole stitch
C	Coral stitch
CF	Closed fly stitch
CS	Crewel stem stitch
FK	French knots
L	Leaf stitch
L&C	Variations of laid and couched work
L&S	Long and short as 'soft shading'
P	Pistil stitch
S	Satin stitch
Sp	Split stitch
WS	Whipped stem stitch
WSW	Whipped spider's web

Wherever you see (D) on the stitch chart, use double thread, otherwise use single thread

Threads

Black cotton thread

Appleton's crewel wool

One skein each of the following:

Reds	Yellows	Blues
221	311	153
222	312	155
223	313	156
224	331	324
714	352	463
753	472	746
754	693	921
755	696	922
756		924
Greys	**Greens**	**Purples**
962	241	603
971	243	604
972	244	605
973	253	606
	293	
	295	
	544	
	647	

Two skeins each of the following:

Reds	Greens	Blues
947	242	324
	255	925
	355	

Beads

4mm (⅛in) black glass bead

Stitching instructions

Begin in the top left corner of the design.

Leaves (top left-hand corner)

1 Begin your design with a single thread, using the simplest version of laid and couched work (see page 154). Next change to a double thread and add decorative French knots in the centre of each square. (Leave the crewel stem outline of this and the next leaf until later.)

2 For the next-door leaf, use trellis stitch in a single thread, making layers of graduated colour with each layer of laid work. The use of the darkest thread as the base colour enhances the beautiful 3D effect of this stitch. Add your couch stitches to the last layer using very little tension on each stitch. This couch stitch in the version of laid and couched work is most easily made as a back stitch, coming up in the square area at the edge of your laid stitches, and then going down between the last laid stitch and its predecessor.

Rose stem and leaf outlines

3 Now, starting at the base of the small pink flower, also at the top left of the design, in single thread, use crewel stem stitch down the outer line of the stem. Work each colour in turn and add extra lines if the drawn design is showing.

Flower 1

4 Use whipped spider's web to create the centre of the same pink flower. The centre is worked first on this occasion, so that your needle does not become entangled while whipping your needle through the web stitches.

Using a double thread for the first colour, and a single thread for the remaining colour, create the petals in long and short stitch. Begin with the lowest left petal as this is slightly behind the other petals. Complete this petal in both colours, then work all the petals in turn, slightly covering the edge of the other petals and, in the lower corner, the top of the rose stem. This should create a 3D effect.

Leaves

5 Stitch the laid and couched work leaves above the bird, outline in crewel stem stitch and similarly, add the stem for the next pink flower.

6 Now stitch the small green leaf above the bird in long and short stitch, again using first a double and secondly a single thread. Try to vary the length of your stitches to prevent a striped effect.

7 Then, stitch the nearby leaf above the branch on the left side of the bird, then followed by the remaining two leaves below the left side of the branch behind the bird, both in long and short stitch. (Depending on where your design is positioned in your frame, you might choose to stitch these two leaves later.)

Flower 2 – largest pink flower

8 Stitch the upper petals in two shades as before in long and short stitch, then work pistil stitch using a single thread over these upper petals, then stitch all of the lower petals, completing all three colours on each petal in turn. Finally, add the rows of French knots, in a double thread, beginning with the upper layer of knots. Complete all other features in this area.

Main branch

9 Beginning in the top left corner of the sawn left-hand 'stump' at the left side of the branch, use layers of split stitch in a double thread to create the main branch, taking your stitches behind the feathers, leaf and bird. Follow the curved lines to create an interesting, rounded effect.

10 Create the stump in crewel stem, in a double thread, worked from the perimeter, and continue in an ever-decreasing spiral of crewel stem stitch.

Blue bird tail feathers and back

11 Now create all the blue and grey tail feathers in single thread. Begin with the far-left feather in leaf stitch and, leaving the largest tail feather until last, work the lower seven feathers to the right in turn, then stitch the largest tail feather in long and short stitch. Change back to leaf stitch for the remaining feathers, working each in turn towards the body of the bird. When you have completed the grey tail feathers, leave the near wing until later and create the far side wing, again in leaf stitch. Then, beginning at the rear of the bird, stitch long and short over the back until you reach the neck ruff.

Blue bird legs

12 Beginning with the feet, work the legs in satin stich in double thread. Repeat satin stitching in a double thread over and over the legs and feet until they are raised and rounded and formed in a 3D shape.

Blue bird wings and body

13 Beginning just under his wing at his rear end, in a single thread, make the first scalloped shape (*a* on chart), creating the thigh and then his belly in buttonhole stitch.

14 Starting at the upper left wingtip, stitch the nearside wing, as before. When you have worked the three rows of leaf stitch, use long and short stitch on the remaining blue neck area. Change stitch direction for each first layer of colour, coming up at the head end and going down over the preceding layer of stitches, so that his ruff has a ruffled appearance! Begin each ruff with a row of stitches that begins in the lower edge of the area and goes down on top of the neck stitches already worked. Continue with long and short stitch over the whole of the grey area, then work irregularly worked satin stitch to create a solid feathered cap of darker blue over the top of his head.

Blue bird beak

15 Add the beak in delicately worked satin stitch in a single thread.

Vine stems

16 Starting at the outer ends, use coral stitch in double thread on the two coiled vine stems and the third below the branch when it is comfortable to do so.

17 Create the interesting laid and couched variation on the leaf below the bird. Note that the second layer of laid work takes the thread over two bars and under one, and is later decorated with French knots on every alternate square.

18 Next, complete the two leaves and the stems below the grapes. Note that one stem has added whipped stem stitch to complement the texture of the grapes.

19 Create each grape with French knots in a double thread, beginning each one with the outer perimeter and ever-decreasing circles until each grape is solidly filled.

Flowers, leaves and stem (top right-hand corner)

20 Now move to the top right corner of the design and use Bayeux stitch and long and short stitch on the small green leaf, then closed fly stitch in double thread on the rosebud sepals. Complete the seed pod in a laid and couched variation and long and short stitch. The largest leaf is worked in another laid and couched variation.

21 The remaining two leaves, stems and flower follow the same rules as before, working the background features before the foreground, and outer before the inner on any parts which feature long and short, crewel stem, and French knot stitches.

22 Now complete all remaining features, referring to the stitch chart and the images here.

8 CONTEMPORARY BLUE BIRD

Like the Eagle, this Blue Bird has been worked from the same drawing as the Traditional Blue Bird (see pages 114–123). This project uses similar threads, colours and stitches to the Contemporary Eagle (see pages 100–113) so that they can be displayed side by side, should stitchers wish to make both. It is worked with stranded and perle cottons rather than crewel wool. The design incorporates bead embroidery, along with stitches and techniques not traditionally associated with crewelwork. These include needle lace techniques and loom weaving patterns modified for use as embroidery stitches.

Dimensions: 31 x 25cm (12¼ x 9¾in)

YOU WILL NEED

Chart

Contemporary Blue Bird chart

Fabric

45 x 45cm (18 x 18in) seeded cotton canvas, in off-white

45 x 45cm (18 x 18in) cotton voile backing fabric, in off-white

45 x 45cm (18 x 18in) 100gsm polyester wadding (batting), optional

Embroidery frame

Two pairs of 35cm (14in) Edmunds stretcher bars

Needles

Embroidery needles, sizes 8 and 10

Betweens quilting needle, size 10

Sharps quilting needle, size 11

Tapestry needle, size 26

Threads

DMC stranded cotton

One skein each of the following:

150	Ultra very dark dusty rose
154	Very dark grape
561	Very dark jade
563	Light jade
564	Very light jade
610	Dark drab brown
611	Drab brown
612	Light drab brown
613	Very light drab brown
676	Light old gold
677	Very light old gold
796	Dark royal blue
798	Dark Delft blue
799	Medium Delft blue
809	Delft blue
961	Dark dusty rose
962	Medium dusty rose
3716	Medium light dusty rose
3781	Dark mocha brown
3834	Dark grape
3835	Medium grape
3836	Light grape
3850	Dark bright green
3865	Winter white

Presencia Finca perle cotton size #16

5g (¼oz) of each of the following:

3000	Ecru
4350	Emerald green
4379	Light Nile green
8060	Very light brown

Beads

Miyuki beads

2g of 15°, 19F matte silver lined, sapphire

2g of 15°, 4248 Duracoat silver lined, dark lilac

2g of 15°, 4266 Duracoat silver lined, hibiscus

2g of 15°, 458 metallic brown, iris

Stitching instructions

Use the chart for the Contemporary Blue Bird in conjunction with these stitching instructions. The numbers on the chart refer to the numbered instructions below.

Main branch

1 The main body of the branch is filled with rows of chain stitch using two strands of thread.

Using 610, work a line of chain stitch up the outside line of the branch, returning down the outside line on the other side. Working towards the centre and using the same thread, work an additional two rows of chain stitch on each side.

Fill in the remaining space in the middle of the branch, working rows of chain stitch backwards and forwards using 611. You will probably work three rows in the lighter colour.

Work outline stitch adjacent to the outside edges of the chain stitch on both sides using a single strand of 3781.

2 Fill the small area that forms the base of the branch with freestyle flower embroidery referring to the guidelines in the embroidery stitch directory.

When you have completed the freestyle flower embroidery, work whipped backstitch on the outline of the oval shape using two strands of 3781.

3 Complete the rest of the main branch following the instructions in step 1.

As the branch narrows on the right-hand side of the head, there will be less space to fill, and you may not work any of the lighter rows.

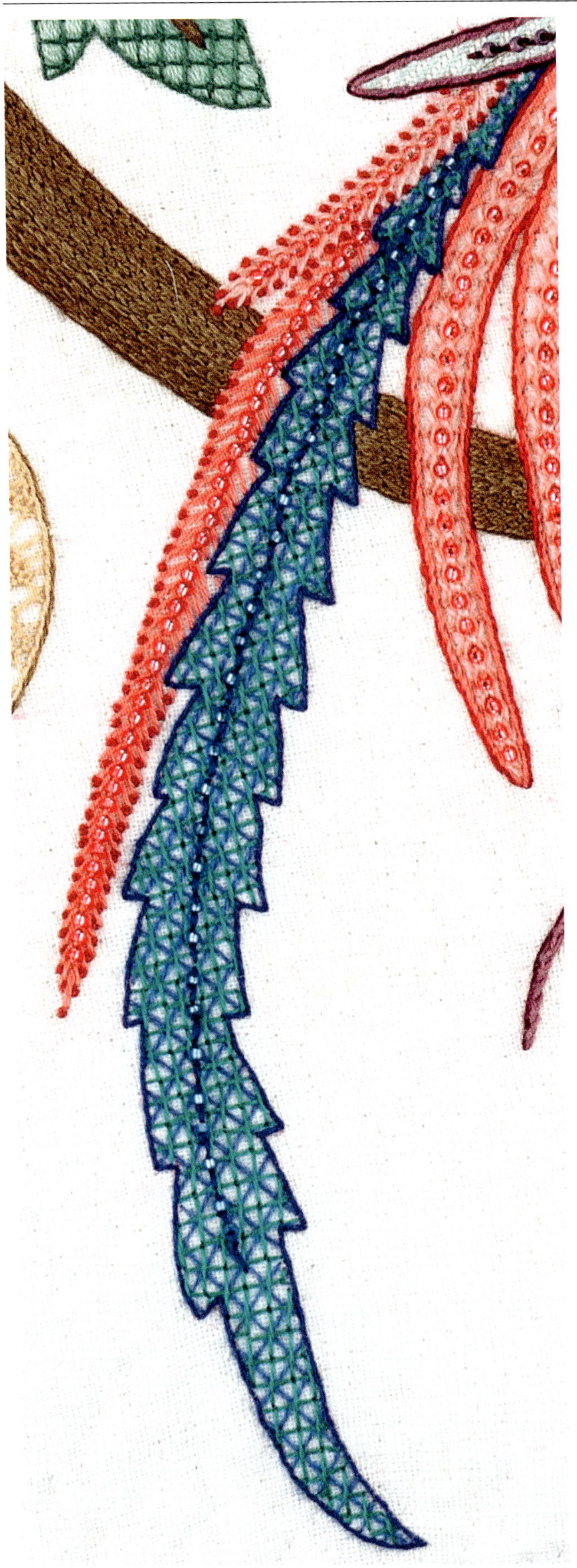

Tail feathers

4 Working from the back of the bird, start with the longest tail feather.

With a heat-erasable pen, draw a diagonal grid on the area that comprises the longest, main tail feather. Place the lines 3mm (⅛in) apart and at right angles to one another.

Working with single strands, fill the feather with trellis with cross stitch couching using 3850 for the trellis and 798 for the cross stitches.

With a doubled-over single strand of 796 and beads 15° 19F, work the vein of the feather with beaded backstitch.

When you have completed the surrounding tail feathers, outline the feather with whipped backstitch using a single strand of 796.

5 Moving to the left, work the two tail feathers with beaded fly stitch (see page 201).

When working the longer of the two feathers, use two strands of 962 and beads 15° 4266 to work the beaded fly stitch. Using a single strand of 150, work single-wrap French knots at the tip and thereafter on the perimeter line on both sides between the 'legs' of the fly stitch.

When working the shorter feathers at the top, use two strands of 3716 and beads 15° 4266 to work the beaded fly stitch. Using a single strand of 150, work single-wrap French knots at the tip and thereafter on the perimeter line on both sides between the legs of the fly stitch.

6 The tail feathers on the right-hand side are filled with beaded interlaced chain stitch.

Using two strands of thread, work the chain and side straight stitches with 962 and the interlacing on both sides with 3716.

With a doubled-over single strand of 961, stitch a bead 15° 4266 into the middle of each chain stitch loop.

Outline each feather with whipped backstitch using two strands of 961 and, with a single strand of 150, work outline stitch adjacent to the outside of the whipped backstitch.

7 Moving up towards the bird, work the additional tail feathers marked 7 on the chart.

Fill the two lighter feathers on the left with needle weaving texture no. 5 (see page 213) using perle #16 3000 for the warp stitches which are worked from top to bottom, and perle #16 4379 for the weft stitches that are worked from the base to the tip of each feather.

The five darker feathers are woven in the same way using perle #16 3000 for the warp and perle #16 4350 for the weft stitches.

Using a doubled-over single strand of 154 and beads 15°4248, work beaded backstitch to depict the vein of each feather, using the lines on the chart to guide you.

Outline each feather with whipped backstitch using two strands of 3835 and thereafter work outline stitch adjacent to the outside of the whipped backstitch using a single strand of 154.

Wing (left-hand side)

8 Moving to the wing feathers, fill the three lighter outside feathers on the left with needle weaving texture no. 5 using perle #16 3000 for the warp stitches which are worked from top to bottom, and perle #16 4379 for the weft stitches that are worked from the base to the tip of each feather. Outline each feather with whipped backstitch using two strands of 3835.

9 The remaining wing feathers are worked with fly stitch using two strands of thread.

The two feathers that form the top row are worked with 3834. The five feathers of the middle row are worked with 3835 and the feathers that fill the bottom row are worked with 3836.

Legs and feet

10 Fill the bird's legs and feet with padded satin stitch.

Using two strands of 613, pad each leg with vertical rows of outline stitch, working into the feet and claws as you get to the bottom.

With a single strand of the same thread, work horizontal satin stitch over the padding.

Outline the visible edges with outline stitch using a single strand of 3781.

Breast

11 Fill each of the scallop shapes that form the bird's breast and thighs with buttonhole stitch semi-circles using single strands of thread.

Starting from the outer circles, work inwards, using the purl edge of the buttonhole stitches to cover the raw edges of the preceding circles.

Referring to the chart, use 809 for the lightest segments, 799 for the medium colour and 798 for the darkest segments.

With a single strand of 796, outline the outside edge of the scallops with outline stitch.

Wing (right-hand side)

12 Fill the wing on the right-hand side of the body with woven trellis couching.

Working with two strands of thread and referring to the guidelines in the embroidery stitch directory, use 3835 for shade 1, 564 for shade 2 and 3836 for shade 3.

Outline the outside edge of the wing with whipped backstitch using two strands of 3835. Work a row of outline stitch adjacent to the outside of the whipped backstitch using a single strand of 154.

Body and head

13 Fill the body with two-tone vermicelli couching.

Work the first series of swirls with two strands of 564 couched down with a single strand of the same thread.

Work the second series with a single strand of 3850 couched down with a single strand of the same thread.

Outline the longer, upper side and the short lower side of the body with whipped backstitch using two strands of 3850.

When you have worked the head, and with a single strand each of 564 and 561 threaded on the same needle, following the guidelines in the embroidery stitch directory, work loose French knots along the intersection of the head and the body and at the base of the fly stitch feathers described in step 9. Allow the loose knots to encroach on the body and the head, or the fly stitch feathers, to create a soft outline.

14 Fill the head with long and short shading using single strands of thread.

Fill the semi-circle within the head by working two rows with 798 and a further row with 799, leaving a ragged edge in the top row.

Leaving out two small areas for the eyes, start at the base of the head with 799. Work two to three rows of shading, until you are about halfway up the semi-circle on each side.

Changing to 809, continue shading towards the top of the head. When you are level with the ragged edge of the top row of the semi-circle, shade in between those stitches, thereby working a continuous row from one side to the other.

Work the last row of shading in the slightly darker 799 to give the impression of the curve.

Using a single strand of 798, work outline around the base of the semi-circle and visible outside edge of the head.

Using two strands of 610, stitch a single bead 15° 458 into each of the spaces left for the eyes. With the same thread, surround each bead with a detached chain stitch.

15 Using two strands of 612, pad the beak with horizontal satin stitch. Thereafter, work long and short stitch shading over the padding.

Start at the bottom tip with 611, shading into 612 to fill the wider part of the beak.

With two strands of 961, work a short line of split stitch to create the pink area on the right-hand side of the beak. Work outline stitch on the outside edge of the split stitch with a single strand of 150.

Outline the shaded area of the beak with outline stitch using a single strand of 3781.

Leaves (top left-hand side)

16 Starting above the main branch on the left-hand side of the project, the green leaf that comes out the stem is filled with diagonal long and short stitch shading using single strands of cotton.

Use 563 closest to the vein, shading out to 564 on the edge of the leaf.

With a single strand of thread 561, work basic trellis couching over the shading (see page 187).

With the same thread, work outline stitch around the perimeter of the leaf.

Fill the vein with rows of chain stitch using two strands of 611. Work up the one side, return to the bottom of the vein and work up the other side, finishing that row when you meet up with the first row.

With a single strand of 3781, work outline stitch adjacent to the outside edge of the vein on both sides.

17 Start with the vein of the colourful leaf above that.

Fill the vein with rows of chain stitch using two strands of 611.

With a single strand of 3781, work outline stitch on both sides of the vein.

Outline the leaf with whipped backstitch using perle #16 4350.

Using a single strand of 561, work outline stitch adjacent to the outside of the whipped backstitch.

Fill the leaf following the guidelines for freestyle flower embroidery (see page 197).

18 The leaf and stem on the left of the branch are worked following the instructions set out in step 16.

Instead of the green, use single strands of 612 and 613 for the long and short stitch shading, with 611 being used for the trellis couching and the outline of the leaf.

19 Move up to the purple flower at the top of the branch.

Work the stem with rows of chain stitch using two strands of 610 and outlining each side with outline stitch using a single strand of 3781.

Fill the centre of the flower with Rhodes stitch using two strands of 3836.

Fill each of the purple petals with long and short stitch shading using single strands of thread. Start at the base of each petal with 3834, shading through 3835 to 3836 at the tip.

Outline each petal with outline stitch using a single strand of 154.

With a single strand of 3834, work a chain stitch circle, stitching in the ditch between the Rhodes stitch centre and the petals. Outline the outside edge of the circle with outline stitch using a single strand of 154.

Pink flower (top centre)

20 The leaf that comes out of the branch is filled with diagonal long and short stitch shading using single strands of cotton.

Use 612 closest to the vein, shading out to 613 on the edge of the leaf.

With a single strand of thread 611, work basic trellis couching (see page 187).

With the same thread, work outline stitch around the perimeter of the leaf.

Fill the vein with rows of chain stitch using two strands of 610. Work up the one side, return to the bottom of the vein and work up the other side, finishing that row when you meet up with the first row.

With a single strand of 3781, work outline stitch adjacent to the outside edge of the vein on both sides.

21 Fill each pink petal with long and short stitch shading. Using single strands of thread, start at the base with 962 shading up to 3716. Outline the visible edge of each petal with outline stitch using a single strand of 150.

Fill the background of the centre of the flower with trellis with cross stitch couching using a single strand of 613. With two strands of 611, stitch a bead 15° 458 into the middle of each circle within the centre of the flower. With the same thread, work a circle of French knots around each bead and thereafter, work whipped backstitch on the upper outline of the centre of the flower. With a single strand of 3781, work outline stitch adjacent to the outside edge of the whipped backstitch.

The calyx of the flower is filled with needle weaving texture no. 2. Starting with the outside leaves, work vertical warp stitches with perle #16 4350. Work the horizontal weft stitches with perle #16 3000.

Work the inside leaf in the same way using perle #16 4379 for the vertical warp stitches and perle #16 3000 for the horizontal weft stitches.

Outline the visible outside edge of each leaf with whipped backstitch using perle #16 4350.

With a single strand of 561, work outline stitch adjacent to the outside of the whipped backstitch.

Work the stem with rows of chain stitch using two strands of 610 and outlining each side with outline stitch using a single strand of 3781, not forgetting the small segment of the branch which lies between the wing feathers of the bird.

22 The leaves that come out of the top of the flower are filled with needle lace stitch no. 8 (see page 207).

Using perle #16 4379 for the green leaf and perle #16 8060 for the golden leaf, work backstitch on the visible outlines of the leaf. Work a horizontal backstitch across the tip.

Familiarize yourself with needle lace stitch no. 8, then fill the leaves. As the shape widens, increase the number of stitches at the beginning and ends of rows. When you reach the base of the leaf, shorten the rows as you work down, attaching the loops of the detached buttonhole stitches where it is appropriate to do so, eventually finishing off by attaching the loops at the bottom.

Using the same thread in each instance, whip the backstitch that forms the visible edges of the leaf.

With a single strand of 561 for the green leaf and 610 for the golden leaf, work outline stitch adjacent to the outside edge of the whipped backstitch.

23 Work all the stems with rows of chain stitch using two strands of 610, outlining each side with outline stitch using a single strand of 3781. Using two strands of 3835, work the tendril that curves away from the colourful leaf with Portuguese knotted stem stitch. With a single strand of 154, work outline stitch on the inside of the curve, adjacent to the tendril.

Leaves and flowers (top right-hand corner)

24 Starting in the top section of the branch, work the brown leaf. Start by filling the centre.

Using perle #16 8060, work backstitch on the outline of the centre of the leaf and thereafter work needle lace stitch no. 10 (see page 209).

When you reach the base of the leaf, shorten the rows as you work down, attaching the loops of the detached buttonhole stitches where it is appropriate to do so, eventually finishing off by attaching the last single loop at the bottom.

Using the same thread, whip the backstitch that forms the visible edges of the leaf.

Fill the outer edge of the leaf with long and short stitch shading overlaid with basic trellis couching and outlined with outline stitch.

Using single strands throughout, work the shading from the inside, using 611, shading through 612 to 613 at the edge.

Using a single strand of 610, work basic trellis couching (see page 187) over the shading and work outline stitch on the outside edge of the leaf with the same thread.

Outline the needle lace centre of the leaf with outline stitch worked adjacent to the whipped backstitch using a single strand of 610.

25 Moving to the right-hand side, fill the petals of the pink flower with woven trellis couching following the guidelines in the embroidery stitch directory.

Starting with the petal at the back and working with two strands throughout, use 961 for shade no. 1, 150 for shade no. 2 and 962 for shades 3 and 4.

Outline the petal with whipped backstitch using two strands of 961. With a single strand of 150, work outline stitch adjacent to the outside edge of the whipped backstitch.

Moving to the front petal of the flower and working with two strands throughout, use 962 for shade no. 1, 961 for shade no. 2 and 3716 for shades 3 and 4.

Outline the petal with whipped backstitch using two strands of 961. With a single strand of 150, work outline stitch adjacent to the outside edge of the whipped backstitch.

Fill each of the calyx leaves with long and short stitch shading.

Working with single strands of thread, start at the base of the leaf with 563, shading to 564 at the tip of each leaf.

With a single strand of 561, work basic trellis couching over the shading and, with the same thread, work outline stitch around each leaf.

26 Moving to the larger colourful leaf, outline the leaf with whipped backstitch using perle #16 4350.

Using a single strand of 561, work outline stitch adjacent to the outside of the whipped backstitch.

Fill the leaf following the guidelines for freestyle flower embroidery (see page 197).

27 Move to the smaller colourful leaf, and following the guidelines in step 26, outline the two sides of the main body of the leaf using the same stitches and thread thereafter, filling it with freestyle flower embroidery.

The tip of the leaf is filled with needle weaving texture no. 2 (see page 211). Work vertical warp stitches, down the length of the space, with perle #16 4350. Work the horizontal weft stitches with perle #16 3000.

Outline the needle weaving with whipped backstitch using perle #16 4350.

With a single strand of 561, work outline stitch adjacent to the outside of the whipped backstitch.

28 Work all the stems with rows of chain stitch using two strands of 610 and outlining each side with outline stitch using a single strand of 3781.

29 Moving to the lower flower, fill the purple petals with long and short stitch shading using single strands of thread. Start with 3834 at the base of each petal, shading through 3835 to 3836 at the tip. Outline the top edge of each petal with outline stitch using a single strand of 154.

Moving down the flower, the leaves of the calyx are filled with needle weaving texture no. 2.

Starting with the outside leaves, work vertical warp stitches with perle #16 4350.

Work the horizontal weft stitches with perle #16 3000.

Work the inside leaf in the same way using perle #16 4379 for the vertical warp stitches and perle #16 3000 for the horizontal weft stitches.

Outline the visible outside edge of each leaf with whipped backstitch using perle #16 4350.

With a single strand of 561, work outline stitch adjacent to the outside of the whipped backstitch

Pink flower (bottom right-hand corner)

30 Fill each pink petal with knotted interlaced chain stitch (see page 176). Using two strands of thread throughout, use 962 for the reverse chain stitches and the small side stitches. Use 3716 to do the interlacing and 961 to work the French knots that are placed inside the loops of the chain stitches.

Outline each petal with whipped backstitch using two strands of 961. With a single strand of 150, work outline stitch adjacent to the outside of the whipped backstitch.

Moving to the centre of the flower, work Rhodes stitch in the inner circle using two strands of 612.

Starting adjacent to the Rhodes stitch centre and working outwards, using single strands of thread, work two chain stitch circles. Work the inner circle with 611. The outer circle is worked with 612.

Outline the outside edge of the outer circle with outline stitch using a single strand of 611.

Work each leaf using two strands of 563. Start at the tip with a straight stitch and then continue down each leaf with fly stitch.

Outline the top, visible edge of each leaf with outline stitch using a single strand of 561.

31 Work the leaves at the base of the branch. Follow the instructions in step 16 for the green leaf, and the instructions in step 18 for the golden leaf.

Leaves and grapes (bottom, centre)

32 Work all the stems below the bird with rows of chain stitch using two strands of 610, and outline each side with outline stitch using a single strand of 3781. Using two strands of 3835, work the curved tendrils with Portuguese knotted stem stitch. With a single strand of 154, work outline stitch on the inside of the curve, adjacent to the tendril.

33 Fill each circle within the bunch of grapes with Rhodes stitch (see page 185) using two strands of 3836.

Using single strands of thread, work three chain stitch circles around the filled circle. This will enlarge each grape, meaning that they will eventually touch one another.

Starting adjacent to the filled circle, work a circle with 3834. Thereafter, work a circle with 3835 followed by a third circle worked with 3836.

Using a single strand of 154, work outline stitch adjacent to each outside chain stitch circle.

34 Moving to the area below the grapes, fill the leaves with needle lace stitch no. 10.

Following the guidelines set out in the first half of step 24, working from the tip to the base of the leaf, use perle #16 4379 for the leaf on the left and perle #16 8060 for the leaf on the right.

In both instances, whip the backstitch around the needle lace with the same perle #16 thread used to work the needle lace.

Work single strand outline stitch adjacent to the whipped backstitch using 561 for the green leaf and 610 for the golden leaf.

Embroidered leaves (bottom, centre)

35 Fill the leaf that curves over the main branch following the instructions set out in steps 26 and 27.

36 Work all the stems with rows of chain stitch using two strands of 610 and outlining each side with outline stitch using a single strand of 3781.

Needle lace leaves

37 Fill the remaining leaves with needle lace stitch no. 10, following the instructions in step 34.

Finishing

This design has been made into a small pillow to make a pair with the Contemporary Eagle on page 100. See page 113 for instructions on quilting the pillow.

Tools and MATERIALS

Whichever crewelwork design you choose to work on, it's essential to have the right tools and materials at hand. In this section we'll explore what is needed for crewelwork and how to prepare your work area for a successful and comfortable stitching experience.

Fabrics

Selecting the right background fabric is important for providing the best finish for your crewelwork projects. It is advisable to pre-wash base fabrics before use.

Project base fabric

Traditional projects

Jacobean pure linen twill is always Phillipa's first choice of fabric, as the density of the threads and the composition of the diagonal weave enable multiple stitches to be made over each area of this ground fabric.

Contemporary projects

Hazel's projects in the book are worked on cotton and cotton/linen blend fabrics. Opt for a fabric that has a tight weave to provide stability for your stitches.

Backing fabric

The contemporary projects have been worked with a backing fabric because the background fabrics are lighter weight than the linen used for the traditional projects. This provides additional stability and gives you a place to finish the threads on the back of your work.

The background fabrics in the contemporary projects are backed with off-white or ecru cotton voile. Voile is a light, sheer, smooth fabric that is perfect for use as a backing fabric. The closest equivalents to voile, if it is hard to find, are batiste or lawn.

To add your backing fabric, cut a piece of voile to the same size as the project fabric, pin it to the back of your project and stitch around all four sides to attach it and prevent fraying. The best machine for this is an overlocker (or serger), or you can use a conventional sewing machine set on a wide zigzag stitch.

Wadding (batting)

The Contemporary Eagle and Blue Bird projects (pages 100–113 and 124–137) were made into small quilted pillows. If you choose to quilt your finished projects, use 100gsm wadding (batting) around 5mm (¼in) thick – often called placemat wadding – to provide extra weight. The embroideries were backed with lightweight wadding (batting), plus an additional layer of cotton voile, and quilted through all layers of fabric.

Needles

Needles are among the most important tools in your embroidery kit. Crewelwork needles are specifically designed for crewel embroidery, allowing you to stitch with precision. Their long, sharp point and broad body makes them ideal for piercing the fabric cleanly, to effortlessly guide the thread through the fabric.

While crewelwork needles may resemble other embroidery needles at first glance, they have distinct characteristics that set them apart, including added strength to withstand the tension and pressure exerted during stitching, and a larger eye size to accommodate crewel wool. The eye, however, shouldn't be so large that it allows the thread to slip out easily. Some needles have elongated eyes, making it easier to thread thicker or multiple strands of thread. Crewelwork needles are commonly made of stainless steel or nickel-plated steel. Both materials are durable and provide smooth movement through the fabric.

Always use needles that are large enough to not only accommodate the numbers of strands that you are using, but also to create a small channel in the fabric. This will mean that your thread will not become too damaged to use.

Crewelwork needles come in a variety of types and sizes, each serving a specific purpose. The most common types of crewelwork needles include:

Standard crewelwork needles are suitable for most embroidery projects. They are available in various sizes, with larger numbers indicating smaller needle sizes, but for use with crewel wool, metric sizes 1 and 2 are ideal. Sizes 7, 8 and 10 crewelwork needles are suitable when working with cotton threads in the contemporary projects.

Crewel/chenille needles have a longer and thicker body compared to standard crewel needles. They are often used for fabrics with a looser weave, or surface woven stitches such as whipped spider's web. Because of their large eye, they are particularly suitable for use with twisted threads.

Milliner's needles, also known as straw needles, have a long, thin body and a round eye. They are excellent for creating bullion stitches.

In addition to crewelwork needles, the contemporary projects in this book use tapestry and bead embroidery needles:

Tapestry needles have a blunt point and are particularly useful when whipping, weaving or going through or under existing stitches. They are used in the needle lace and needle weaving techniques.

Bead embroidery needles are steel needles that have a slim shank but, more importantly, a small eye. This allows them to pass through small beads and they should be used for all of the bead embroidery stitches in the contemporary projects.

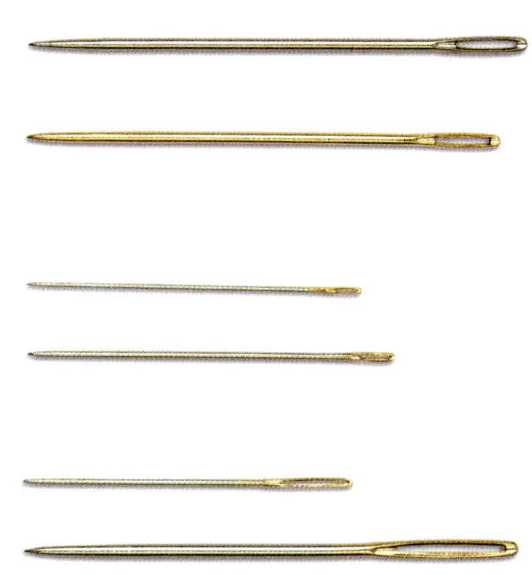

Above, top to bottom: crewel needles for crewel wool (silver size 1, gold size 2); crewel needles for cotton thread (sizes 7 and 10); tapestry needle; and chenille needle.

When to replace your needles

A favourite rule of ours: new design, new needles! However, if you prefer to keep your needles for slightly longer, ensure you replace them before they become too dull. If your needle doesn't glide smoothly through the fabric or struggles to penetrate, it's time to replace it.

Using fresh, sharp needles ensures clean and precise stitches and makes your crewelwork experience more enjoyable.

Threads

When it comes to threads, crewel wool is the traditional choice, offering a rich texture, vibrant colours and easy blending of long and short stitches – the essential stitch in most crewelwork designs. However, you can also add other threads such as stranded cotton or silk, depending on the nature of the design or your personal choice.

Crewel wool

All of Phillipa's traditional designs are worked in Appleton's two-ply crewel wools. Appleton's wool comes from the British sheep sold at the Yorkshire wool markets, and is scoured, spun and dyed in Yorkshire, the next-door county to Phillipa's home in Westmorland. Appleton's began as a company in 1885, and the dye colours used on the embroidery wools in her four projects replicate the historic colours from the era of original design.

Work with lengths of wool no more than the smoothness of the thread allows, around 30–38cm (12–15in). Wool thread has a slight stretch, and the stitches can be placed gently on the linen with less tension on each stitch than one would employ when using a cotton thread. Wool threads can be very forgiving and when, for example, working long and short stitch, if you miss a stitch or the stitch is not at the correct angle, stitching over the incorrect angle or the filling in a gap is very easy to do. This can be preferable than pulling out a thread, which can twist the wool making it unusable.

Stranded cotton

Cotton threads are easy to use and, provided you work with reasonable lengths of thread on your needle, are not likely to knot or tangle. A reasonable length of thread to work with is, for ease of calculation, from the tip of your fingers to your elbow, or around 35cm (14in).

Supplied in skeins and usually six-stranded, cotton is ideal for fine work, and DMC stranded cotton is used in Hazel's contemporary projects. It has a lustrous sheen and you can embroider with as many strands as you like, depending on the texture you wish to achieve. Use size 8 or 10 embroidery needles when stitching with stranded cotton.

Perle thread

This twisted thread is available in a variety of sizes and colours, with a sheen that is remarkably effective for the contemporary projects. It is easy to work with and provides alternative texture to your work. It is ideal for many of the weaving and needle lace stitches featured and the contemporary projects, which use perle thread from the Presencia Finca #12 and #16 ranges. Because of the twist it is inclined to tangle, so run it through a thread conditioner to prevent this. Use a size 7 embroidery needle, a size 26 chenille or a size 26 tapestry needle when stitching with perle thread.

Fine cordonette thread

DMC Special Dentelles 80 is used for the finer needle lace and weaving stitches in Tiny the Tabby (page 62). Similar to perle, it is a twisted thread with a light sheen. As with perle thread, use a thread conditioner to prevent twisting. Use a size 7 embroidery needle or a size 26 tapestry needle when stitching with Special Dentelles.

Beads and crystals

Use the best beads that you can find to improve the effect of your work. Look for seed beads with even sizes and holes than are central in the bead. Hazel's contemporary crewelwork projects use beads from the Miyuki range of Japanese seed beads. The contemporary projects use size 15°, 11°, 8° and 5° round rocailles beads.

When incorporating beads into your embroidery stitches, attach them to fabric using stranded cotton in a similar shade to the bead. Because the holes in the beads are small and you will need to pass the needle through, sometimes more than once, use a size 10 or 12 bead embroidery needle or a size 11 Sharps needle. Hazel's preference is for the quilting needles; they are short and bend less. Use only one strand of thread, doubled over for extra strength.

The sizing of crystal rhinestones and beads indicates either the diameter or the length of the glass. Preciosa flat-back crystals are used for the eyes of Tiny the Tabby (see page 62) and also to create interest in the small flowers and buds of Summer Jewels (see page 44). Instructions for attaching these crystals are included on page 203.

Pictured opposite: (1) sharp embroidery scissors; (2) curved-tip embroidery scissors; (3) Jacobean pure linen twill; (4) cotton twill fabric; (5) 80% cotton, 20% linen fabric; (6) Osnaburg seeded cotton fabric; (7) cotton voile backing fabric; (8) black glass beads; (9) sewing pins; (10) Miyuki 15° beads; (11) crewel needles in various sizes; (12) Prescencia Finca perle threads; (13) DMC stranded cotton skeins; (14) Appleton's two-ply crewel wool skeins.

1
2
3
4
5
6
7
8
9
10
11
12
13
14

Essential tools

Embroidery hoops

Embroidery hoops are indispensable for crewelwork. A 'hands free' seat or floor frame with three interchangeable sizes of hoop is ideal. Choose hoops that are appropriate for your project size, keeping in mind that smaller hoops offer more control and are good for accessing the corners of the design, while larger hoops accommodate more sizeable designs.

Wooden stretcher bars

Stretcher bars hold your print taut to improve the quality of your work. Fabric is attached to the sides of the bars with a staple gun or drawing pins in a square or rectangle around the design. When using stretcher bars, make sure you have a wide margin of fabric around the design so that attaching it to a frame does not damage the area close to your stitching. The contemporary projects are worked using Edmunds stretcher bars in sizes varying from 12in (30cm) to 17in (43cm).

Stretcher bars are not suitable for Jacobean linen twill as they cannot hold the heavy fabric taut in place for an extended length of time.

Slate frames

These frames are perfect for using with Jacobean linen twill, or any lighter fabric. When working a larger design, or one with much raised embroidery, you may prefer using a slate frame supported by trestles or with a clamp. The advantage with this type of frame is that you do not need to block your work afterwards.

Scissors

Small, sharp embroidery scissors are essential for cutting threads neatly and precisely. Use large dressmaking scissors for cutting fabric.

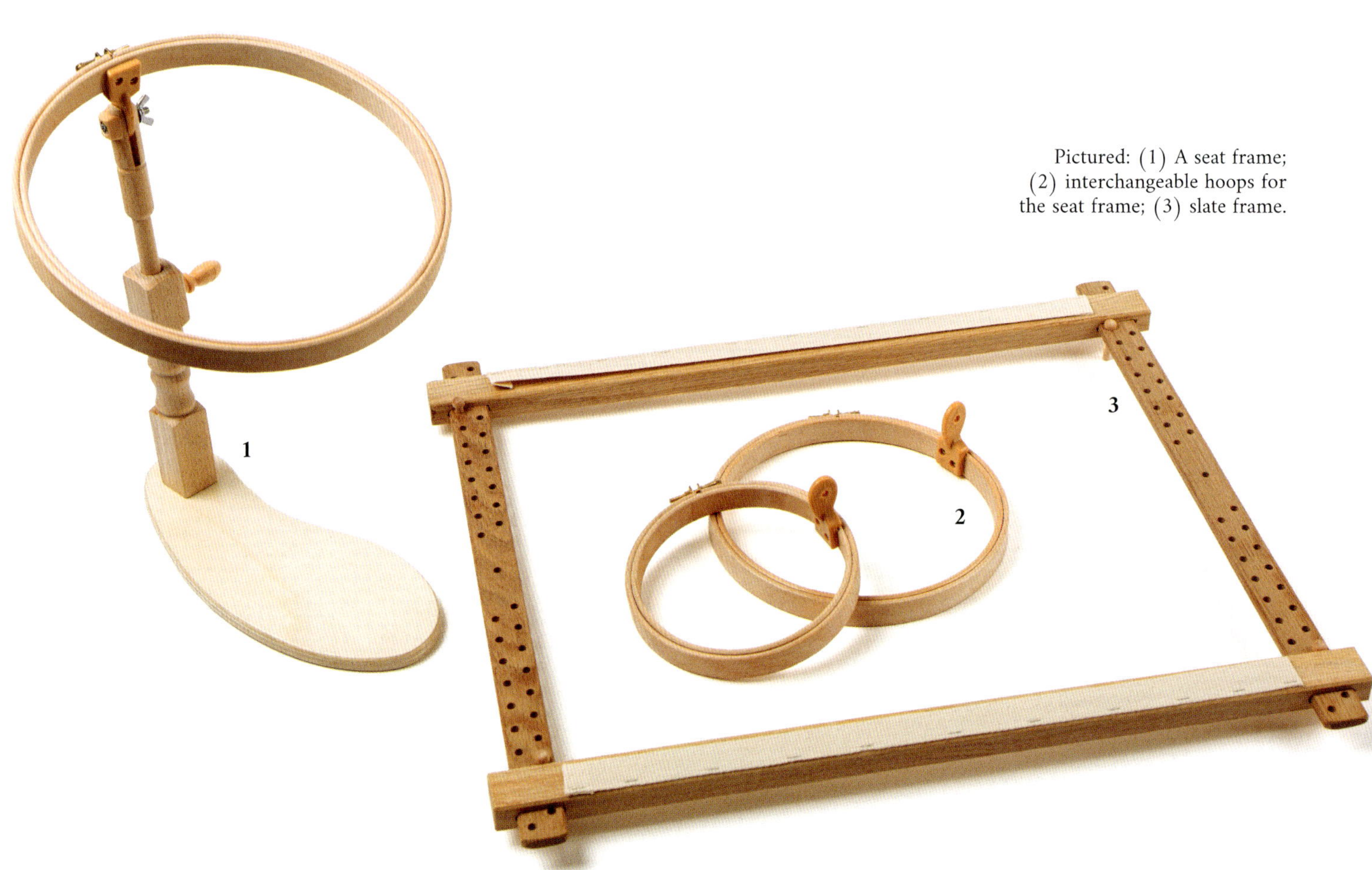

Pictured: (1) A seat frame; (2) interchangeable hoops for the seat frame; (3) slate frame.

Other items

Pins

Sewing pins are useful for attaching the backing fabric to your design, and pinning your background fabric in place before sewing to your chosen frame (if using a slate frame). You will also need drawing pins if using stretcher bars.

Thimble

A thimble protects your finger while pushing the needle through the fabric. Choose a thimble that suits your preference, whether it's a traditional metal thimble or a more modern, ergonomic design.

Light box

Use a light box when tracing the designs onto fabric. Alternatively, you could use a glass surface and a lamp.

Pencil or a heat-erasable pen

For tracing the design onto your background fabric.

Thread conditioner

Silicone thread conditioners and beeswax are often useful, particularly if you live in a humid environment. Run cotton thread through a thread conditioner or beeswax block to prevent tangles and knots and to strengthen the thread. Note that thread conditioner is not suitable for use with wool thread.

Beading mat or tray

A small velour mat – or a small tray lined with velour – is vital for keeping beads together when working on bead embroidery stitches.

Spinster twisting tool

Used in the contemporary projects only for twisting threads, for example Summer Jewels and Tiny the Tabby.

Embroidery charts

A full-size chart is provided for each of the eight designs, folded into the pocket at the back of the book. See 'General project instructions' on pages 14–15 for more information on how to use the charts. Note that the presentation of the charts differs slightly between the traditional and contemporary projects.

The charts are also available to download from the Bookmarked Hub, where you can print extra copies and scale them to a different size, if preferred. Visit www.bookmarkedhub.com and search for this book by title or ISBN: the files can be found under 'Book Extras'.

Transferring the designs to fabric

Before you start stitching, you will need to transfer the outline from the chart onto your background fabric. The easiest method to do this is by using a light box or a flat glass-topped table with a lamp positioned underneath the glass.

First, tape the four corners of the paper design, right side up, onto the lightbox or glass. Next, tape your fabric directly over the paper design, again onto the glass, making sure that they are both securely taped and will not move.

Next, switch on the light box or lamp underneath the glass and, using a sharp pencil or heat-erasable pen, draw the main lines in the design while angling your pencil at a 45-degree angle to the surface of your fabric. The pencil lines will not disappear with use but they will not harm your fabric. If you are less confident, then draw your lines lightly.

Keep an even pressure and try to draw with a continuous line. You may wish to practise drawing on your fabric on the edge of the linen to discover the ideal amount of pressure and the pencil angle needed to produce a clean line. A tip for achieving this is to rest your drawing arm firmly on the table for stability.

Add the smaller details to the design and, when you think it is completed, switch off the light to check that you have included all the lines you need and that the pencil line is clearly visible. If you make an error, then the pencil marks might be removable by gently rubbing with a soft eraser.

Stitch directory

In this chapter you will find the instructions for all of the stitches used in the book, separated into traditional and contemporary stitches. If a particular stitch is worked differently in the traditional and contemporary designs, it is included in both sections of the stitch directory; other stitches are listed only once. You can use the list opposite to help you find the correct stitches.

Crewelwork was, and still is, worked mainly using woollen threads, and is ideally embroidered onto tightly woven Jacobean linen twill and uses a slightly different technique than when using cotton or silk threads. Onto an evenweave fabric, the needle and threads will usually pass without too much of a challenge, even if the needle angle is positioned at a slant. However, when using wools and a twill fabric, the angle of the needle is all important, and using a stabbing action will result in the needle entering the linen twill cleanly, creating a hole where the wool thread then passes cleanly through the linen. If you slant your needle at an angle to the linen then the wool will abrade, and you will find that the consequent fluffiness of the wool will make it unusable. The crewel needle needs to be wide enough to create this hole and will be smooth enough to pass cleanly through the linen and make a large enough hole to accommodate a smooth passage.

The introduction of silks with crewelwork started in about 1750 and was mainly used for French knots or bullion stitches in the centre of flowers. Later, in the nineteenth century onwards, silk was used for edging the long and short stitched areas, thus giving an extra luxurious sheen to depictions of floral displays.

Using resources in castles, country houses, museums and her own collection of historic crewel work, Phillipa has looked to the past, and referenced stitches in her designs in this book to continue this legacy. Hazel has expanded the crewel view in her designs, with her extensive range of threads and beads, bringing the work of past embroiderers into the twenty-first century.

Long and short stitch and pistil stitch are worked in crewel wool in the Greedy Squirrel design (see pages 16–25).

TRADITIONAL STITCHES 147

Backstitch 147
Bayeux stitch 147
Block shading 147
Buttonhole stitch – single thread 148
Closed fly stitch – single thread 148
Closed fly stitch – double thread 149
Coral stitch – double thread 150
Crewel stem stitch – single thread 151
Crewel stem stitch – double thread 151
Fan stitch – single thread 152
Fern stitch – double thread 152
French knots – double thread 153
Laid and couched work 154
Variation 1: single thread, three layers 154
Variation 2: single thread, four layers 155
Variation 3: couched with detached fly 156
Variation 4: trellis 157
Variation 5: four layers of laid work and three layers of couching 158
Variation 6: laid and couched work with double thread 159
Leaf stitch – single thread 160
Long and short stitch: two colours 160
Long and short stitch: three colours 161
Long and short stitch as soft shading – pointed leaf 162
Long and short stitch as soft shading – hummock 163
Long and short stitch as soft shading – oak leaf 164
Long and short stitch – vine leaves 165
Pistil stitch – double thread 166
Satin stitch – double thread 167
Satin stitch, raised – double thread 167
Seeding – single thread 168
Split stitch 168
Whipped spider's web – single thread 168
Whipped stem stitch – single thread 169

CONTEMPORARY STITCHES 170

Embroidery stitches 170
Backstitch 170
Backstitch – whipped 170
Blanket stitch – padded and striped 170
Blanket stitch and buttonhole stitch 171
Bullion knots 171
Burden stitch 172
Buttonhole stitch – flower 173
Buttonhole stitch – layered 174
Chain stitch 175
Chain stitch and backstitch combination 175
Chain stitch – detached 175
Chain stitch – interlaced 176
Chain stitch – interlaced variation (knotted) 176
Chain stitch – interlaced variation 177
Chain stitch – reverse 177
Eye stitch filler 178
Fly stitch 178
Fly stitch – whipped 179
French knot – loose 179
French knot – single wrap 179
Heavy chain stitch 180
Herringbone stitch – interlaced 181
Herringbone stitch – raised 181
Long and short stitch shading 182
Long and short stitch shading – diagonal 182
Outline stitch 183
Outline stitch padding 183
Portuguese knotted stem stitch 184
Raised stem stitch 185
Rhodes stitch 185
Satin stitch – small leaves 185
Satin stitch – padded 186
Split backstitch 186
Trellis couching – basic 187
Trellis with cross stitch couching 187
Trellis couching – woven 188
Tufting – scruffy 189
Twisted thread 189
Twisted thread couching 190
Twisted long and short stitch 190
Up and down buttonhole stitch 191
Vermicelli couching 192
Vermicelli couching – two tone 192
Wheatear stitch 193

Continued overleaf

Freestyle embroidery 193
Freestyle embroidery – random 193
3-petal lazy daisy bud 194
9-petal lazy daisy flower 194
Buttonhole bud 194
Buttonhole stitch half flower 195
Eye stitch variation 196
Sheaf stitch 196
Single weaving filler stitch 196

Bead embroidery stitches 199
Attaching a single bead 199
Attaching a smaller bead with a larger bead 199
Beaded backstitch 200
Beaded backstitch picot line 200
Beaded circles around a bead/crystal 201
Beaded fly stitch 201
Beaded picot (attached) 202
Beaded wheatear stitch 202
Caged crystals 203
Chain stitch – interlaced and beaded 204
Covering a large bead 205

Needle lace stitches 205
Needle lace bars 205
Needle lace stitch no. 7 206
Needle lace stitch no. 8 207
Needle lace stitch no. 9 208
Needle lace stitch no. 10 209

Needle weaving patterns 210
Basic: double weaving 210
Basic: triple weaving 210
Needle weaving texture no. 2 211
Needle weaving texture no. 3 212
Needle weaving texture no. 5 213
Needle weaving checks and stripes no. 1 214
Needle weaving checks and stripes no. 9 215

Needle weaving and beaded embroidery are used in the Summer Jewels design (pages 44–61).

Long and short shading is worked in cotton threads in the Contemporary Blue Bird design (pages 124–137).

Traditional stitches

Backstitch

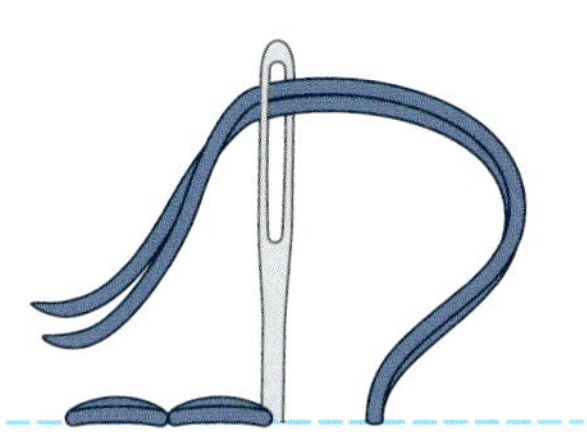

1 Bring the needle up through the fabric and back down at the start of the line.
2 Bring the needle up through the fabric another 6mm (¼in) further along the line and then pass it back down at the end of the first stitch. Keep your needle upright at a 90 degree angle to the fabric at all times.
3 Continue along the line in the same way, stitching against the last stitch. Repeat this process until you have completed the stitch line.

Bayeux stitch

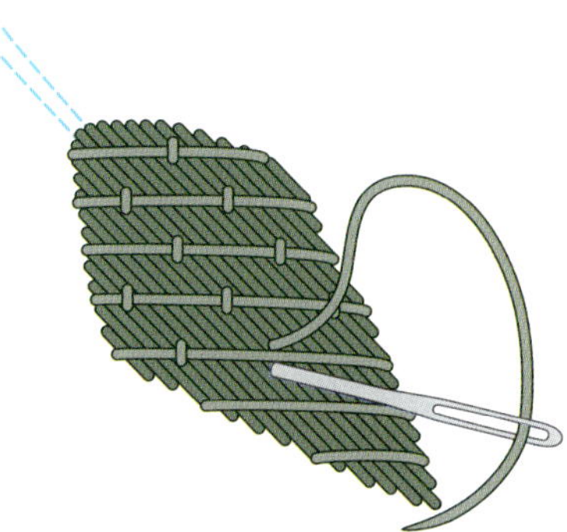

This ancient stitch is used on many historic embroideries, including the Bayeux Tapestry. Please note that the printed diagonal lines on the linen in the illustration indicate the top layer of stitching.

1 Lay a base layer of satin stitch in double thread. Begin with a stitch down the centre of the shape and work one half at a time. Use straight lines to cover the shape.
2 Next, in single thread, lay the contrasting colour at intervals diagonally across the shape. If you wish, use a ruler to judge the spaces between each stitch. Continue with the same thread and couch this single laid thread at intervals.

Block shading

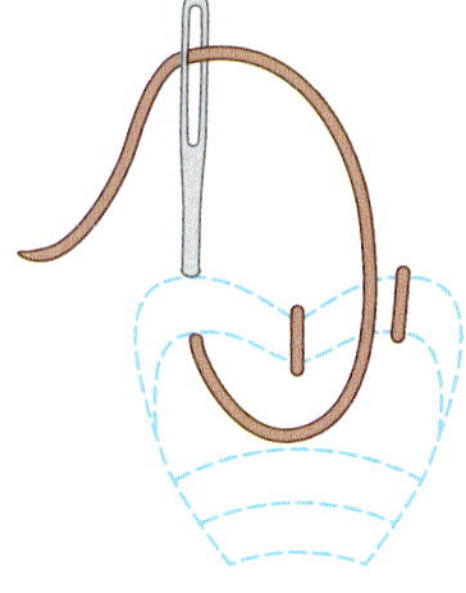

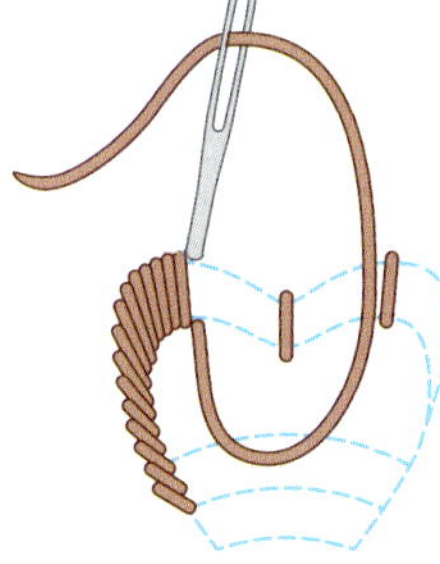

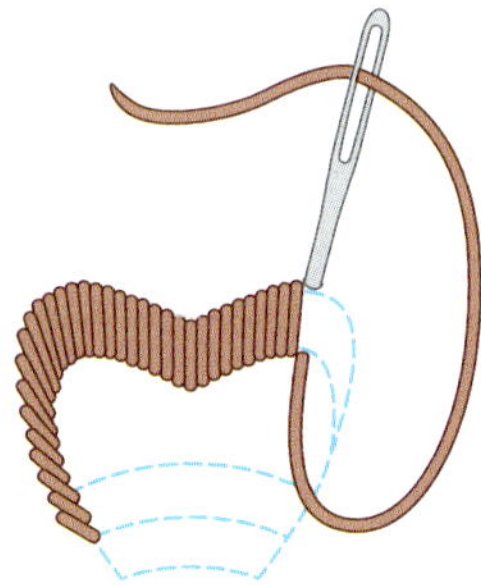

This technique, also known as block stitch, is similar to long and short shading, but uses satin stitches all in similar length, worked in rows.

1 First row: add three straight stitches, at the lowest and highest points of the first row to be stitched, these will determine the angle of the stitches in this area.
2 Coming up at the base of the first row, begin with a straight stitch dividing this area of the petal in half and then quarters. Work across one quarter before returning to the original direction stitches to complete the next.
3 Always take your needle down through the linen just beyond the printed line. Continue by stitching each quarter with close stitches to densely cover the fabric.

Buttonhole stitch – single thread

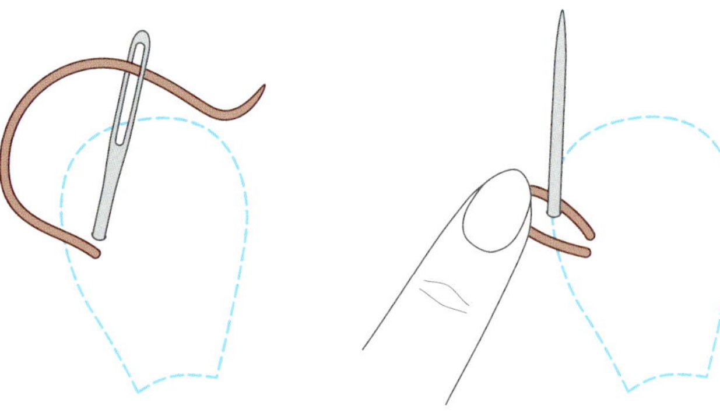

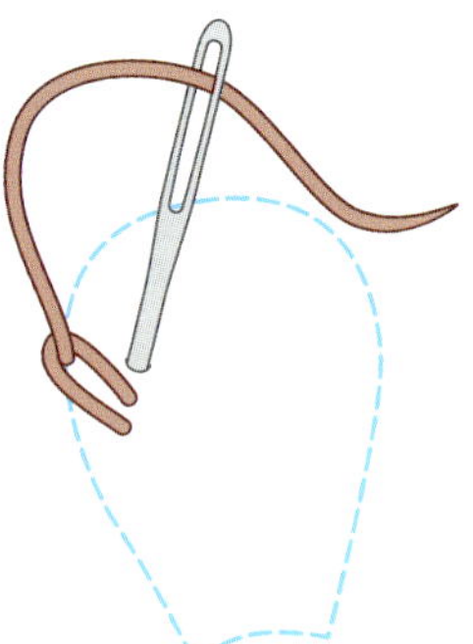

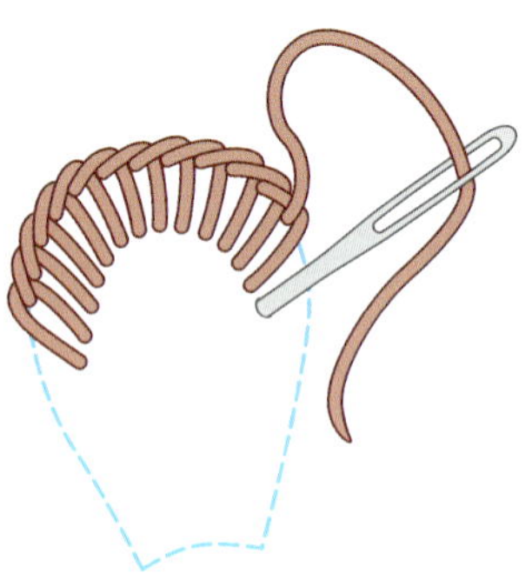

1 Begin by coming up through the side edge of the petal, then take your needle down through the linen just to the side of this stitch. Do not pull your wool tight at this point but leave a loop.

2 Bring your needle up on the outline of the petal, inside the loop of thread. Pull the needle gently to create enough tension on the first stitch. Then, take your needle back down through the linen beside your last stitch.

3 Again, remember to leave a small loop to enable the creation of the next stitch. Tension this second stitch and continue along this line until the tip of the petal is covered, securing your last stitch with a small couching stitch.

Closed fly stitch – single thread

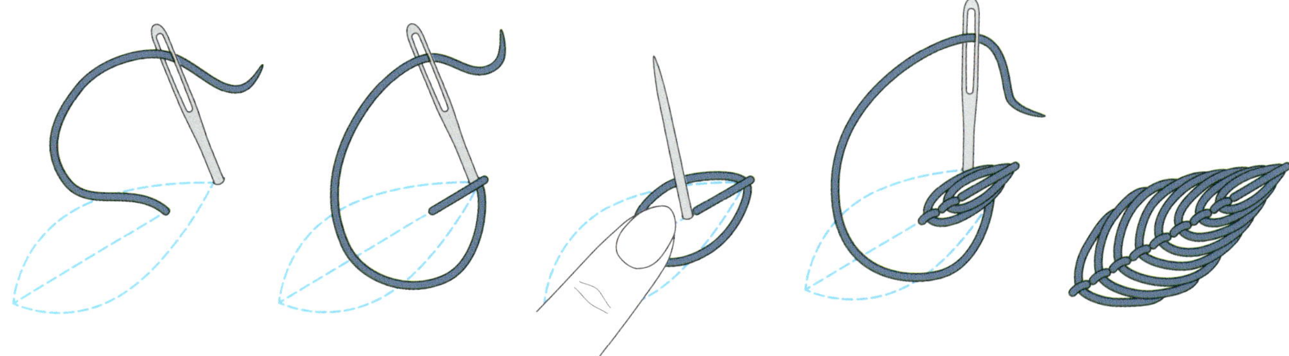

1 Bring your needle up through the fabric in the centre of the leaf, then take it back through just beyond the leaf tip, making one straight stitch.

2 Next, bring the needle back up just to the right of the leaf tip and go back through the fabric on the opposite side to your original stitch, holding the loop down the leaf. Come back up through the fabric again at the end of your original stitch and gently pass your needle through the loop.

3 Pull the thread taut until the loop closes. Then, still on the centre line, couch over the loop. Come back up through the fabric slightly behind the first stitch, and back down again on the other side of that first stitch. As before, leave a loop hanging down the shape resting on the fabric. Come back up through the fabric at the end of the first couching stitch and pass the needle up inside the loop. As you did before, couch this loop.

4 Repeat this process and come up very close below the last stitch through the blue printed outline, just below where you came up for the last stitch, and go down again equally close to the left side. Repeat the actions above all the way down the leaf forming a deep V shape.

Closed fly stitch – double thread

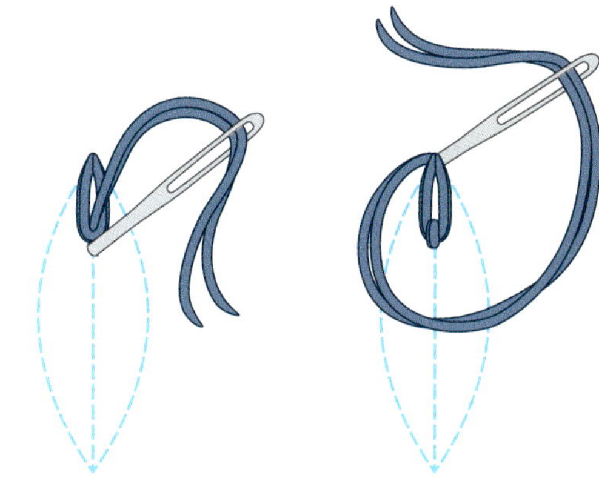

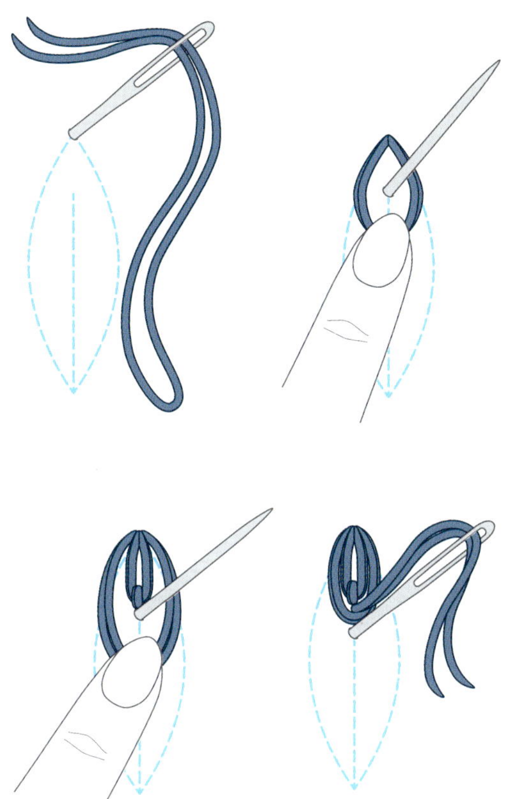

1 When working this stitch in double thread, the thread is secured by the first stitch. The loop created by the threading process removes the need to secure your thread. Fold and thread the wool through your needle as shown.

2 Take your needle down through the fabric 4mm (⅛in) beyond the tip of the leaf, then hold the loop down the leaf. Come back up through the fabric at the top of the printed central line, and up through the loop. Pull the needle and thread down the shape until the loop closes. Then, still on the centre line, 'couch' over the loop, with a 4mm (⅛in) stitch.

3 Come back up through the fabric slightly behind and underneath the top of the first stitch, and go back down again on the opposite side of that first stitch. Again, hold the loop hanging down the shape on the fabric. Come back up through the fabric at the end of the first couching stitch and pass the needle up though the loop. 'Couch' this loop, as you did before.

4 Repeat this process and come up very close below the last stitch, through the blue printed line, approximately 4mm (⅛in) below where you came up for the first stitch, then go down again equally close to the opposite side. Repeat the actions above all the way down the leaf forming a deep 'V' shape.

Coral stitch – double thread

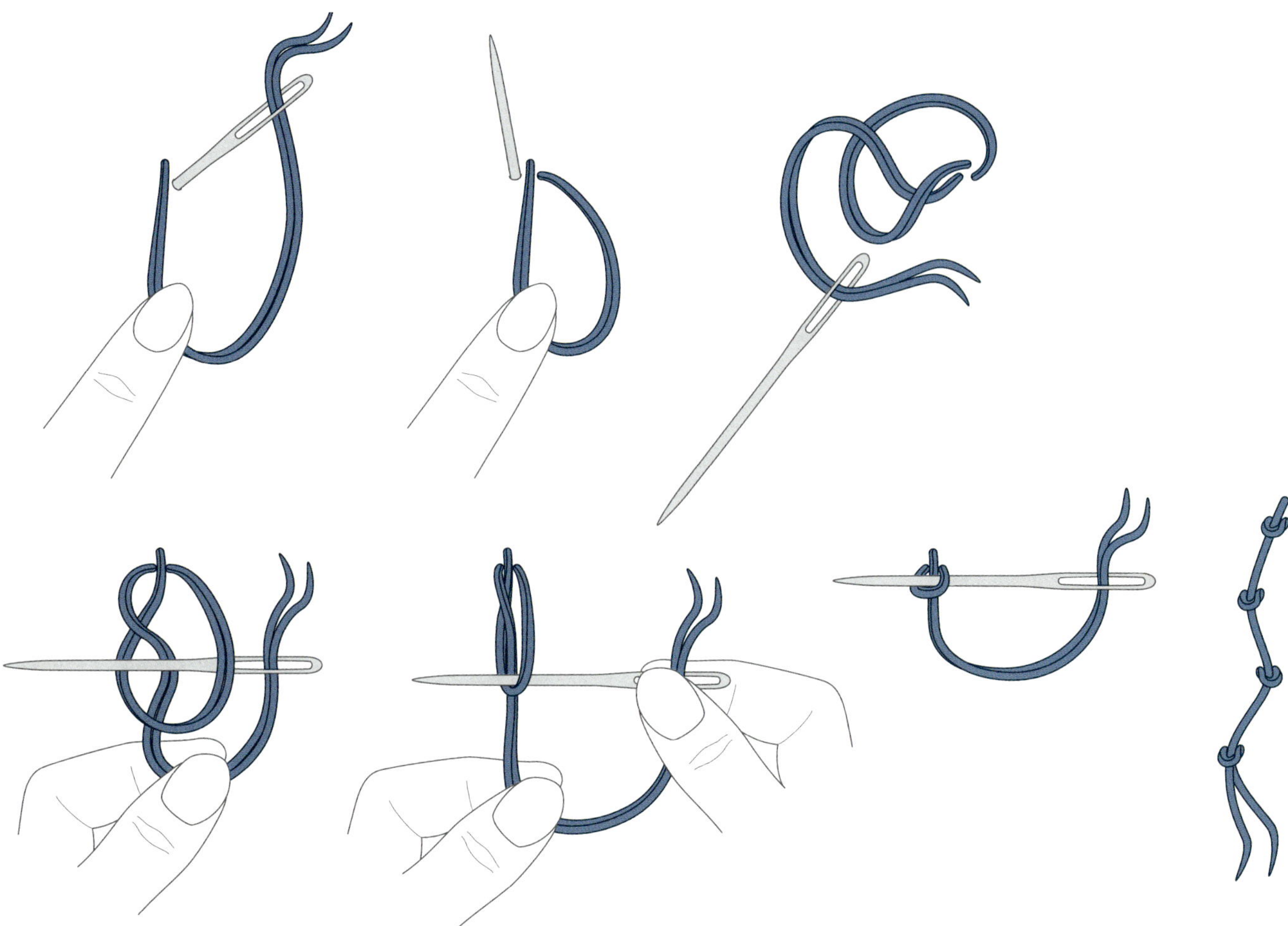

1 Bring the needle up and lay the working thread down where you would like the stem to be. Hold it in place with your finger and take the needle down through the fabric just below and to the right of the top of the first stitch.

2 Bring only the point of the needle back up again on the opposite side of the stitch.

3 Still holding the loop on top of the linen, and with the needle halfway through the fabric, bring the loop over the needle and pull the needle through.

4 Before you tension your stitch, insert your needle halfway into the loop. Then pull gently on the thread while tensioning the loop against the needle.

5 Now use the needle to place this ever-decreasing loop onto the fabric, creating a consistently perfect knot. Repeat this step at regular intervals along the line, until you reach the base of the line.

Crewel stem stitch – single thread

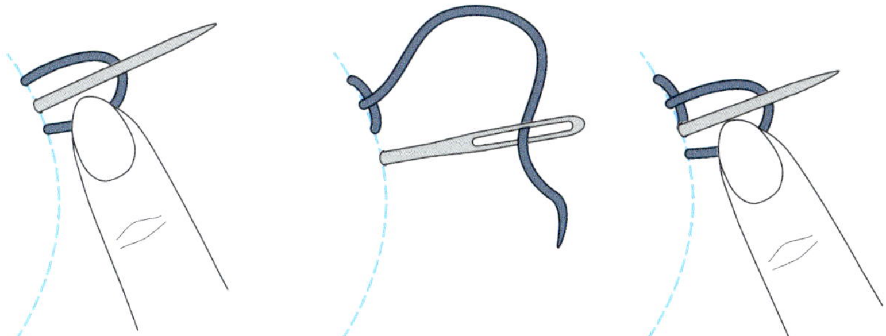

Tip

Where several lines of stitching are worked on a stem, begin at the top of each line, using each colour in turn.

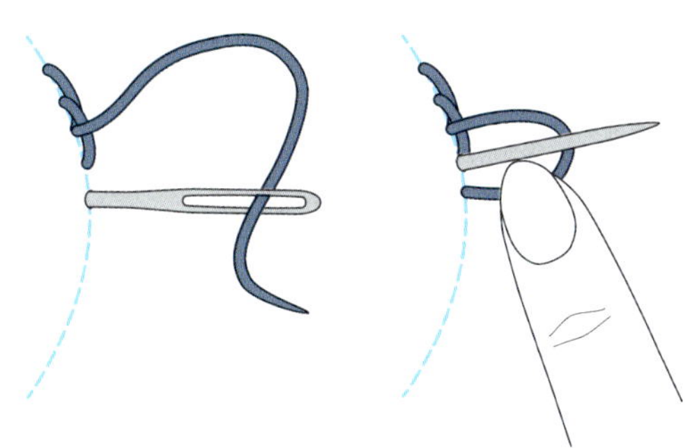

1. Begin by coming up at the top and going down again 6mm (¼in) along the line, leaving a loop on top of the fabric. Hold the loop with your finger and bring the needle up and halfway back along the first stitch. Release the loop as you pull the needle and thread up through the fabric. Pull until the looped thread is flat.
2. Continue stitching in a line by taking your needle down a further 6mm (¼in) along the line, once more creating a loop.
3. Again holding the loop in place, come back up through the fabric at the end of the first stitch, then once more pull until the loop is flat. Continue by taking your needle down another 6mm (¼in) along the line and repeat this same sequence until you reach the end.

Crewel stem stitch – double thread

Follow the steps above for crewel stem stitch worked in single thread, but holding your thread double.

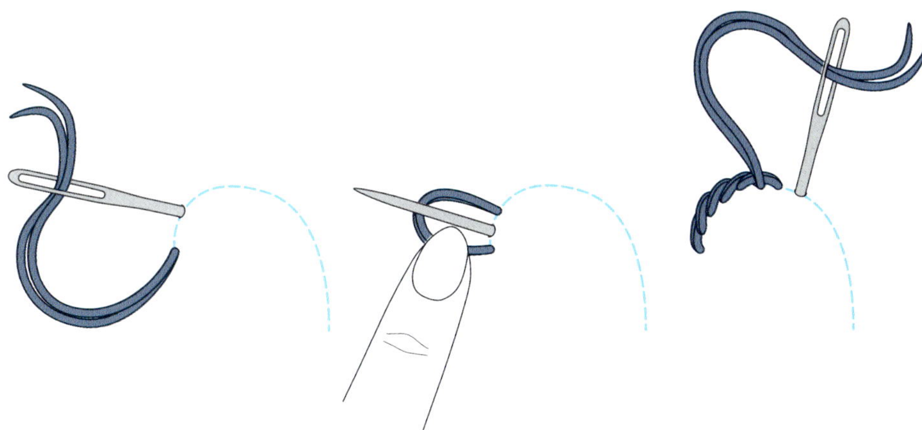

Tips

Remember that the loop should always be held away from the outside of the curve, so when the curve changes direction, so does the side you hold the loop.

When working rows of stem stitch, always begin with the colour on the outer side of a curve and make smaller stitches when negotiating tight corners.

Fan stitch – single thread

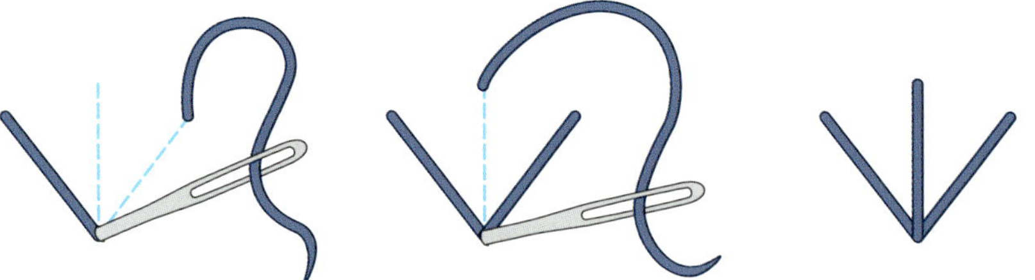

This decorative stitch was used extensively in crewelwork during the seventeenth century.

Make straight stitches to create a 'V' shape, then work a slightly longer central stitch.

Fern stitch – double thread

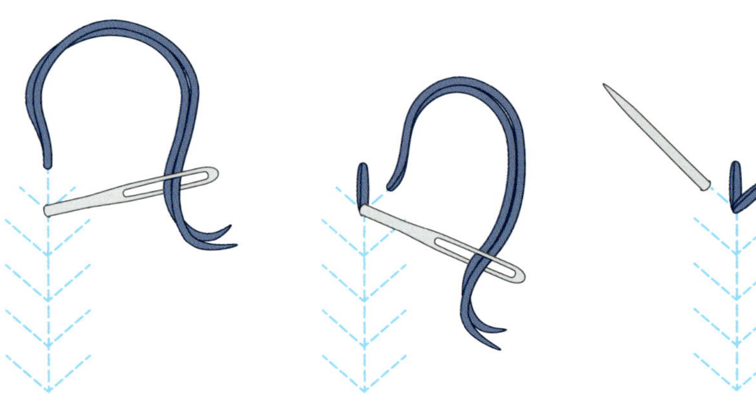

1 Bring your needle up at the top of the line, then take it back down at the point where the first set of lines branch off. Next, bring your needle up through the tip of the right-hand branch, and then down into the same hole as the base of the first stitch.

2 Come up again through the tip of the left branch and create another stitch coming back down through the same hole as before.

3 Progress down the line by bringing the needle up through the fabric at the point where the next branches are formed, and take it back down through the same hole as your previous stitches.

4 Repeat until your line is complete.

French knots – double thread

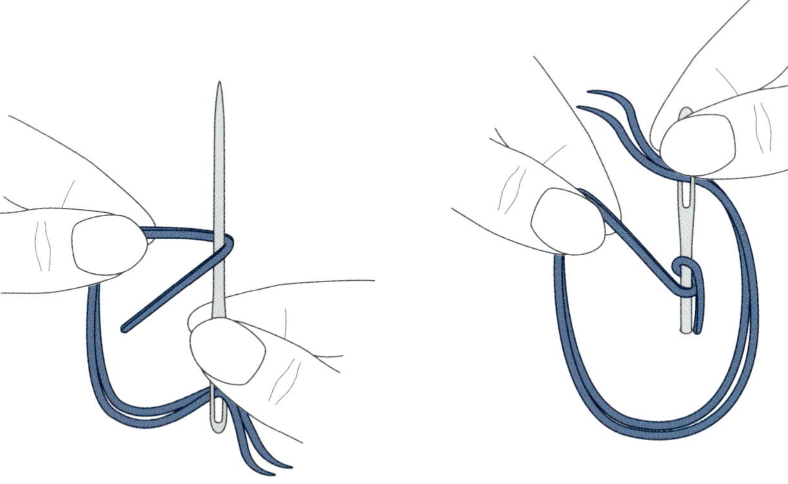

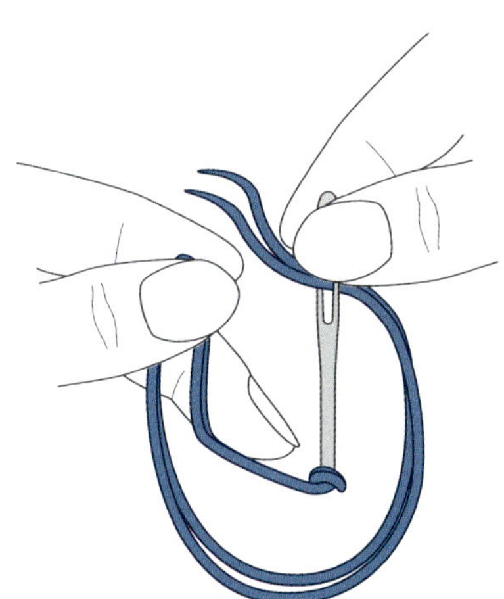

1. Having come up through the fabric, hold the wool taut a little way above the fabric with one hand. Using your other hand, hold the eye of the needle, with its tip pointing away from the fabric. Wind the wool anti-clockwise (or clockwise for left-handers) once around the needle. Keep the wool pulled tightly and keep this 'wool' hand above your needle.
2. Turn the point of the needle away from you, then push the point of your needle into the fabric, 3mm ($^{1}/_{8}$in) or so away from where you came up.
3. Firmly hold your needle in this position, and use your first or second finger of your 'wool' hand to slide the turned wool down the needle, until it rests on the fabric. Lock the knot in place by pulling firmly on the wool.
4. Still keeping hold of the needle, let go of the wool and then pull the needle through from underneath to complete the knot.

Laid and couched work

This historic stitch has been widely used from the late seventeenth century to the present day, being particularly useful for organizing informal shapes into calming and pleasingly ordered areas of interest.

From the Bayeux stitch to the variations used today, laying one thread across a whole feature seems to be just too quick and easy to be true! The wonderful feature of this stitch is that it can be as simple or as complicated as you wish, with squares or diamond shapes making up the grid, then lightly decorating as you couch the junctions where two threads cross, before adding extra decoration to this stable base.

Variation 1: single thread, three layers

Laid work – first layer

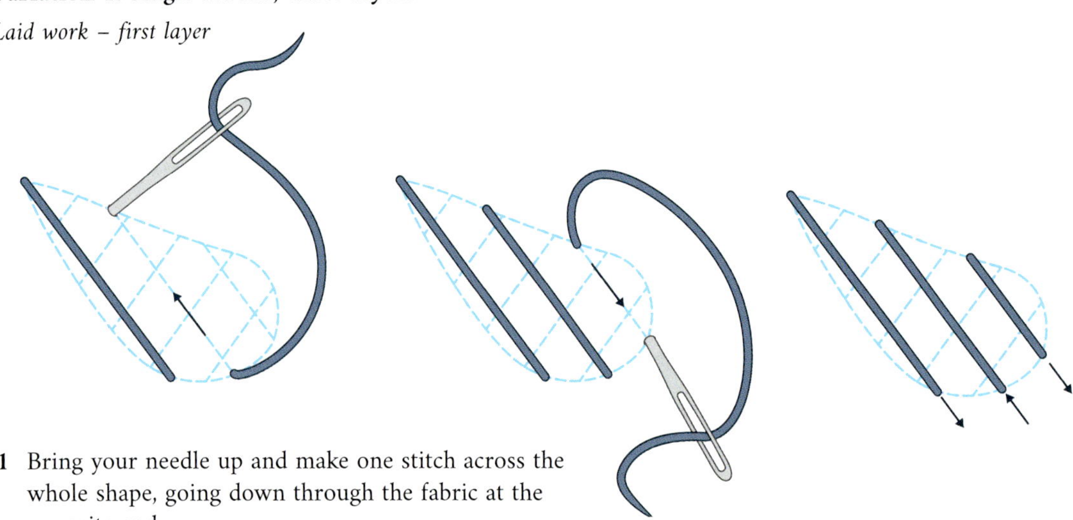

1 Bring your needle up and make one stitch across the whole shape, going down through the fabric at the opposite end.

2 Next, bring the thread up at the same end of the adjacent line, and go down at the opposite end. Continue stitching up and down over the shape.

Laid work – second layer

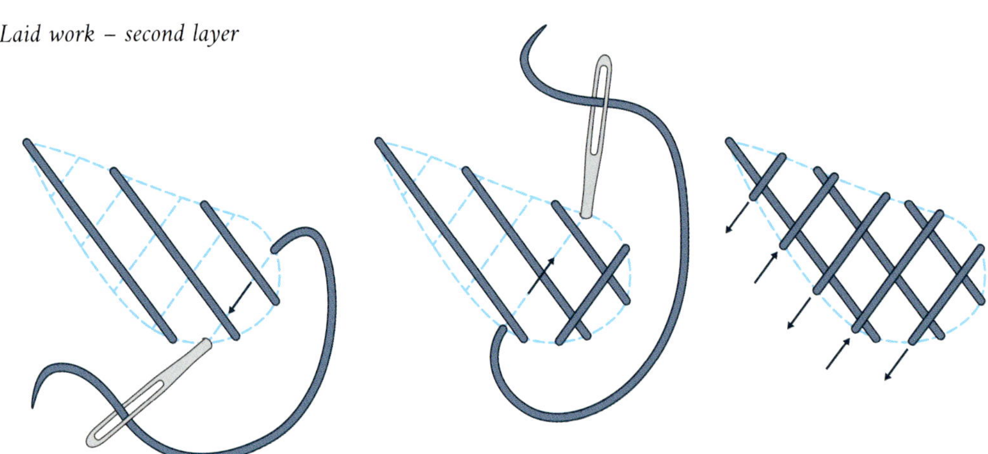

3 To create the second layer, use the same colour and work in the opposite direction at evenly spaced intervals.

Couching – third layer

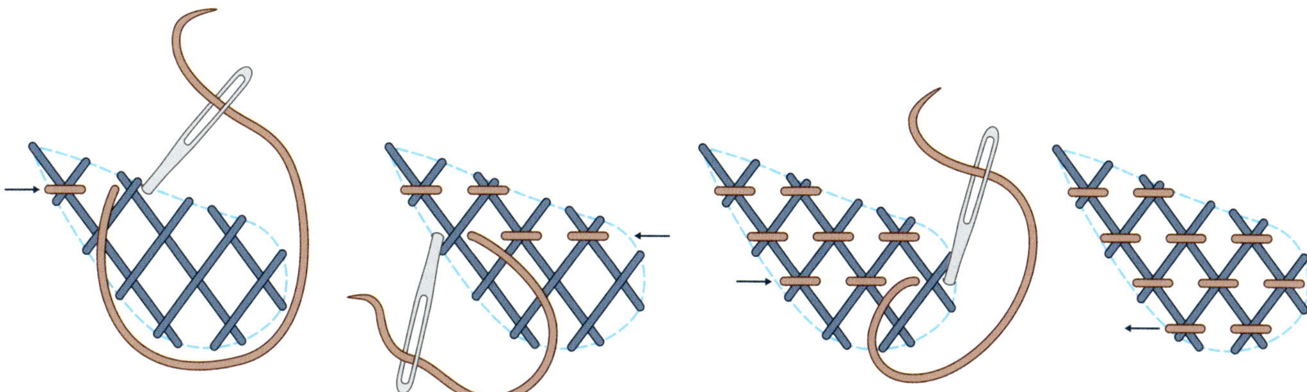

4 Using a contrasting colour, 'couch' with small straight stitches over every point where the laid stitches overlap.

Note that each 'couching' stitch travels across each diamond shape. This maintains the exact shape of the laid work below.

Variation 2: single thread, four layers

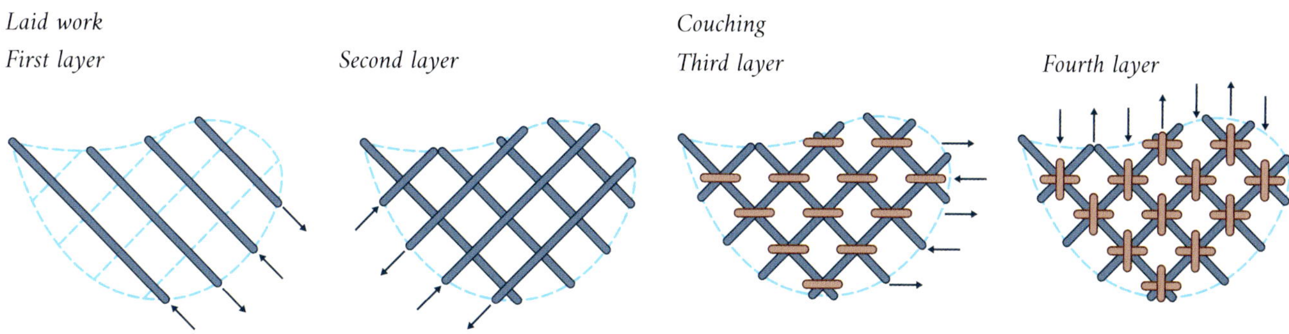

Worked with the same basic laid work in two layers of one colour, but instead of using a single straight couching stitch, it is couched with two layers of straight stitches.

Create your 'laid' work as before.

In a contrasting colour, 'couch' in two layers, first horizontally and then vertically over every point where laid stitches overlap, with small straight stitches.

> **Tip**
>
> Take care not to tension couching stitches too much or the stitching will 'dimple'.

Variation 3: couched with detached fly

First colour – single thread

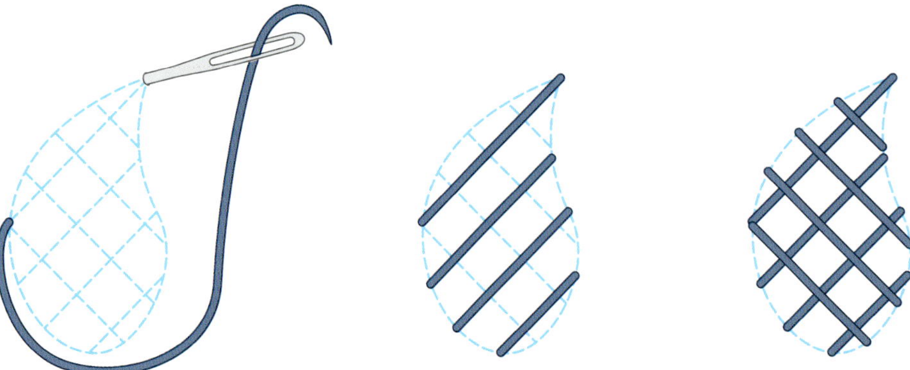

1 Lay straight lines with your wool across the shape and follow this first layer of stitches, with a second layer worked in the opposite direction.

Second colour – single thread

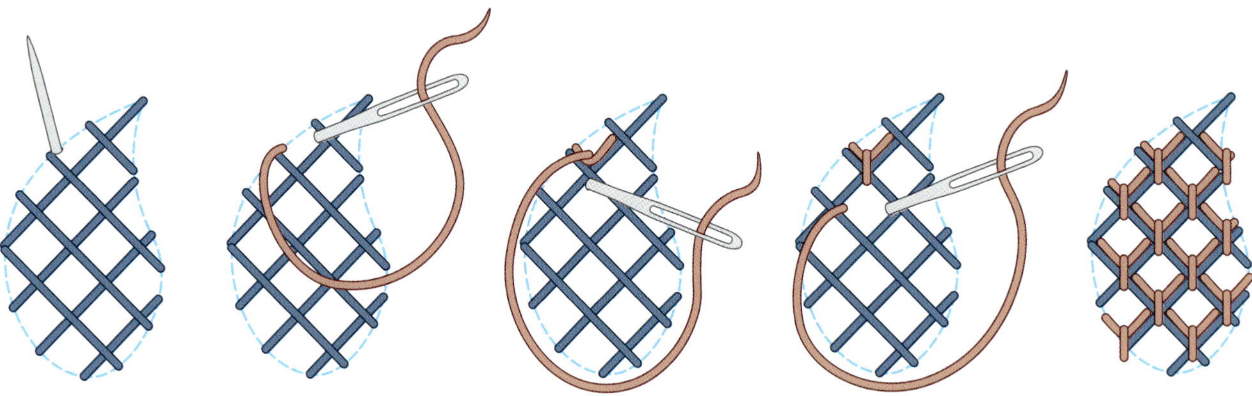

2 Using a second colour, create a detached fly stitch inside the diamond shapes you have just created. To do this, come up through the fabric inside the left corner of an empty diamond, and go back down again just inside the right corner. Hold the loop on top of the fabric, then come back up through the fabric just above where your laid lines cross below, before passing your needle up inside the loop.

3 Continue adding detached fly stitches in each square, adding only part of the stitch in areas where the shape of the leaf does not allow for a whole stitch.

Variation 4: Trellis

First colour – single thread

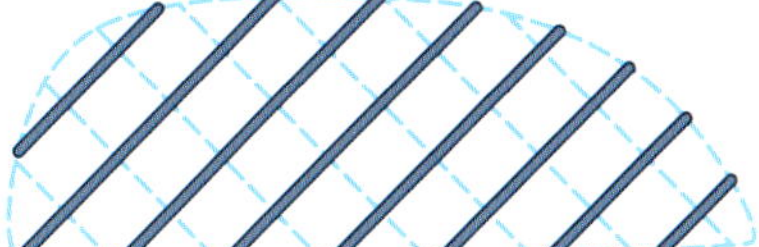

1 This time, in single thread throughout, stitch the first two layers of laid stitches as before.

2 To create the second layer, use the same colour and cover the lines in the opposite direction.

Second colour – single thread

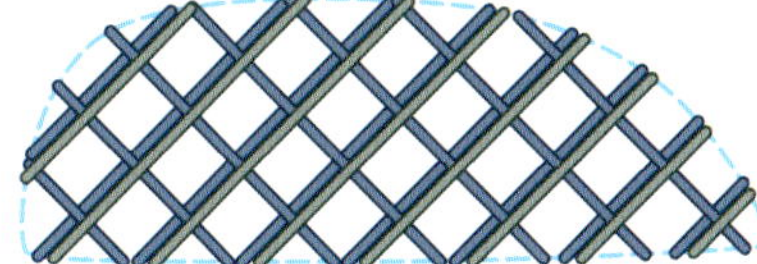

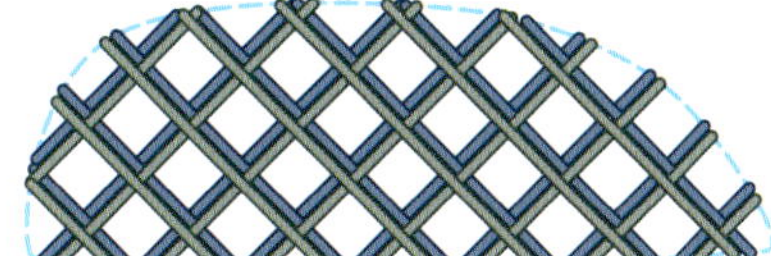

3 The second colour is then carefully laid alongside and touching the first colour, and immediately below it to the right.

4 Then, stitch this colour in the other direction, below and to the left of the first colour.

Third colour – single thread

5 Then create the final layers of laid work in the same way.

Fourth colour – single thread

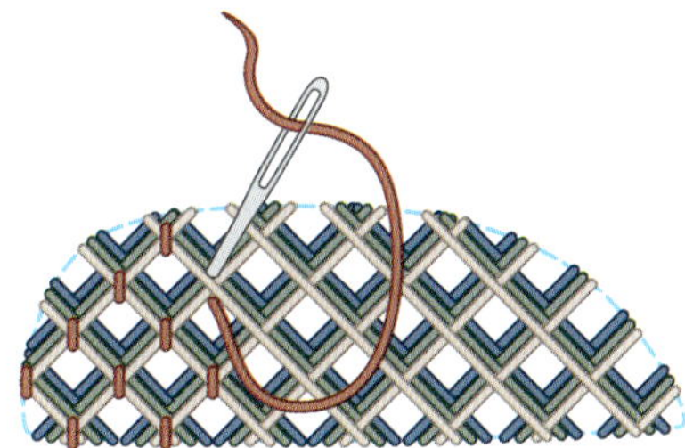

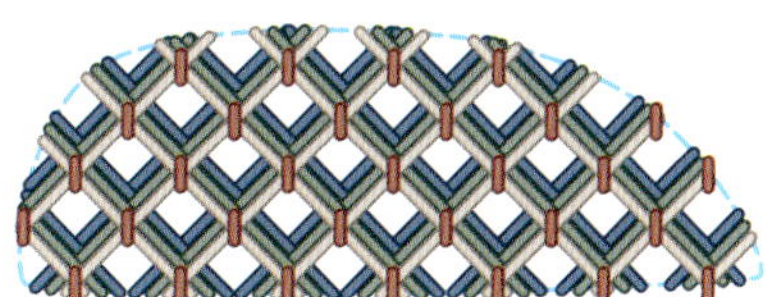

6 Finally, using the contrasting colour indicated on the stitch chart, couch by making a stitch vertically over the previous colour only, anchoring each point where the laid lines cross each other.

Variation 5: four layers of laid work and three layers of couching

All layers of this variation are worked in a single thread.

Laid work – first colour

Create the first two layers of laid stitches.

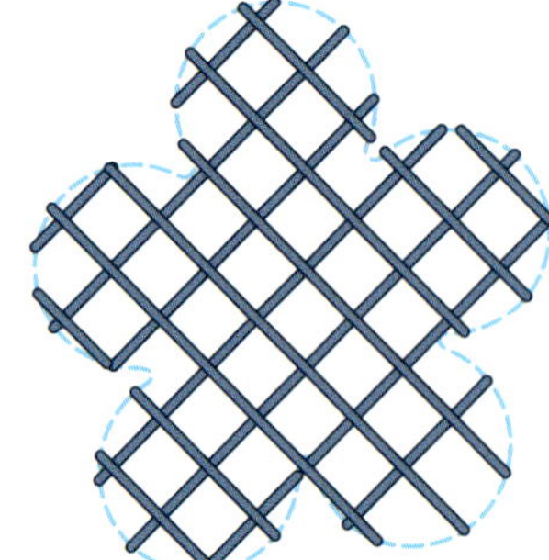

Laid work – second colour

Stitch the third and fourth layers in a second colour, running horizontally and then vertically over a row of intersections from the previous layer. Each row of stitches will skip a row.

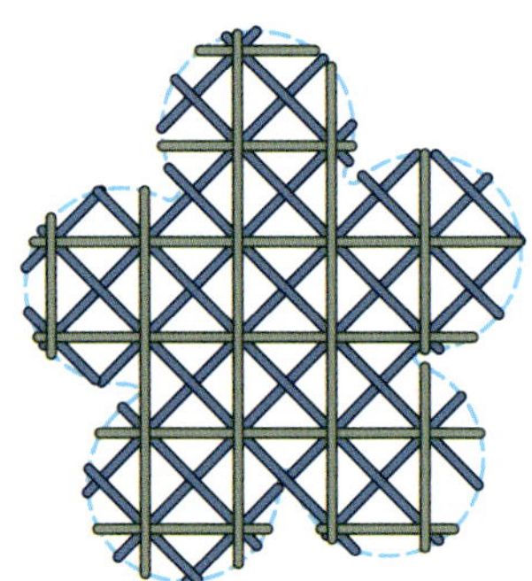

Couching – third colour

The first and second couching layers are then stitched diagonally, creating a cross stitch effect over all four laid layers.

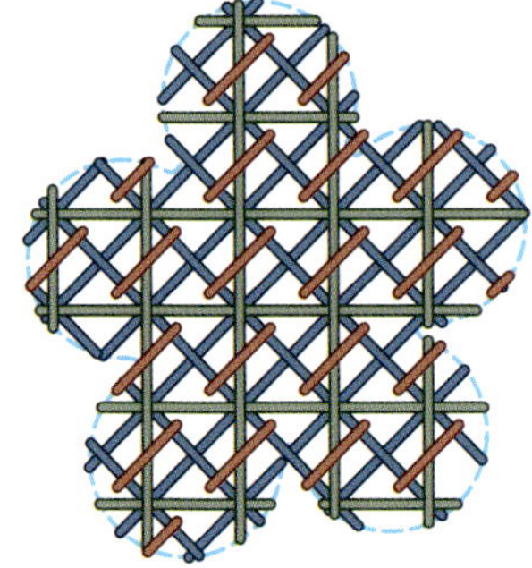

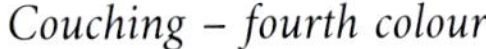

Couching – fourth colour

Finally, couch the intersection of all but the first two layers (the centres of the last crosses made).

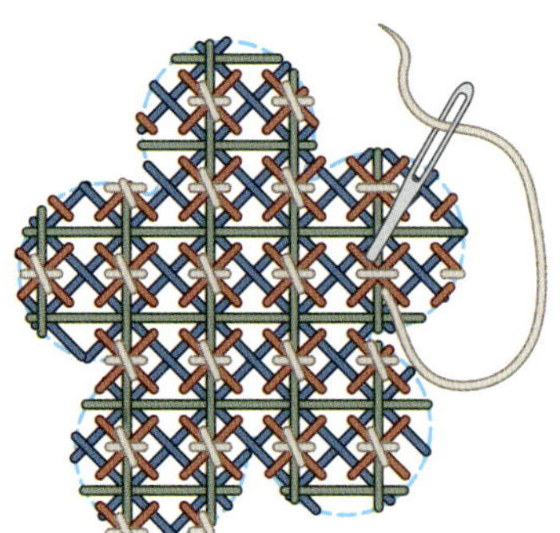

Variation 6: laid and couched work with double thread

First colour – double thread

Create your first layer of laid work in double thread.

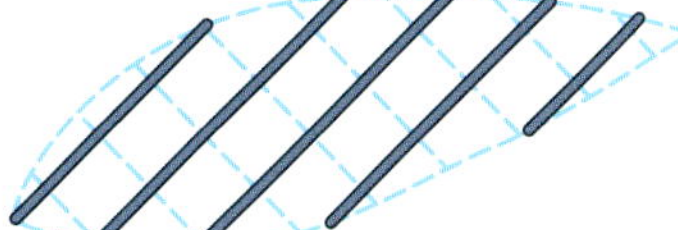

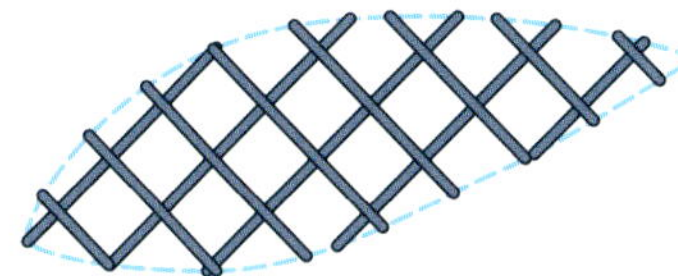

Second colour – double thread

Couch every other square diagonally with two parallel rows of running stitches to form double crosses over every other square.

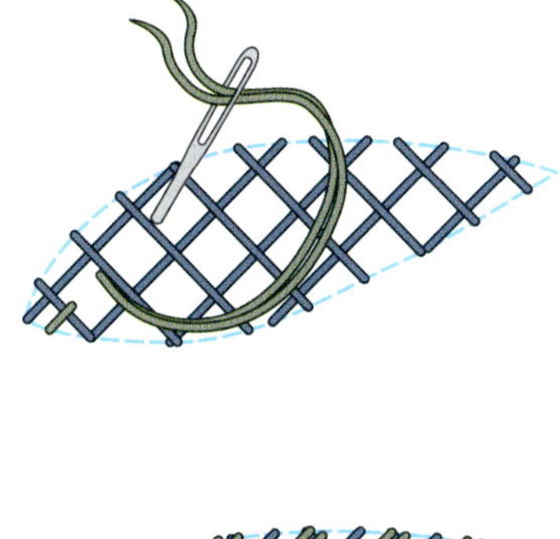

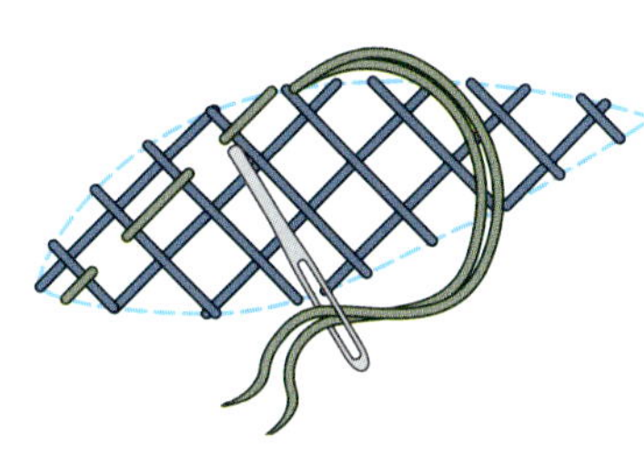

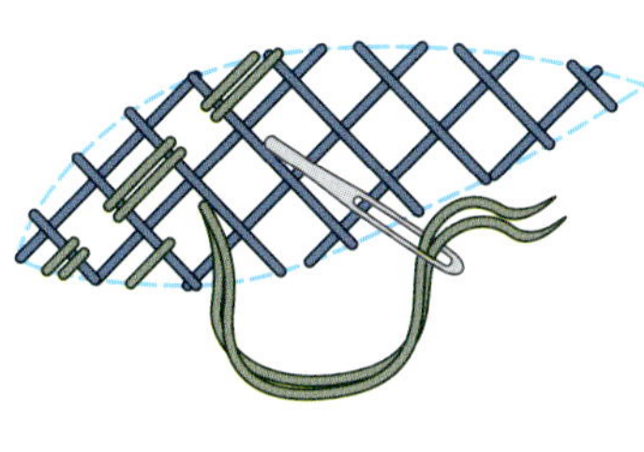

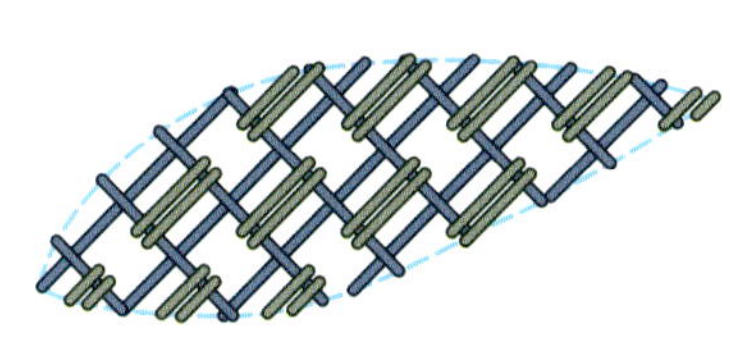

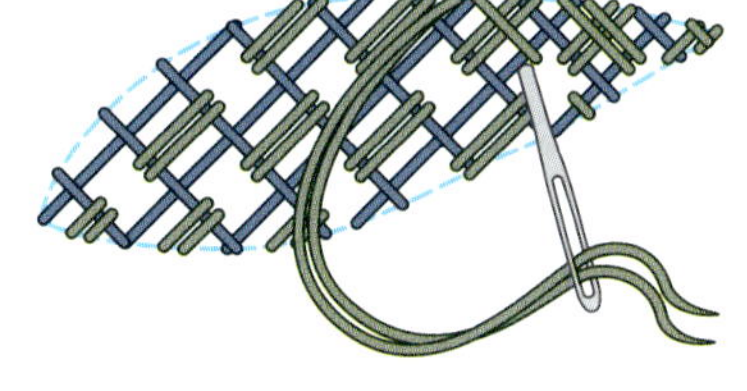

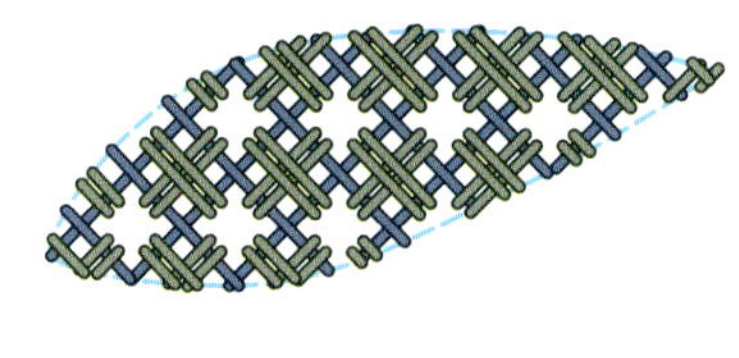

Third colour – double thread

Using a third colour, couch in one direction, followed by the next to create crosses.

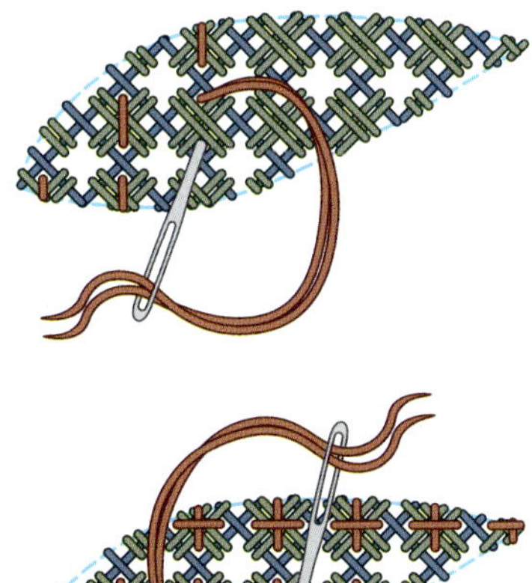

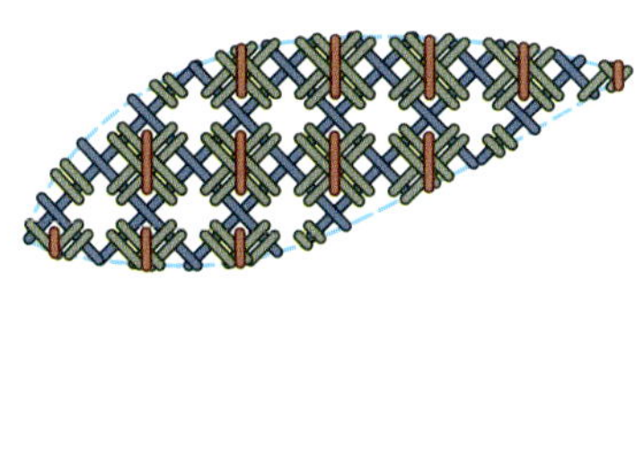

Leaf stitch – single thread

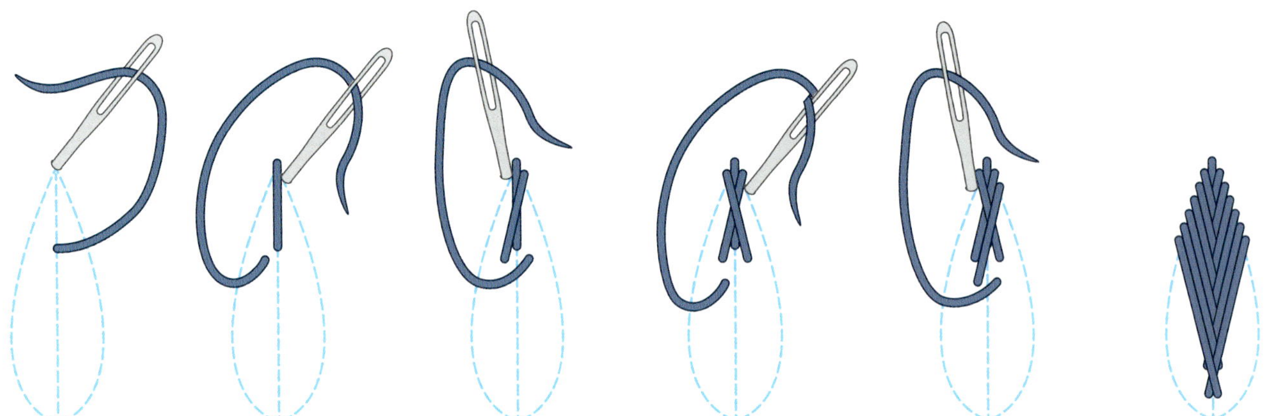

1 Start by bringing your needle up through the fabric at the top of the central line of the feather and taking it back down again just past the tip.

2 Next, bring your needle up again through the fabric on the left-hand side of the base of the original stitch and then cross the first stitch, bringing the needle down on the opposite side next to the tip. Your third stitch should mirror your second stitch.

3 Repeat this sequence all the way down the petal edge, moving each pair of stitches down the shape.

Long and short stitch: two colours

Long and short stitch is a classically beautiful crewelwork technique in which the wools are blended together to create a gradual change of colour. Begin with the top of the shape you want to fill and work across and then downwards. Variations of long and short stitch as 'soft shading' include using two or three colours and single or double thread.

First colour – double thread

1 Secure your thread in the lower area of the petal, then bring the needle up and go down just beyond the tip. Stitch across the bud to the left with alternating long and slightly shorter stitches to densely cover the area, stitching very close together.

2 Next, come up alongside the original stitch, and work towards the right in the same way, all the way to the side of the bud.

Second colour – single thread

3 Again making your first stitch halfway across the bud, come up through the first colour and stitch in the opposite direction, down towards the sepals with alternating long and short stitches.

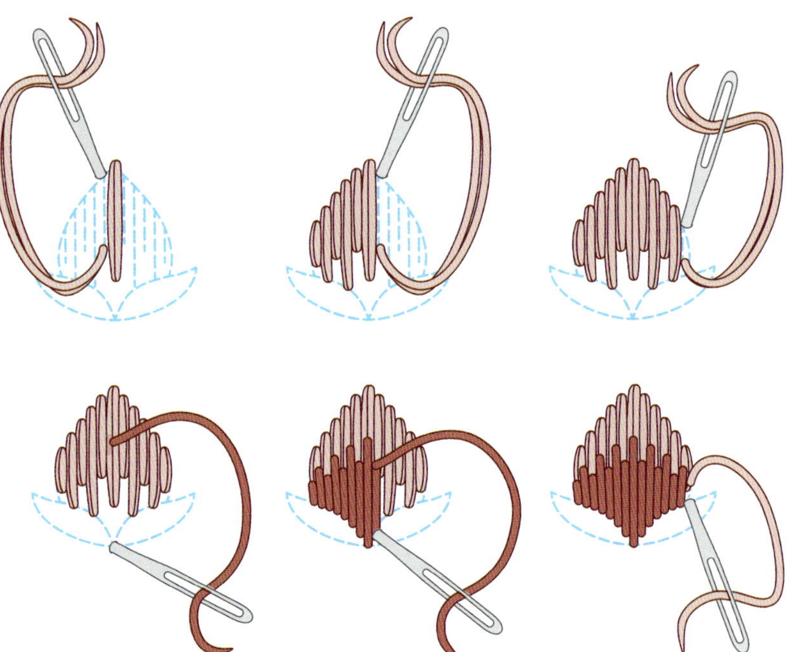

Long and short stitch: three colours

First colour – double thread

1 Come up in the centre of the petal and stitch down just beyond the outline. Then stitch across the petal to the edge of the section, with alternating long and slightly shorter stitches. Cover the area by keeping the stitches very close together.

2 Take the thread across the back of your work and begin the opposite side of the petal, completing the first colour.

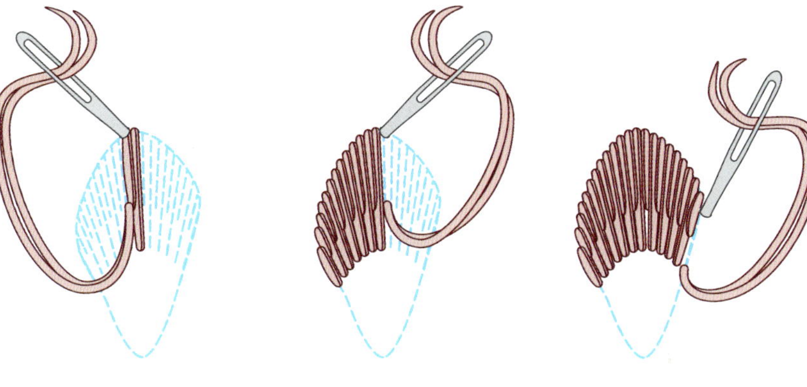

Second colour – single thread

3 Using a second colour, bring your first stitch up through the first colour near the tip of the petal and stitch down the centre line towards the base of the petal. Continue to come up through the first colour with alternating longer and shorter stitches (shorter at both ends). As before, once you have completed this first half, return to the middle before completing the other side of the petal in this second colour.

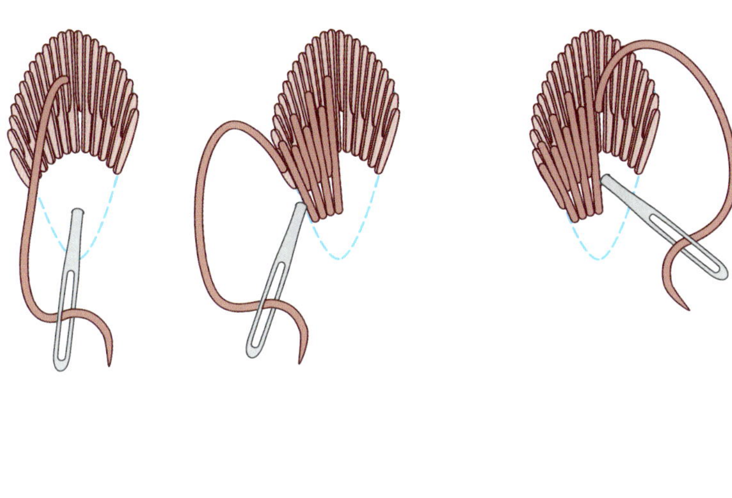

Third colour – single thread

4 The third colour is also stitched in exactly the same sequence, first one half and then the other. Starting again halfway across the petal, and using the third colour, come up through the stitches of the second, and sometimes even the first, and stitch down onto the base of the petal and through the blue line. Varying the length of your stitches as you come up through these previous colours is the key to achieving the 'soft shading' effect.

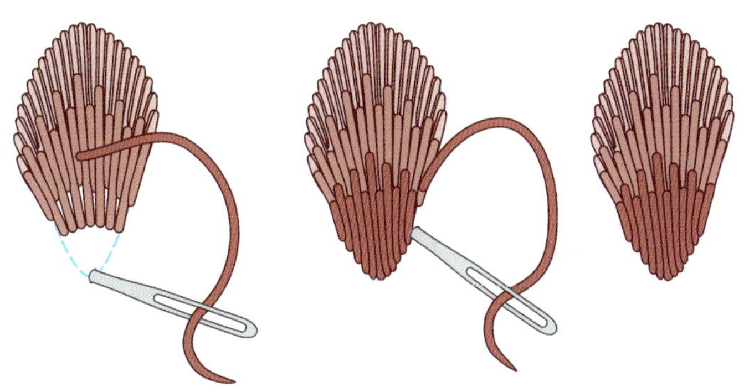

Tip

Use the angle of the stitches of the first colour as your guide for the angle of the second and third colours. Blend the colours by varying the length of your stitches and do not be afraid to come up deep into the first colour with the occasional stitch.

Long and short stitch as soft shading – pointed leaf

First colour – double thread

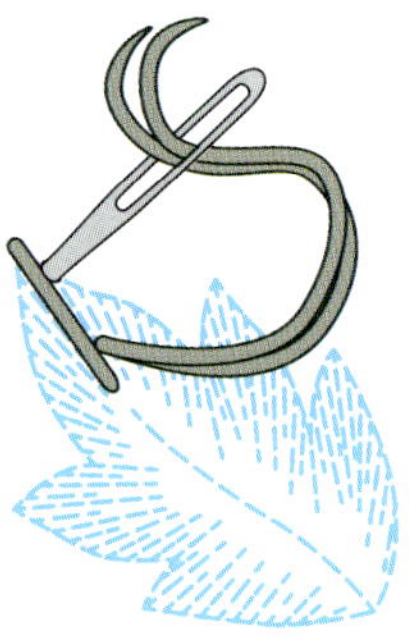

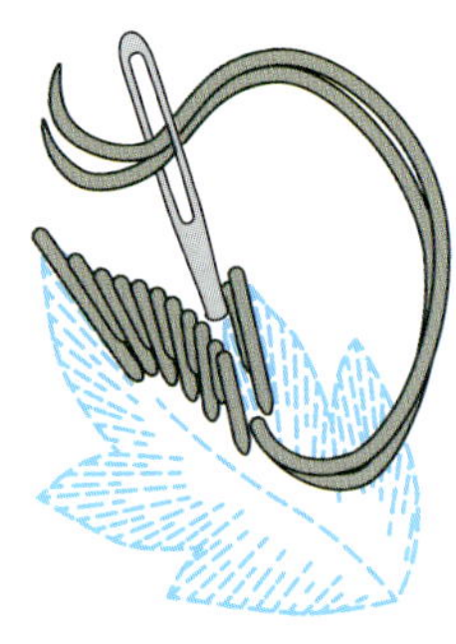

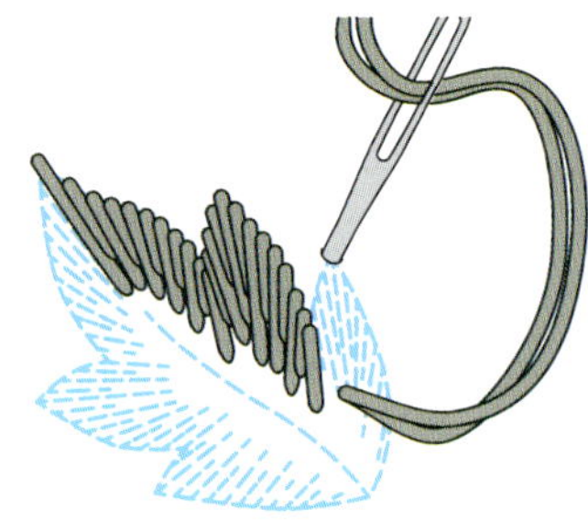

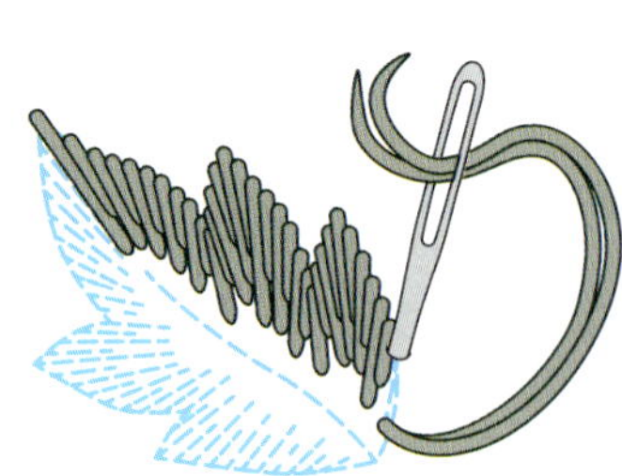

1 Secure your thread within the lower half of the leaf, then bring your needle up through the fabric, halfway across the leaf tip, and go down just beyond the tip of the printed leaf outline. Follow this with a three-quarter-length stitch. Mentally divide each side of the leaf into the sections; this will help you to achieve the correct angle for your stitches.

2 Continue stitching across the section with alternating long and slightly shorter (three-quarter-length) stitches, all the way to the side of the first section.

3 Densely cover the area, keeping the stitches close together and adding extra stitches where needed. Begin the next section by coming up midway across the area, and go down again just over the leaf outline, then work back towards the previous section. Next, come up alongside your original stitch in this section with a three-quarter-length stitch and work the remaining half of this section.

4 Work down this part of the leaf section by section, before returning to the tip of the leaf and completing the first colour of the opposite side in the same way.

Second colour – single thread

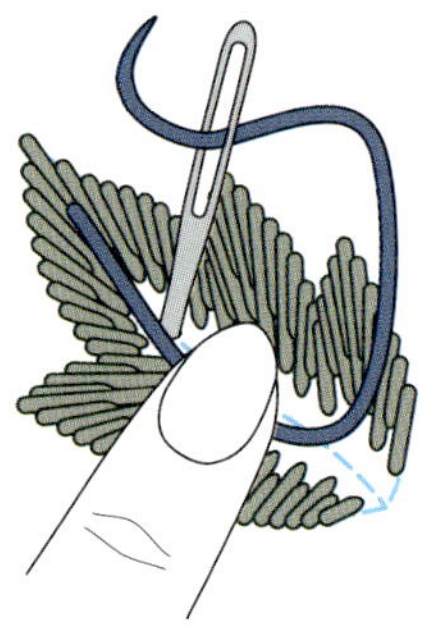

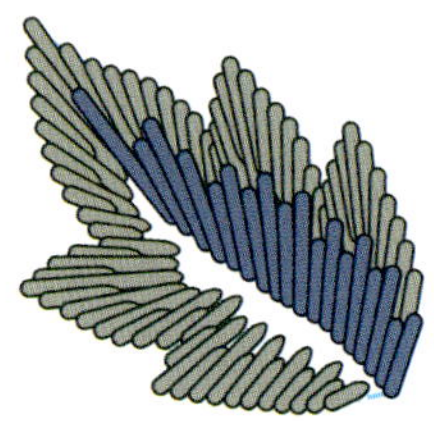

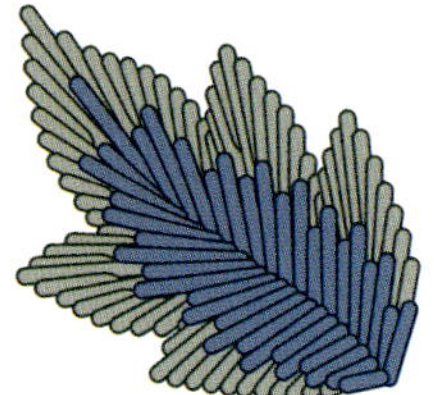

5 All the stitches in this second colour end on the central vein of the leaf. Bring your needle up halfway across the tip, through the stitches of the first colour, then down again at the top of the printed leaf vein. To find the correct angle for the first stitch in each area, 'lay' the thread down over the first colour to create the same angle as the first layer of stitches.

6 Work alternately one long stitch followed by one short stitch (approximately half-length).

7 Continue stitching this second colour in sections. The 'soft shading' effect is achieved by varying the length of your stitches, particularly in this second colour.

8 Complete this leaf by adding crewel stem stitch down the central vein, then continue this stitch all the way down the stem.

Tips

Use the angle of the stitches of the first colour as your guide for the second.

Don't be afraid to come up deep into the previous colour with the occasional even longer stitch to achieve the full 'soft shading' effect.

Long and short stitch as soft shading – hummock

First colour – double thread

1 To make your first stitch, come up halfway across the hummock and go down through the fabric just beyond the outline. Next, bring your needle up alongside your first stitch and take your needle back down just beside the top of this stitch.

2 Stitch across one side of the area with pairs of long and then slightly shorter stitches. Densely cover the area, keeping the stitches very close together.

3 Next, carry the thread across the back of your work and come up again alongside your original stitch, before working across the other half of the hummock, using the same technique.

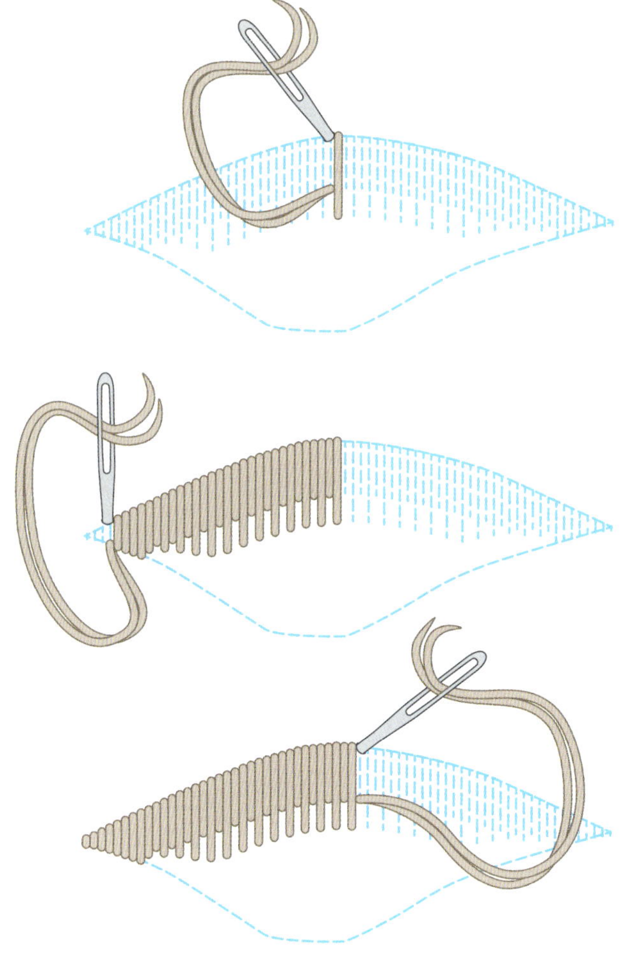

Second colour – single thread

4 Use fewer stitches and single thread for the remaining layers of colours. Using the second colour, bring your first stitch up through the first colour and stitch down towards, but not over, the base of the hummock. Continue to come up through the first colour with alternating longer and shorter stitches (shorter at both ends). As before, once you have completed this first half, return to the middle, and complete the other side of the hummock in this second colour.

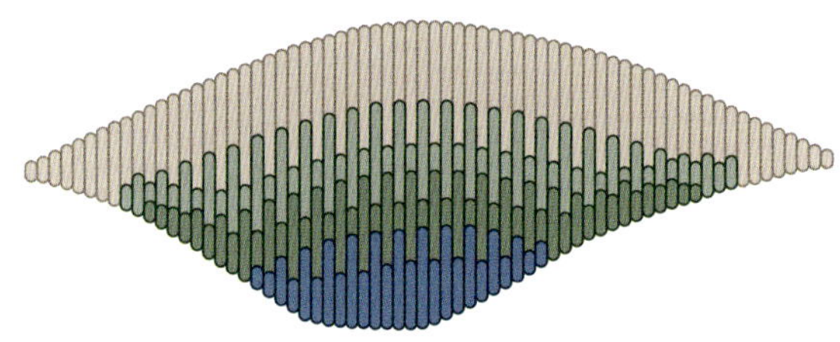

Third colour – single thread

5 The third colour is also stitched in exactly the same sequence, first one half and then the other. Starting again halfway across the hummock, and using the third colour, come up through the stitches of the second, and sometimes even the first.

Fourth colour – single thread

6 For the fourth colour, stitch down onto the base of the hummock and through the blue line with long and half-length stitches.

Long and short stitch as soft shading – oak leaf

First colour – double thread

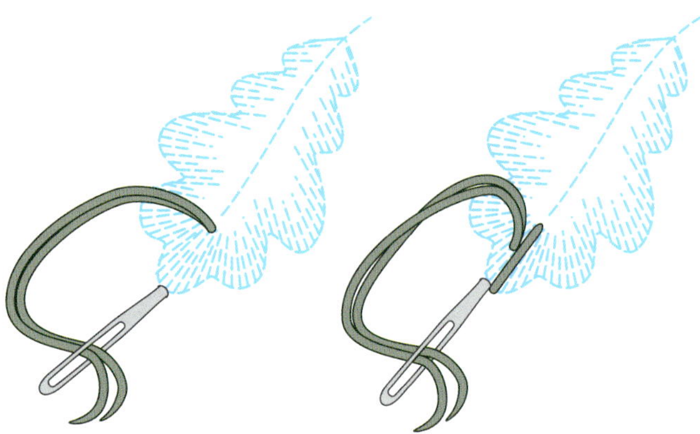

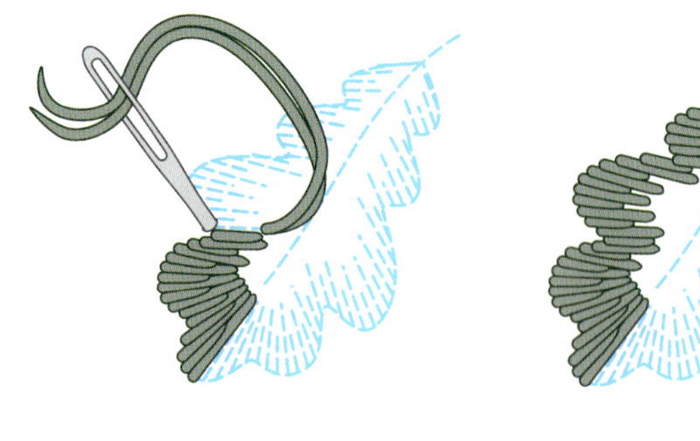

1 Mentally divide the leaf into the sections to help you to achieve the correct angle for your stitches. Using double thread, come up at the tip of the leaf vein and go down over the edge of the leaf. Follow this with a three-quarter-length stitch.

2 Continue stitching across the section with alternating long and slightly shorter (three-quarter-length) stitches, all the way to the side of the first section. Densely cover the blue outline by keeping the stitches close together, adding extra stitches where needed to create a densely stitched leaf edge.

3 Begin the next section by coming up midway across the area, and go down again just over the blue outline, then work back towards the previous section. Next, come up alongside your original stitch in this section with a three-quarter-length stitch and work the remaining half. Work down one side of the leaf section by section, before returning to the tip of the leaf and completing the first colour of the opposite side in the same way.

Second colour – single thread

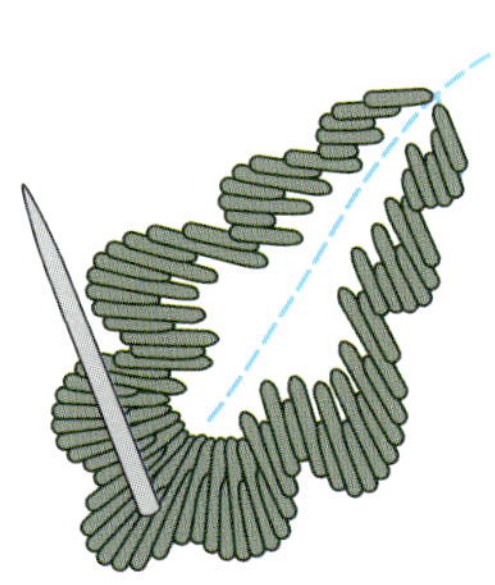

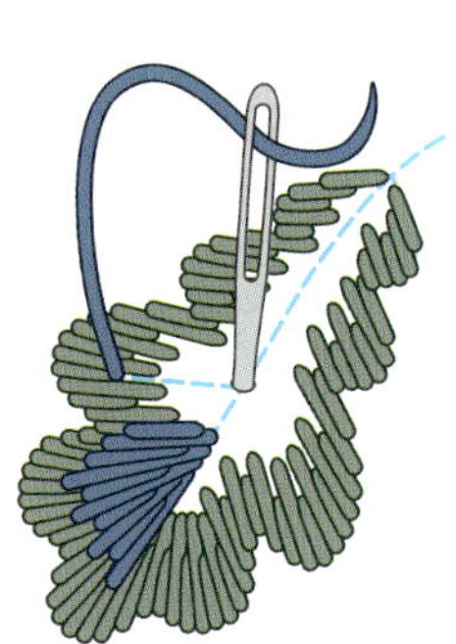

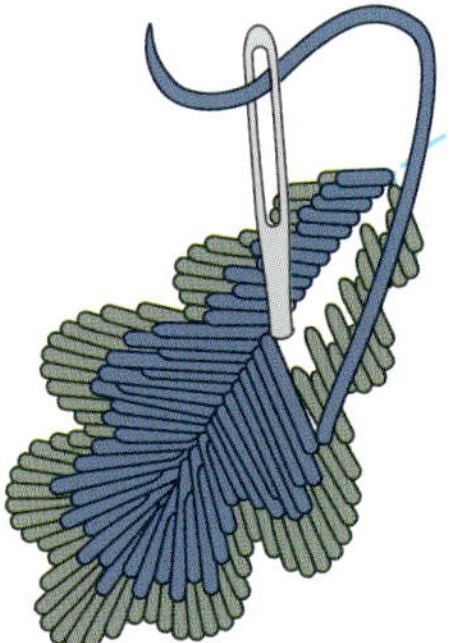

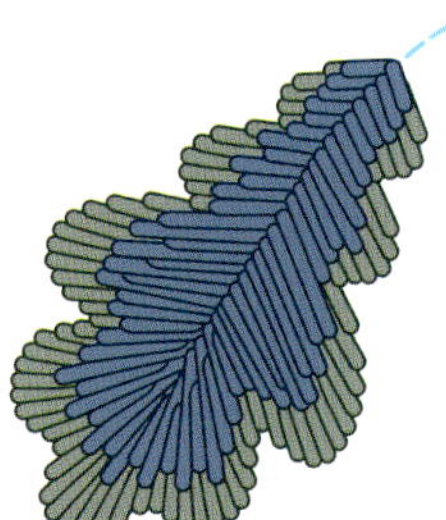

4 All the stitches in the second colour end on the central vein of the leaf. Bring your needle up halfway across the tip, through the stitches of the first colour, then go down again at the tip of the printed leaf vein.

5 To find the correct angle for the first stitch in each area, 'lay' the thread down over the first colour to create the same angle as the first layer of stitches. Work alternately one long stitch followed by one short stitch (approximately half length).

6 Continue stitching this second colour in sections. The 'soft shading' effect is achieved by varying the length of your stitches, particularly in this second colour.

Long and short stitch – vine leaves

First colour – double thread

1 Work the vine leaves in much the same way as the oak leaf, but work in sections. Come up halfway across the leaf tip and go down over the outline. Continue stitching across the section to the right with alternating long and slightly shorter (three-quarter-length) stitches, all the way to the side of this section.

2 Bring your needle up halfway across the next section and take it down again over the tip of this area. Work towards the left, all the way to the previously stitched area. Then, coming up alongside your original stitch in this section, work the remaining section.

3 Complete the remaining side in the same colour, using the same method. Starting at the central tip of the leaf, work the first section to the left before coming up at the tip on the left-hand side and working back towards the last stitched section. Return to the last tip and stitch the final section of the leaf.

Continued overleaf

Tips

To create a raised edge similar to the original seventeenth-century crewelwork, use a generous amount of double thread in this first colour.

If any of the outer edges show gaps in your stitches, add more over the top of this layer in a single thread in the same colour to correct this.

Long and short stitch – vine leaves *continued*

Second colour – single thread

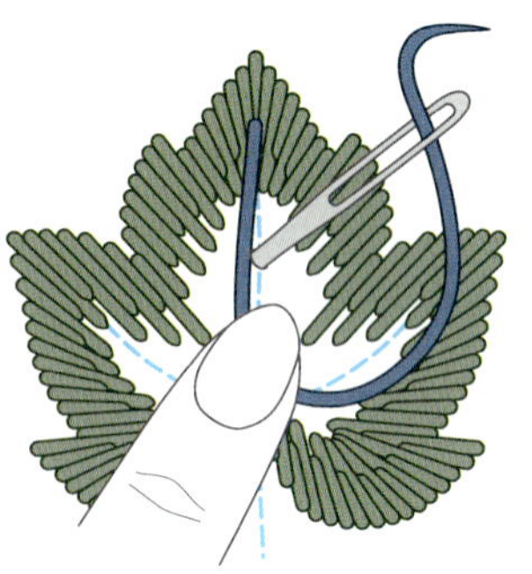

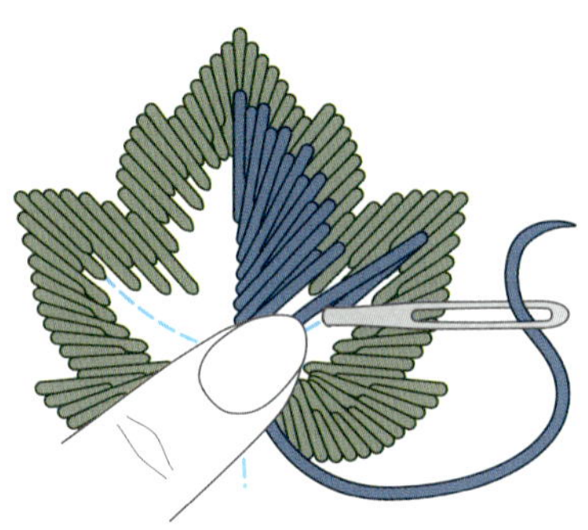

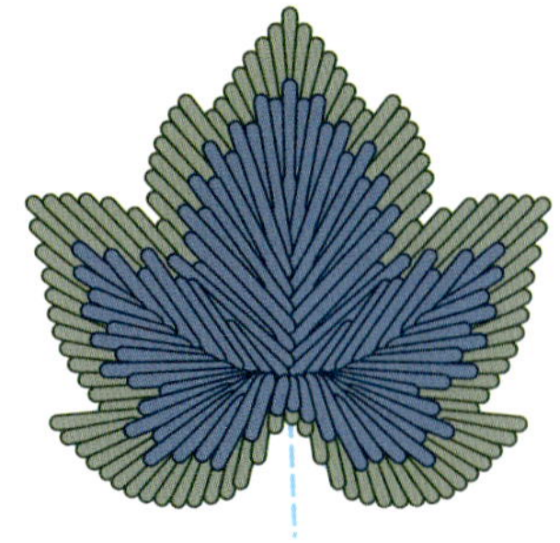

4 When using this second colour, to maintain your stitch direction, use your finger to 'lay' each long stitch in place before you make these stitches. Stitch the second colour also in sections, coming up through the first colour and stitch down onto the leaf vein.

Pistil stitch – double thread

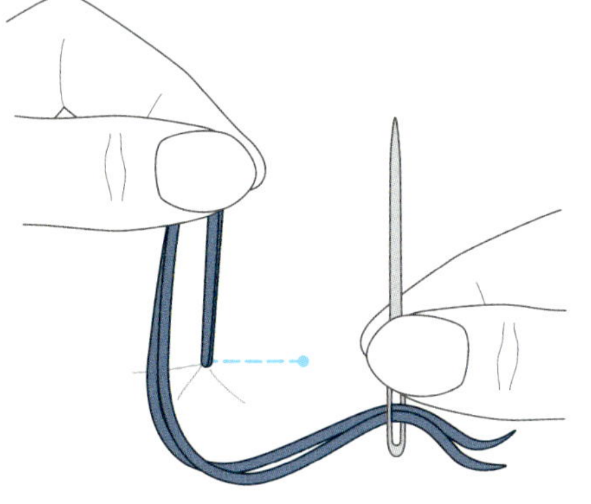

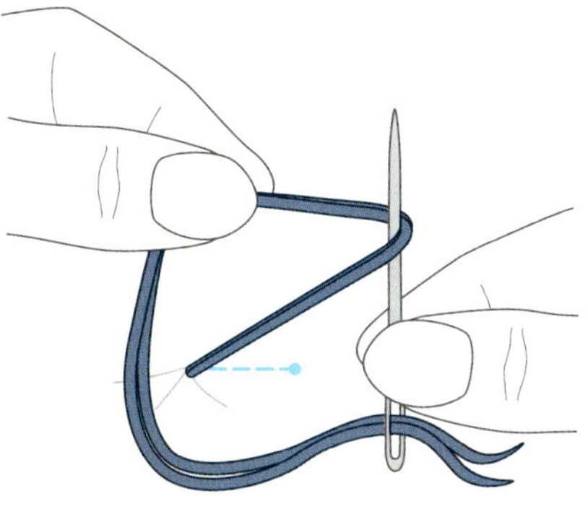

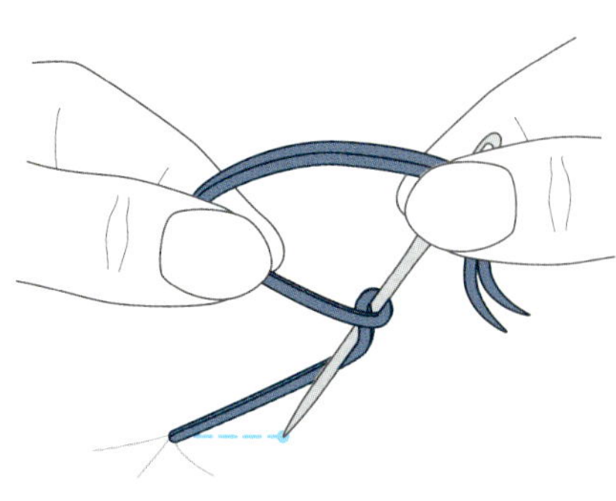

1 Bring your needle up through the fabric and hold the wool taut a little way above the fabric. Hold the needle with your other hand, the tip pointing away from the fabric, parallel with the taut wool. Now wind the wool anti-clockwise (or clockwise for left-handers) once around the needle.

2 Keeping your 'wool' hand high and the wool taut, turn the point of the needle away from you, and push its point only down into the fabric, through the blue circle printed dot on the fabric.

3 Now press your middle finger on your 'wool' hand, down on the taut wool and slide the wool down the needle until it rests on the fabric. Next slide the thumbnail of your 'needle' hand down the shaft of the needle to hold the knot in place. Then holding the needle and the knot in place with your 'needle' hand, and keeping the knot in place with your thumbnail, release your 'wool' hand and use this to pull the needle from underneath your frame, down through the fabric to complete the stitch.

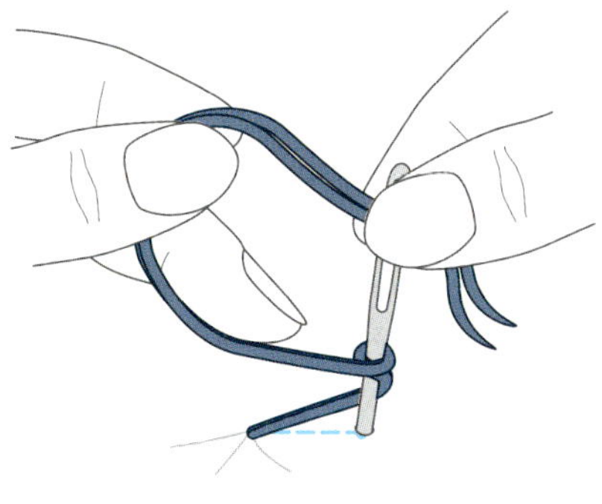

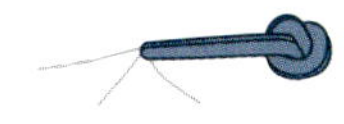

Satin stitch – double thread

Satin, or raised satin stitch, is always worked in one direction when stitching in wool threads, coming up and going down as illustrated.

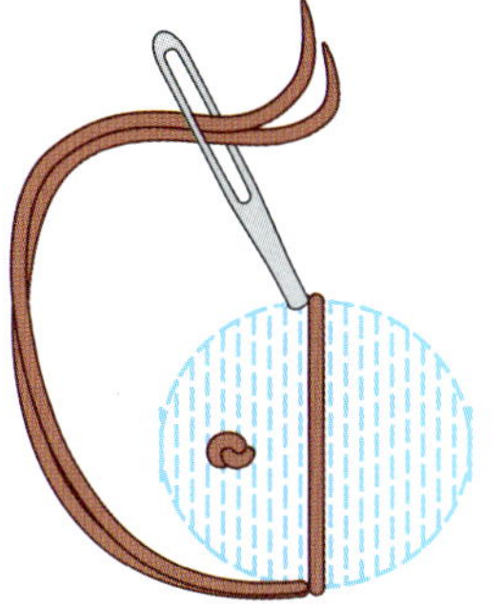

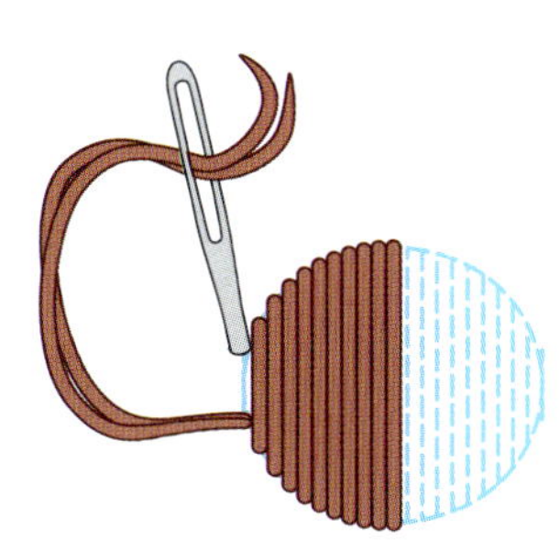

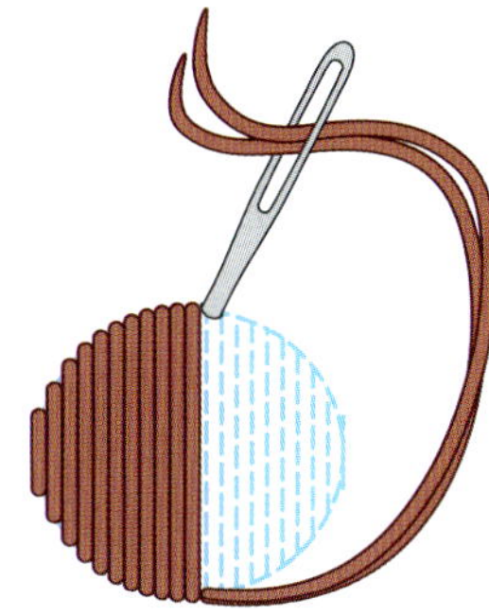

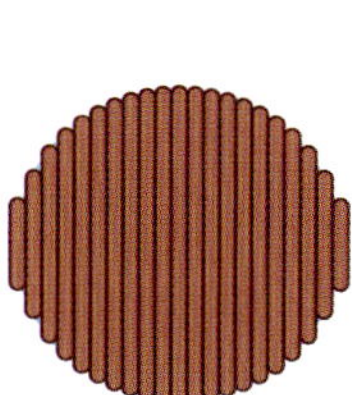

1 To maintain the perfect stitch angle, your first stitch must divide the area in half. Bring your needle up at the base of the cherry and take it down just over the printed outline. Then, stitching from this centre line, use the straight lines printed on the fabric to fill the shape, laying the threads closely alongside each other and always ensuring that the printed outline is covered.

2 Work across one half before returning to the centre. To complete the second half, cover the entire area with closely worked straight stitches.

Satin stitch, raised – double thread

To create a raised satin stitch, first work the shape in satin stitch (see below), then repeat the same sequence to cover the area with subsequent layers of stitches.

Second layer

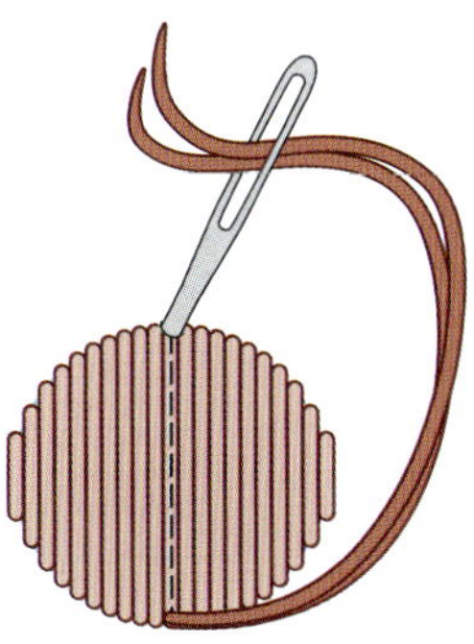

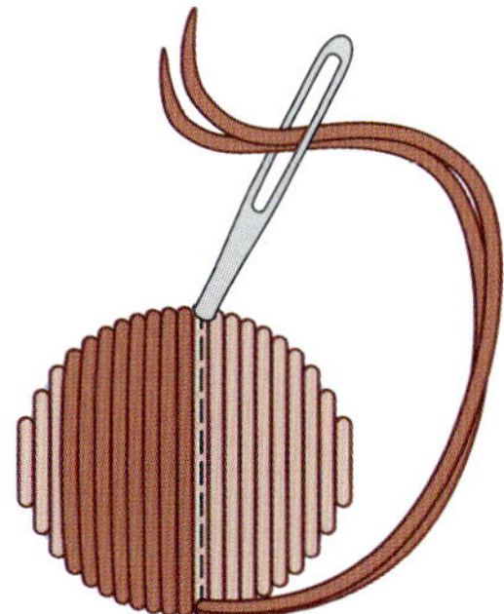

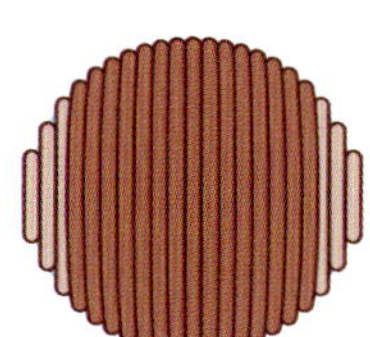

1 Repeat the 'centre out' sequence of stitching described below. Cover exactly the same area, but, with each layer of stitching stop just one stitch short of each side of the shape. Do not venture beyond the holes created around the perimeter by the first layer of stitching.

2 Continue with more layers – up to four layers – reducing the sides of each layer of stitches as before. This will create a pleasing 'domed' effect. The raised effect this creates is typical of Jacobean needlework, of the late seventeenth century.

Seeding – single thread

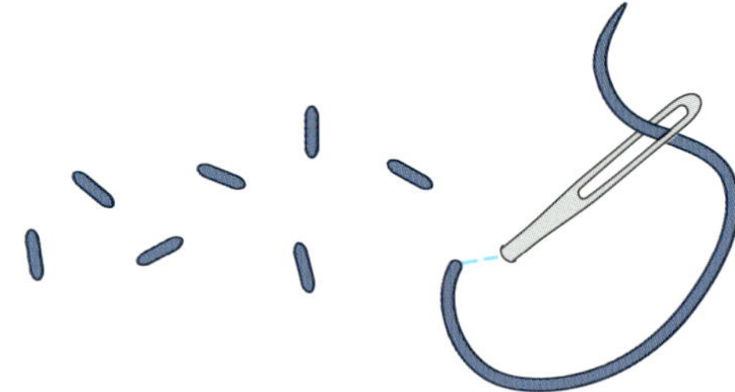

Often used for decoration, randomly placed seeding stitches create a pleasing effect.

To create each stitch, bring your needle up through the fabric and back down to create a short straight stitch. To achieve the required 'random' effect, scatter the stitches at different angles.

Split stitch

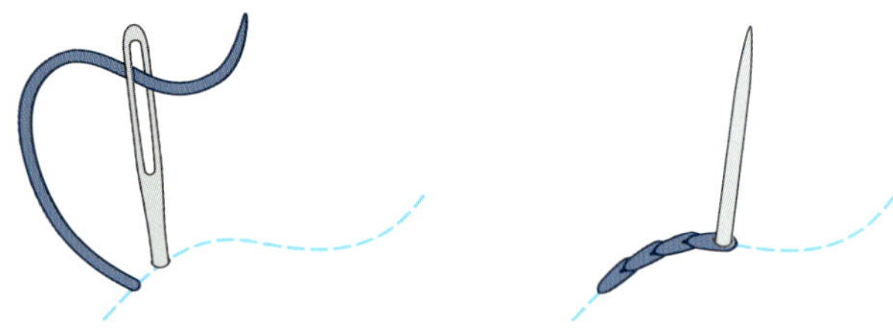

1 Come up through your fabric and take your needle down again 6mm (¼in) along, making a straight stitch. Then come halfway back along this stitch and bring your needle up through the middle of the stitch, splitting the thread.
2 Go down another 6mm (¼in) along the line, and again bring your needle up through the previous stitch.
3 Repeat until you have covered the desired area.

Whipped spider's web – single thread

This stitch creates a 3D effect and neatens itself as it grows.

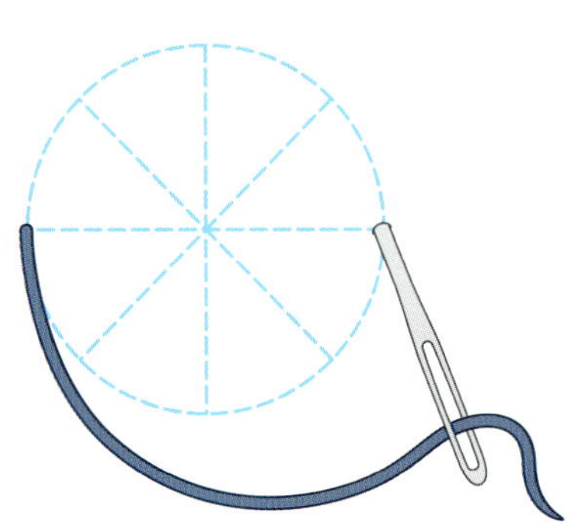

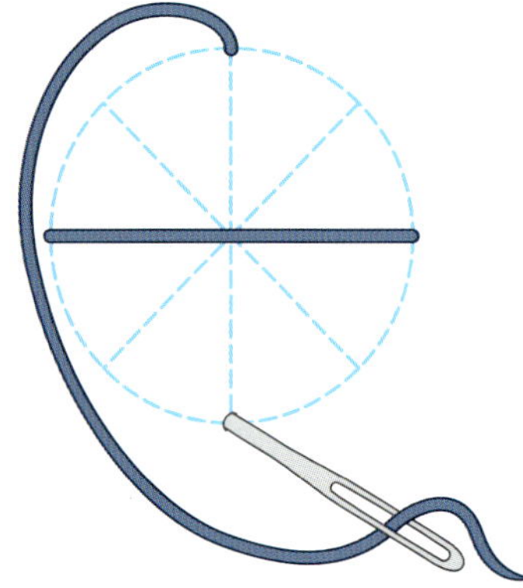

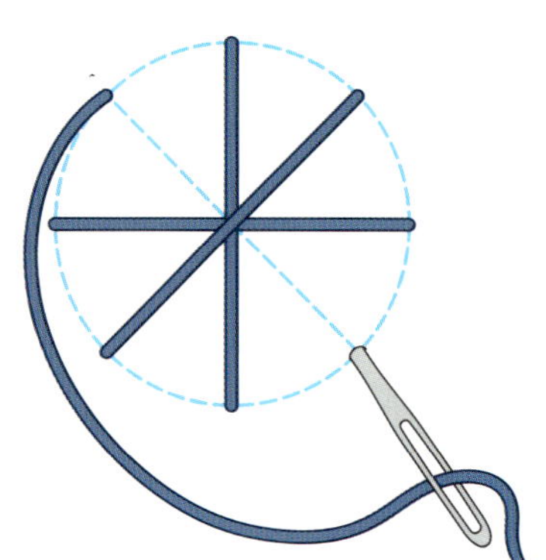

1 Begin by stitching straight stitches over the shape.

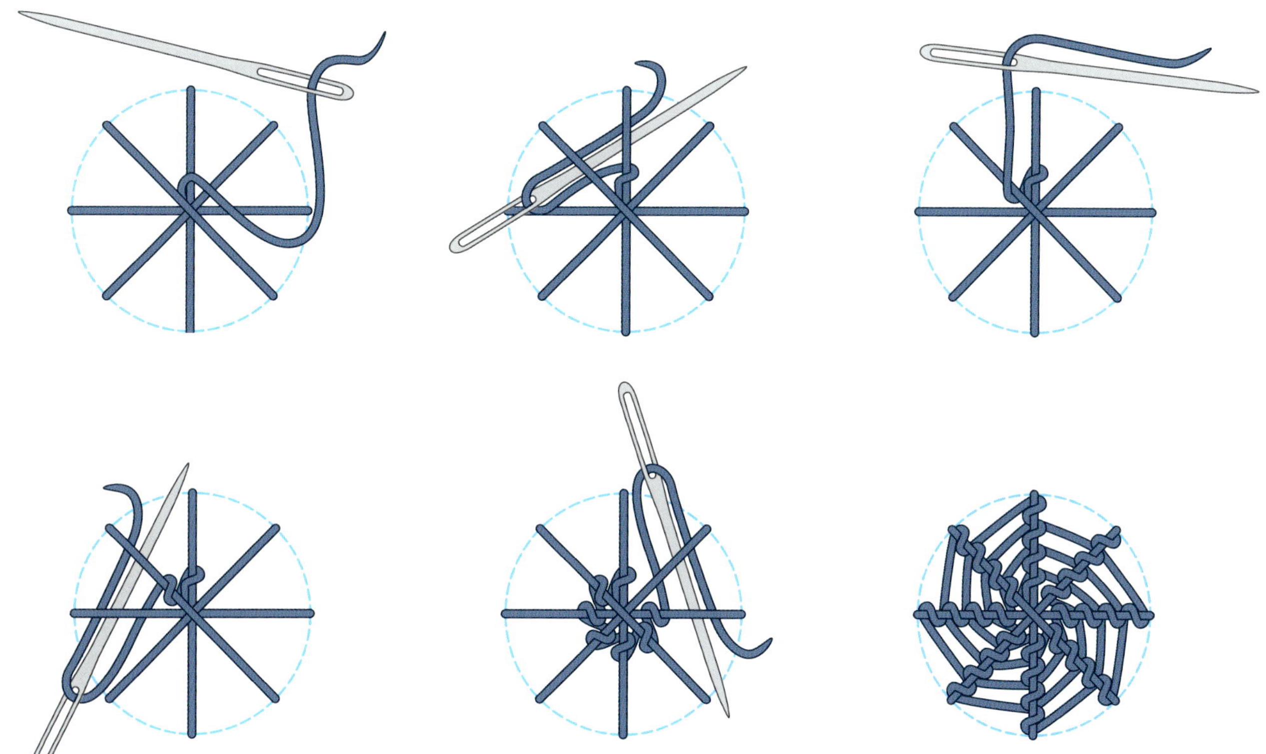

2 Next, after gently moving these stitches aside with your finger, come up between two stitches in the centre of the web. Rotate your needle so that the eye end travels first and bring your needle back over one thread, then post your needle, eye first, under the same thread and the next one. Push the needle and thread under these two threads, then bring the needle back over one thread, before pushing the needle and thread under the next pair of spokes in the wheel of satin stitches. Repeat this method of 'back one and forward two' around the spider's web, until it forms a raised mound.

Whipped stem stitch – single thread

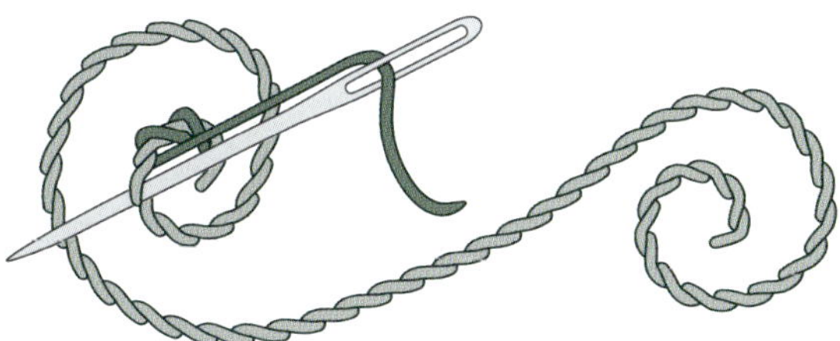

1 Work a line of crewel stem stitch (see page 151).

2 Change colours and whip each stitch. Start whipping at the tip of the line, as shown, and crewel stem stitch away from the curve, keeping the tension even when working with crewel wool.

Contemporary stitches

Embroidery stitches

Backstitch

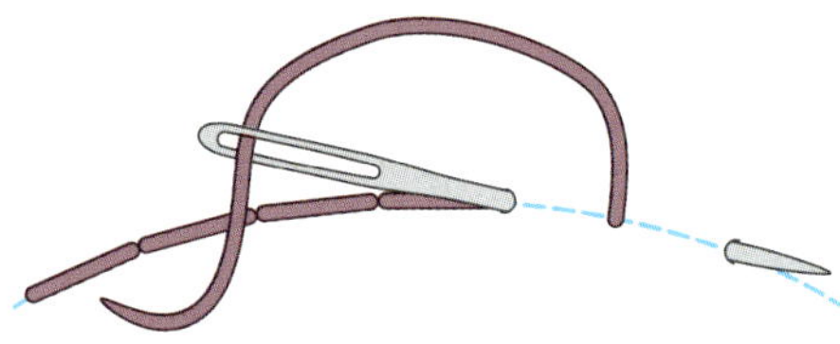

1 Bring the needle up a stitch length beyond the beginning of the line.
2 Go in at the beginning of the line, coming up again a stitch length beyond the beginning of the stitch you are working.
3 Repeat as necessary, keeping your stitch length as even as possible.

Backstitch – whipped

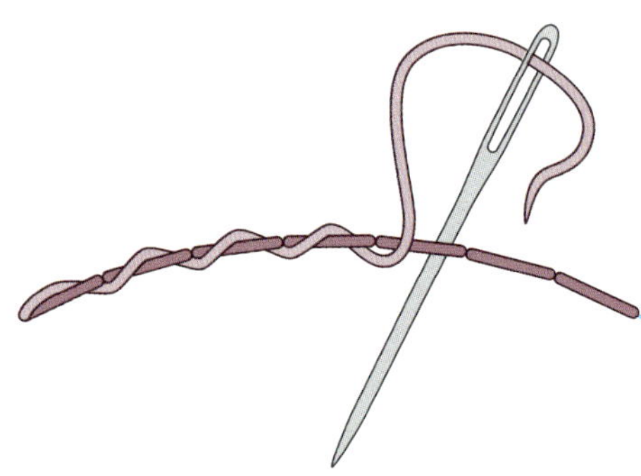

To whip backstitch, bring your needle up out of the same hole as the first stitch, and weave your needle and thread over, then under, each backstitch.

Tip

It is advisable to use a tapestry needle when whipping.

Blanket stitch – padded and striped

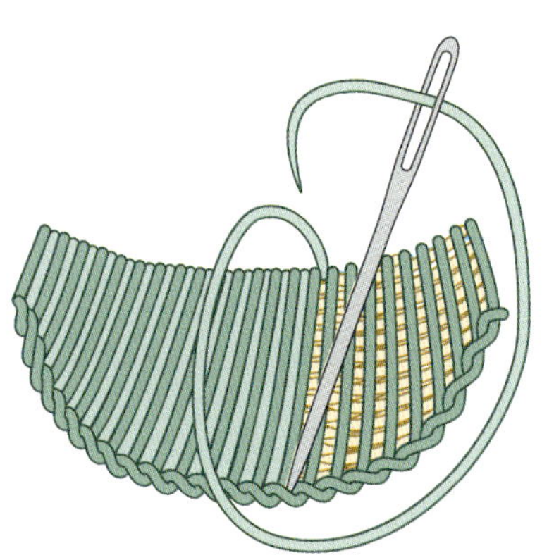

1 Pad the shape (see outline stitch padding, page 183) with horizontal outline stitch.
2 Start on the left-hand side with straight stitch. Working on the outside of the padding, come out on the outside line, going in on the inside line. Come out of the same hole on the outside line.
3 Leaving space for a small straight stitch, go in on the inside line without pulling through, leaving a loop. Leaving the space needed to accommodate a straight stitch, come up on the outside line, catch the loop and pull through. As you tighten, allow the purl to form on the line outside the padding.
4 Repeat steps 2 and 3 until you have filled the space. Secure the final blanket stitch with a small couching stitch.
5 Thereafter, using a different colour thread, work straight stitches in the gaps. Work from outside the padding on the inside line, burying the end of the straight stitch under the ridge (or purl) of the blanket stitch.

Blanket stitch and buttonhole stitch

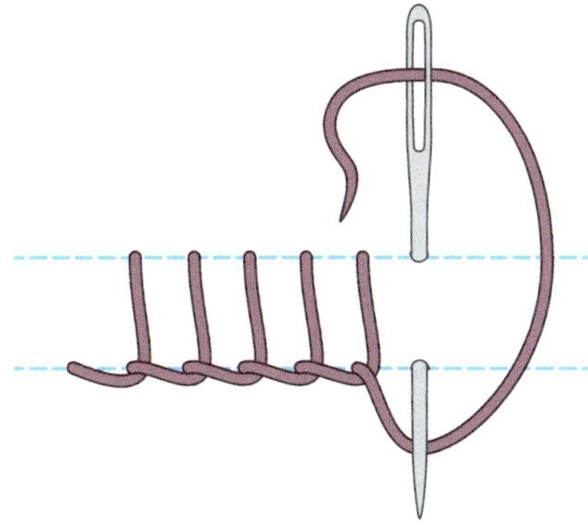

The only real difference between these two stitches is the spacing between them.

1 Working from left to right, bring the needle up where you require the purl edge.
2 Go in on the top line and, without pulling through, come out again directly below on the bottom line, with the thread looped under the needle. Pull through.
3 Continue in this way. If you are creating blanket stitch, make sure that the gaps you leave between the stitches are even.

   If you are working blanket stitch, leave a gap when you go in at the top edge and again at the bottom edge when you come up to catch the loop and pull through to finish the stitch.

   If you are working buttonhole stitch, leave only enough space to form the stitch without pushing the existing stitches out of place. While not quite as close, your spacing is similar to satin stitch so that the finished product looks like satin stitch with a purl on the one edge.
4 Secure at the end with a small couching stitch over the last loop.

Tip

If you are working the stitch on a curve with the purl on the outside of the curve, you will leave a slightly smaller, evenly spaced gap on the top line so that the stitch fans around evenly. Sometimes you will need to put the needle into the same hole.

Bullion knots

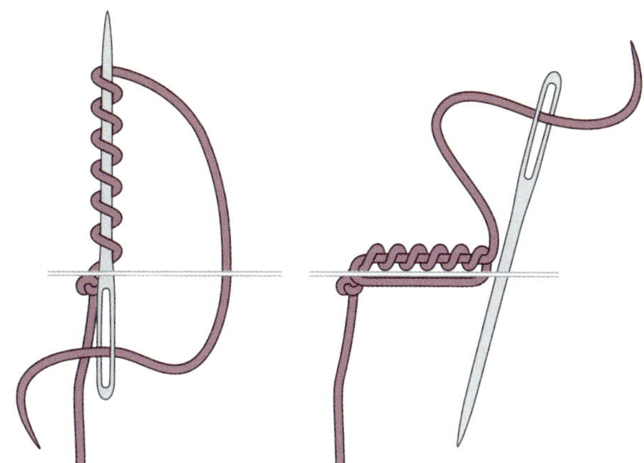

1 Come out of the fabric at the start of the space you wish to fill, and go in again at the end of that space.
2 Come out again at the start of the space, leaving a loop of thread on the top; don't pull the needle all the way through the fabric.
3 Twist the thread around the needle as many times as you require.
4 Holding the twists between your thumb and forefinger, pull the needle through.
5 Pull the working thread until the knot lies flat, then take the needle back into the fabric at the start of the space.

Burden stitch

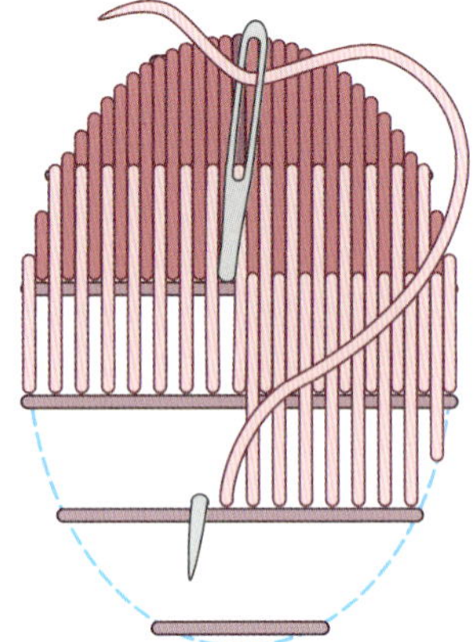

1 Work horizontal lines at 3mm (⅛in) intervals across the shape you wish to fill.

2 Working with the darkest thread and starting on the middle line of the shape, work the first two rows simultaneously, placing the vertical stitches next to one another.

3 Come up above the top horizontal stitch and go in just above the second horizontal stitch (first row). Moving to the left, come up above the top horizontal stitch and go in just above the third horizontal stitch (second row).

4 Repeat step 3 to complete the left side of the shape. When you get beyond the top horizontal line, use the perimeter of the shape as the starting point when you come out of the fabric.

5 Going back to the centre, complete the right side of the shape in the same way.

6 Using the same darker thread, work the third row of vertical stitches. Bearing in mind that the stitches on the sides of the shape may be shorter, bring your thread up just above the fourth horizontal stitch and go into the fabric just above the second horizontal stitch. Go into the same hole that you went into when you were working the stitches of the first row. Leaving a space the width of a stitch (to accommodate the stitches of the next row), come up above the fourth horizontal stitch, repeating the stitching process to the end of the row.

7 Change to the lighter thread and, working from side to side, bring your thread up just above the fifth horizontal stitch, going into the fabric just above the third horizontal stitch. Go into the same hole that you went into when you were working the stitches of the second row.

8 Keep adding rows in this way. As you start each row, you will drop down, coming up just above the next horizontal stitch and going into the fabric having missed the next two horizontal stitches, always going into the fabric using the same hole that you went into when you worked the penultimate row.

9 In the very last row, you will work short straight stitches from the bottom perimeter line, going over the horizontal stitch that is showing and going into the base of the stitch that goes into the fabric immediately above that last horizontal stitch.

Tip

If you are working on this particular shape, you will need to work two more rows with the lighter thread after step 8 and then go back to working rows with the darker thread until you reach the bottom.

Buttonhole stitch – flower

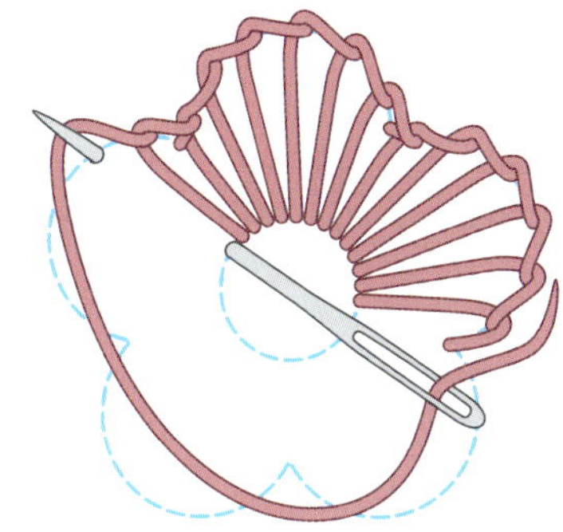

1 Bring your needle up on the line that depicts the outside of the flower and go back into the fabric on the line that depicts the outside of the centre circle.

2 Without pulling through and working up the first petal, come up a little further along the outside line, making sure that the working thread loops under the sharp end of the needle.

3 Pull through to create the first buttonhole stitch. Pull outwards, away from the flower, keeping a firm tension.

4 Holding the thread outwards with your non-working hand, take the needle through the fabric on the line that depicts the outside of the centre circle to create the next stitch.

5 Once again, without pulling through and working up the petal, come up a little further along the outside line, leaving a similar space for each stitch.

6 Make sure that the working thread is under the sharp end of the needle and pull through to form the second stitch.

7 Keep working buttonhole stitches in this way, working up towards the tip of the petal and then working down to the next valley that is the end of the petal and start of the second petal. Keep the spaces between the stitches as even as possible.

8 As you work downwards, make sure that the stitch which will catch the last loop of the petal will come out in the valley, the lowest point.

9 When you have caught the loop, work a couching stitch over the thread, as if you were finishing off the line of buttonhole stitch.

10 Come up again in the space within the last stitch and continue working the second petal in the same way as the first.

11 Continue working the petals in this way, working the couching stitch in the dip at the end of each petal.

12 As you work the last petal and get close to where you started, space your stitches in a way that ensures your last loop is caught by a stitch which comes out of the fabric where your first stitch started in the valley at the beginning of the first petal.

13 Catch the last buttonhole stitch with a small couching stitch that comes out on the outside line of the circle, catches the loop, and goes back into the same hole.

Tip

In instances where there is no central circle, each stitch will be worked into the same hole in the middle of the flower.

Buttonhole stitch – layered

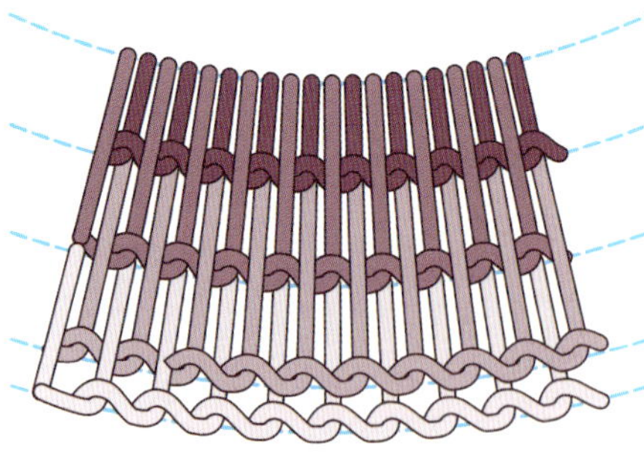

1 To work the first row, start on the second line working into the top line and pulling through towards yourself. If you are working with a shaded range, use the darkest thread.

2 When you work the first stitch leave a gap big enough to accommodate the first stitch of the second row.

3 As you work the subsequent stitches, leave gaps that are large enough to accommodate the stitches of the second row – these will be worked into the gaps.

4 The last stitch is completed with a small couching stitch that holds it in place.

5 Using a lighter shade, start the second row on the third horizontal line.

6 Come up in line with the gap before the first stitch in the first row and work a straight stitch, going into the fabric on the top horizontal line.

7 Come up on the third line, out of the same hole that you came out of when you started the straight stitch.

8 Thereafter, work buttonhole or blanket stitches (see page 171) going in on the top line between the stitches of the first row and coming out on the third line, in line with where you went in on the top row, catching the loop and pulling through.

9 When you get to the end of the row, work a couching stitch that is long enough for the row to end in line with the end of the first row.

10 As you did in the first row and working with a lighter shade on the fourth horizontal line, start the first buttonhole stitch in line with the beginning of the first row and indeed, in line with the straight stitch that started the second row.

11 Filling the gaps created by the second row, go into the fabric in line with the stitches of the first row, tucking your needle under the purl of the first row buttonhole stitch, coming back up in line with where you went in, catching the loop and pulling through.

12 Continue working the row in the gaps between the stitches of the second row and when you get to the end, catch the last buttonhole stitch with a longer stitch, as you did in the first row.

13 Working with the darkest shade to give the impression of an outline, work the final row on the perimeter line, immediately adjacent to the purl of the previous row, filling in the gaps between those stitches.

Tip

This guideline is for a four-row block of layered buttonhole stitch. You can add extra rows at this point, depending on the space you need to fill. You should finish these rows a little below the perimeter line.

Chain stitch

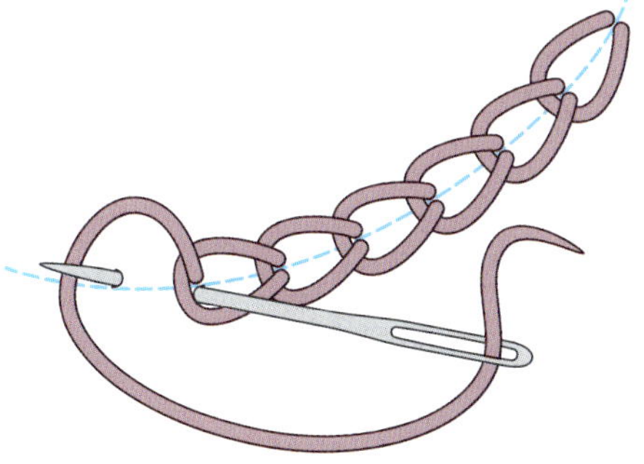

1 Bring the needle up on the line and pull through.
2 Take the needle back into the same hole and come up again where you want the chain stitch to end, loop the thread under the needle and pull through.
3 Staying inside the loop, go back into the same hole, loop the thread under the needle and pull through.
4 Repeat as required, then catch the last loop with a small couching stitch.

Chain stitch and backstitch combination

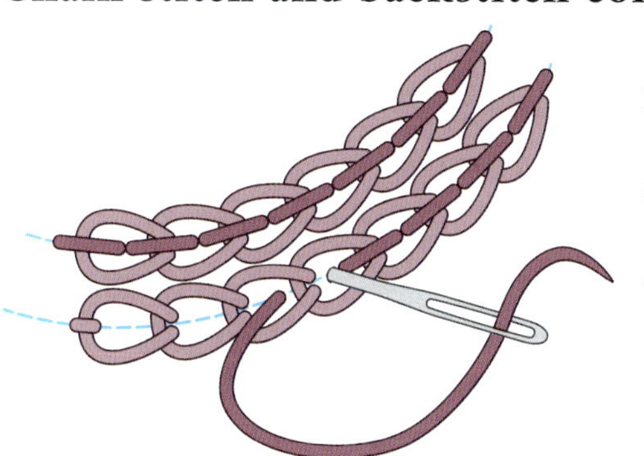

1 Work a row of chain stitch.
2 Work backstitches from the middle of the first chain stitch to the space just before the start of the chain stitch.
3 Follow with backstitches that start in the middle of the next chain stitch and go into the start of the backstitch in the previous chain stitch.
4 Continue working backstitch in this way, finishing on the outside of the last chain stitch.

Tip

When you work multiple rows of this stitch combination, it is sensible to complete the backstitch in the row before moving on to the next row of chain stitch, otherwise it can be difficult to see where you should stitch if you have done all the chain stitch before you start on the backstitch.

Chain stitch – detached

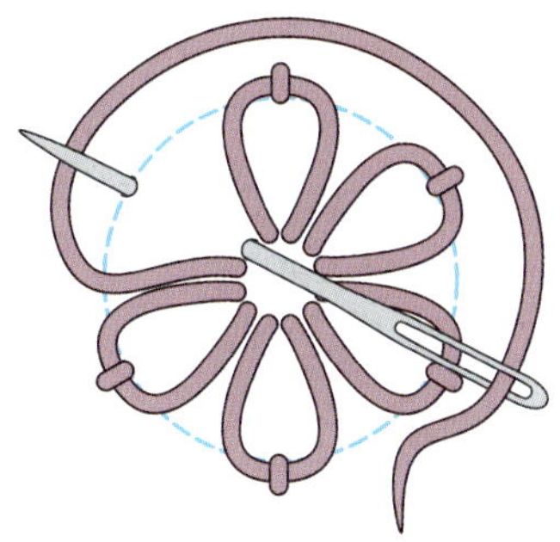

1 Bring the needle up at the base of the stitch and pull through.
2 Take the needle back into the same hole and come up again where you want the stitch to end, loop the thread under the needle and pull through.
3 Catch the loop with a small couching stitch.

Chain stitch – interlaced

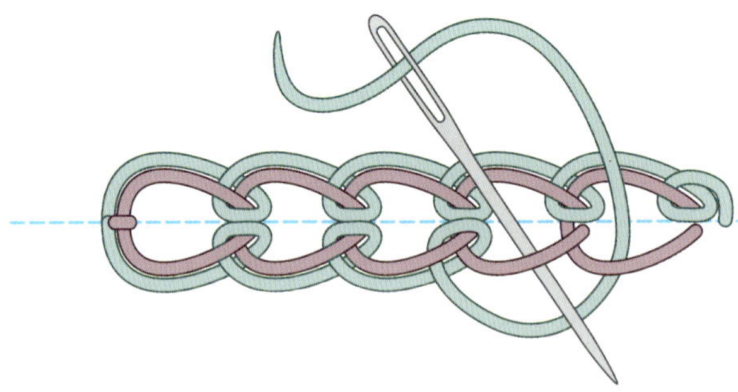

1 Starting at the tip of the straight line on the side, work a straight stitch. Come up the length of a chain stitch below the straight stitch.
2 Take your needle under the straight stitch and go back into the fabric in the same hole that you came out of.
3 Come up the length of a chain stitch below the straight stitch.
4 Take your needle under the loop that creates the previous chain stitch and go back into the fabric in the same hole that you came out of. Continue in this way to the end of the line.
5 Starting on the left, come up at the beginning of the line, usually out of the same hole that accommodates the straight stitch at the beginning of the reverse chain stitch. Take the needle under one side of the second chain stitch.
6 Working backwards, go under the same side of the first chain stitch, go over the working thread that comes from the left, and go under the one side of the third chain stitch.
7 Working backwards, go under the same side of the second chain stitch, go over the working thread and go under the one side of the fourth chain stitch. Continue in this way to the end of the row.
8 Go into the fabric at the base of the last chain stitch.
9 Starting from the beginning of the line again, interlace the other side in the same way.

Chain stitch – interlaced variation (knotted)

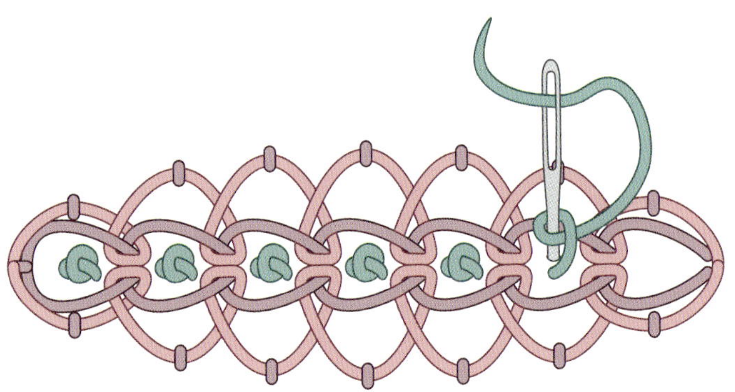

1 Following the guidelines above, work the interlaced chain stitch variation making the loops of the reverse chain stitch slightly longer, usually 3–4mm (around ⅛in) in length.
2 Work a single-wrap French knot (see page 179) into the spaces within the loops of the reverse chain stitch.

Chain stitch – interlaced variation

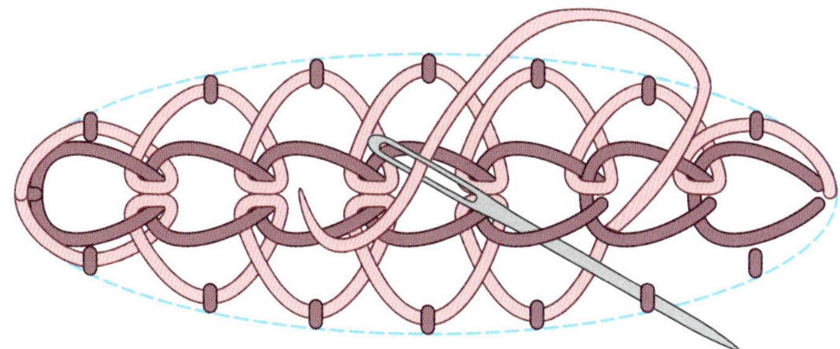

1 Working in a straight line down the middle of the shape and starting at the tip, work a short, straight stitch. Come up the length of a chain stitch below the straight stitch.
2 Take your needle under the straight stitch and go back into the fabric in the same hole that you came out of.
3 Coming up on the outline of the perimeter approximately level with the middle of the corresponding chain stitch loop, work a short straight stitch in towards the chain stitch.
4 Work an identical straight stitch on the other side.
5 Come up the length of a chain stitch below the previous chain stitch and repeat the process, including the straight stitches on both sides, following the line of the shape. Continue in this way to the end of the line.
6 Starting on the left, come up at the beginning of the line, usually out of the same hole that accommodates the straight stitch at the beginning of the reverse chain stitch.
7 Take the needle under the straight stitch on the left and then under one side of the second chain stitch.
8 Working backwards, go under the same side of the first chain stitch, then go over the working thread that comes from the top.
9 Go under the next straight stitch on the left side and then under the one side of the third chain stitch.
10 Working backwards, go under the same side of the second chain stitch, go over the working thread, under the next straight stitch on the left side, and go under the one side of the fourth chain stitch. Continue in this way to the end of the shape.
11 Go into the fabric at the base of the last chain stitch.
12 Starting from the beginning of the line again, interlace the other side in the same way.

Chain stitch – reverse

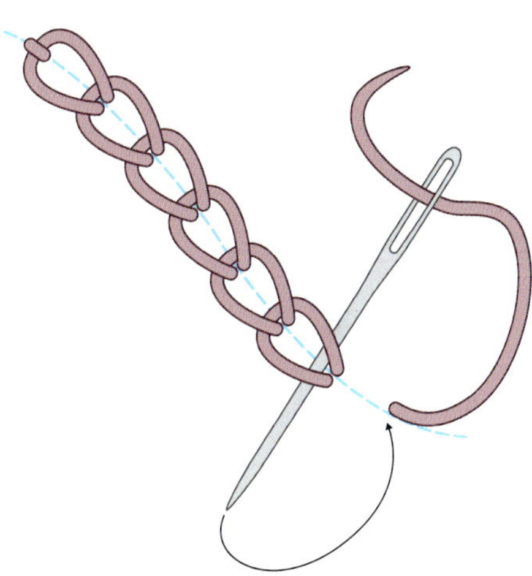

1 Start with a short straight stitch.
2 Come up on the line slightly further down. Take your needle under the straight stitch and go back into same hole.
3 Continue by coming up on the line slightly further down.
4 Take your needle under both threads of the previous loop and go back into same hole.
5 Continue in this way finishing off by just going back into the same hole for the last loop.

Eye stitch filler

1. An eye stitch is made up of straight stitches that all go into the same hole in the middle. Come up on the outside of the chosen area for the stitch, and work in a clockwise direction to make straight stitches of varying lengths into the same central hole.
2. Pull reasonably tight so that the hole in the middle becomes a visible hole which creates the 'eye'. The finished eye stitch should not be too circular or too square. You are aiming for a reasonably irregular shape.
3. Work your way around the area you want to fill. As you add further stitches, fit these irregularly shaped eye stitches together like a jigsaw puzzle.
4. There will be small areas that are not filled with any part of the eye stitches so, to fill those in and also to add texture, work single wrap French knots (see opposite) in small, intermittent groups or as single knots here are there. Try to get an even spread of French knots over the area of the shape.

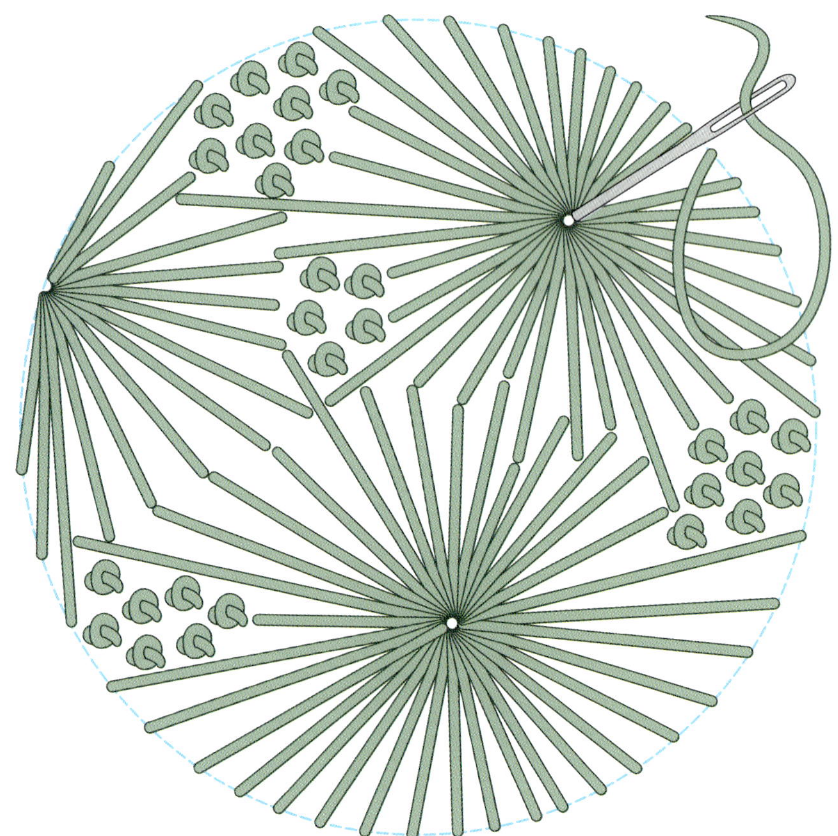

Fly stitch

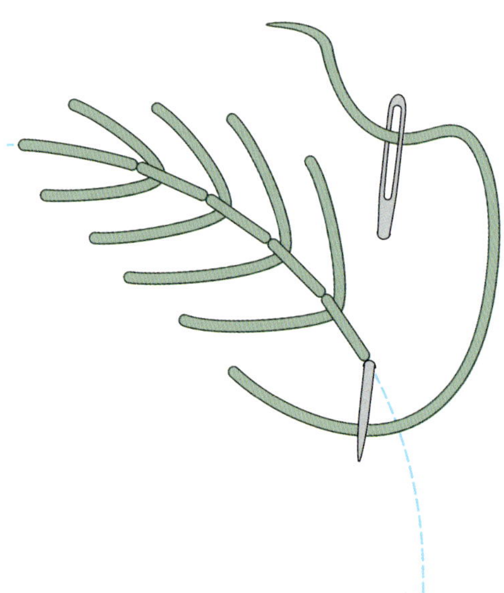

1. Start at the tip of the shape with a straight stitch. Come up on the left of that stitch, then go in at the same level on the right, leaving a loop.
2. Come up in the bottom hole of the straight stitch. Catch the loop and pull through.
3. Make a straight stitch. For extended fly stitch you make a longer stitch; for close fly stitch it is shorter, about the length of a couching stitch.
4. When you start the next loop, leave a gap if you are working extended fly stitch. Start close to the previous stitch if you are working close fly stitch. Continue making a line of stitches in the same way.
5. At the end of the line, catch the last loop with either a long straight stitch or a short couching stitch.

Fly stitch – whipped

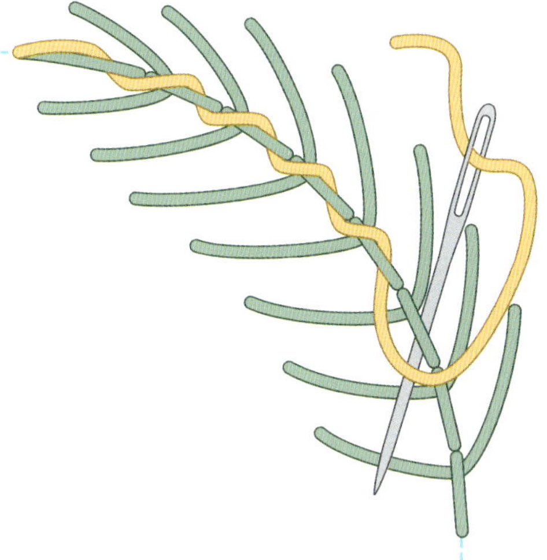

1 Work a line of extended fly stitch, following the directions opposite.
2 Using a different colour thread, start at the tip and (referring to the yellow thread in the diagram) come up through the same hole where you started the straight stitch when you worked the basic fly stitch. From right to left, go under that straight stitch.
3 Thereafter, working from right to left every time, go under each of the straight stitches that form the spine of the fly stitch.
4 When you reach the bottom of the line, go into the hole that you went into when you worked the last stitch of the basic fly stitch.

French knot – loose

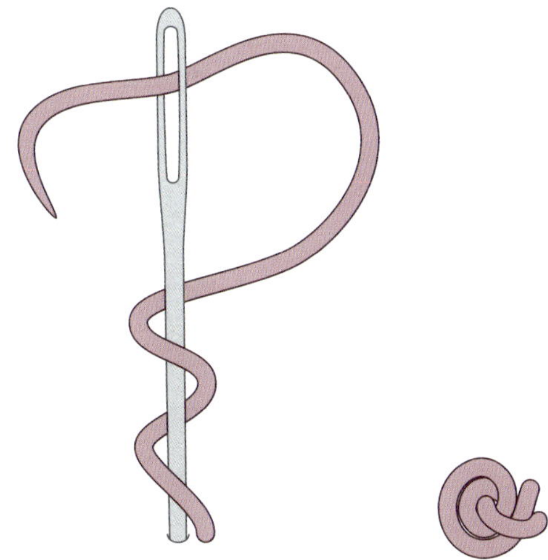

1 Bring the needle up through the fabric. Loosely twist the thread around the needle two or three times.
2 Tighten only slightly and go back into the fabric just next to where you came out. Pull the needle through controlling the twists as you do so, the aim being to achieve two or three loose loops of thread held down by the thread that goes into the fabric.
3 Working a group of these together to fill an area creates the impression of feathers, foliage or flowers seen in the distance.

French knot – single wrap

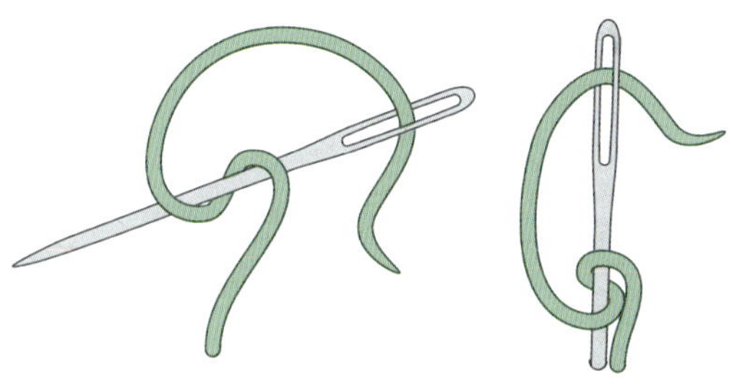

1 Bring the needle up through the fabric. Twist the thread around the needle once and tighten.
2 Go back into the fabric just next to where you came out.
3 Pull the twist that is around the needle down to the bottom so that it touches the fabric.
4 Hold the thread and pull the needle through to form the knot.

Heavy chain stitch

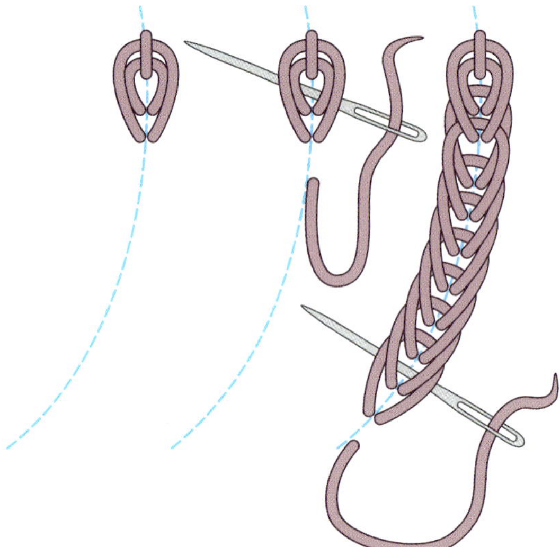

1 Start at the tip of the line with a straight/backstitch.
2 Leaving enough space for a stitch, 3–4mm (⅛in) with perle #5 thread and about 2–3mm (1/16in) for finer thread, come up below the straight stitch on the line.
3 Take the needle and thread under the straight stitch and go back into the hole that you came out of when you started.
4 Come up a few millimetres below and go under the straight stitch a second time. This is the start of the stitch.
5 Come up a stitch length below the last loop that you made – the second loop that started the stitch. Go under, not the previous loop, but the one before that. So, in other words, the first loop that went through the straight stitch at the start.
6 Come up a stitch length below the last loop that you made. Take your needle under, not the previous loop, but the one before that.
7 Continue working this way, taking the needle under the second last loop every time, until you reach the end of the line.
8 You end by going back into the same hole that you came out of when starting the very last loop.

Herringbone stitch – interlaced

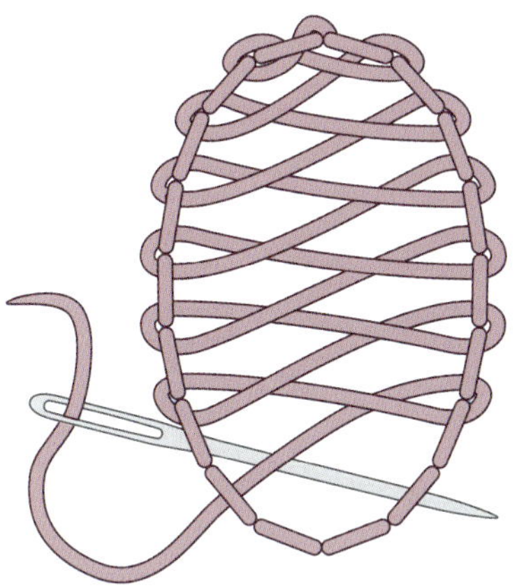

1 First, work backstitch around the shape. It is important that not only should the size of the stitches be approximately even but that they should be worked in pairs that lie opposite and level with one another.

2 The threads are then laced through the backstitches. Begin at the top of the shape, bring your needle up from under a backstitch on the outside of the shape. Go under the stitch to the left.

3 Still working to the left, miss a backstitch and go under the next one, moving outwards.

4 Moving inwards, go under the backstitch that you missed and, moving to the right, miss a backstitch at the top and go under the second stitch, moving outwards.

5 Moving upwards, go under the backstitch that you missed on the right and moving to the left, go under the loop of thread and go under the third backstitch on the left.

6 Moving upwards, go under the second backstitch on the left and moving to the right, go under the loop of thread and go under the third backstitch on the left.

7 Continue in this way until you reach the bottom.

Tip

The easiest and most effective way to achieve the outline backstitches opposite one another is to work each pair together. Work one side then the other, before moving to the next pair, allowing the thread to travel along the back of the work.

Herringbone stitch – raised

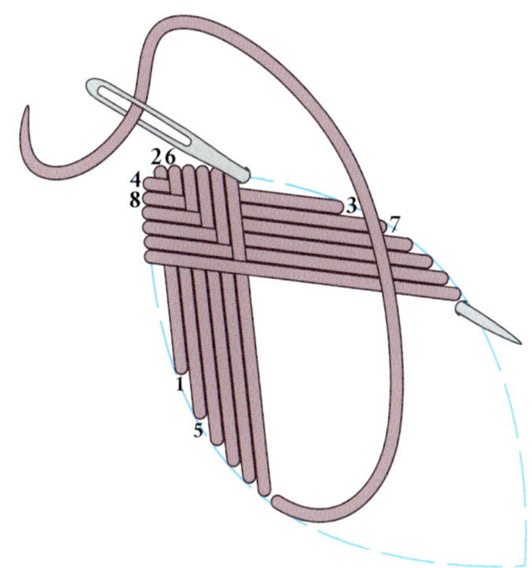

1 Bring your needle up on the left at the point marked 1.

2 Go into the fabric on the right at the point marked 2.

3 Bring your needle up on the right at the point marked 3.

4 Go into the fabric on the left at the point marked 4. Points 2 and 4 are close together so that they resemble the point, or tip of a leaf.

5 Bring your needle up on the left at the point marked 5 and keeping with the sequence that you have started, go in on the right.

6 As you work the stitches, start inside the lines of the shape and finish on the line of the shape on the other side. This will ensure that your outside edge is formed by the end of each stitch, when you go into the fabric, and you should try to keep that even so that you get a smooth edge.

7 As you move down the shape from tip to base, watch how much empty space you have left on both sides of the shape. If one side is larger than the other, you need to start your stitches slightly further apart on that side.

8 You finish the leaf by making sure that the last stitch on either side covers the start of the stitches that are below it.

Long and short stitch shading

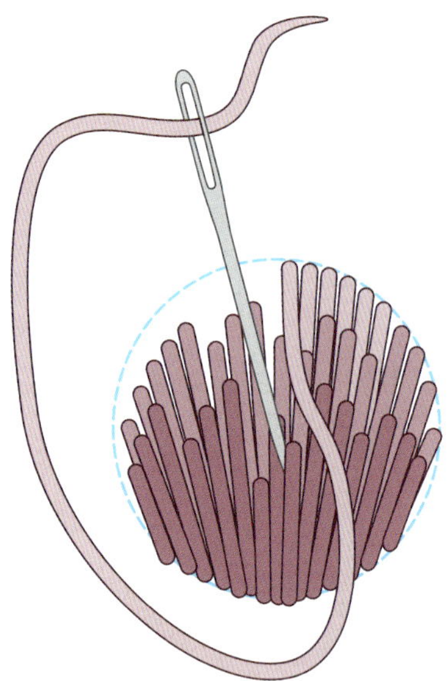

1 Start in the centre of the shape a little over halfway up. Use a single strand of the darkest thread. Work a vertical straight stitch, going in on the bottom outline of the shape.

2 Working to the right, continue working straight stitches of varying lengths going into the perimeter line at the bottom of the shape and fanning them slightly. This means that you will make them further apart at the top and closer together at the bottom, sometimes going into the same hole.

3 Each stitch should be a different length to the others that are close to it. These lengths should be random to give a more natural look.

4 Use lighter thread as you work up towards the tip. The second and subsequent rows comprise similarly random straight stitches that have differing lengths at both the bottom and the top.

5 Glide the needle between the stitches of the previous row, going into the fabric between the threads.

6 The top row follows the perimeter line at the tip of the shape. It is worked in the lightest shade of thread and the stitch lengths differ at the bottom. Like the second (and subsequent) rows, glide the needle between the stitches of the previous row, going into the fabric between the threads.

Long and short stitch shading – diagonal

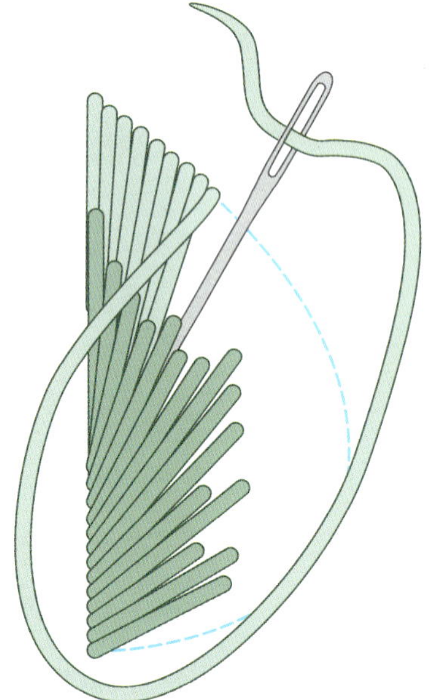

1 Start below the tip on the vein or straight edge, using a single strand of the darkest thread.

2 Work a vertical straight stitch, going into the line.

3 Working to the right, continue working straight stitches of varying lengths, fanning around the shape as you go.

4 Come up on the outside leaving a small gap between the stitches and go in on the line leaving no gap or even going into the same hole. Once the stitches reach the angle you would like them to be, work the stitches parallel to one another as you work towards the bottom of the shape.

5 Each stitch should be a different length to the others that are close to it. These lengths should be random to give a more natural look.

6 Grade the colours of the threads, going lighter as you work outwards to the edge in the second and subsequent rows.

7 Glide the needle between the stitches of the previous row, going into the fabric between the threads.

8 The outside row follows the perimeter line at the tip of the shape. It is worked in the lightest shade of thread and the stitch lengths differ at the bottom. Like the second (and subsequent) rows, glide the needle between the stitches of the previous row, going into the fabric between the threads.

Outline stitch

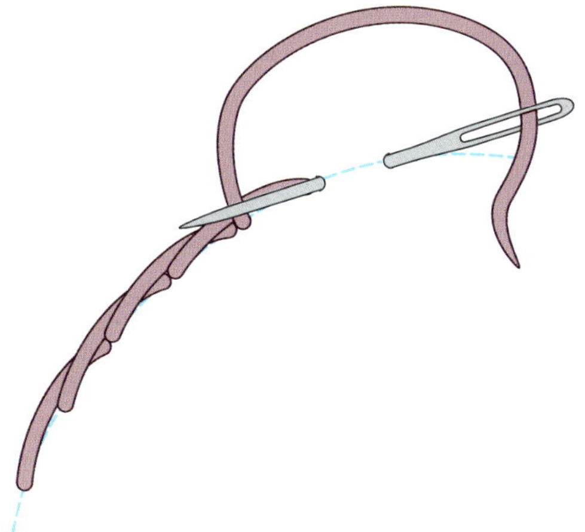

1 Working from left to right, come up at the beginning of the line.
2 Go in on the line and before pulling the thread through, come up halfway back on the line. Pull through.
3 Go into the fabric halfway further and come up just a little past halfway back, so that you are not coming up in the same hole as where the first stitch finished.
4 Continue to the end of the outline.

Outline stitch padding

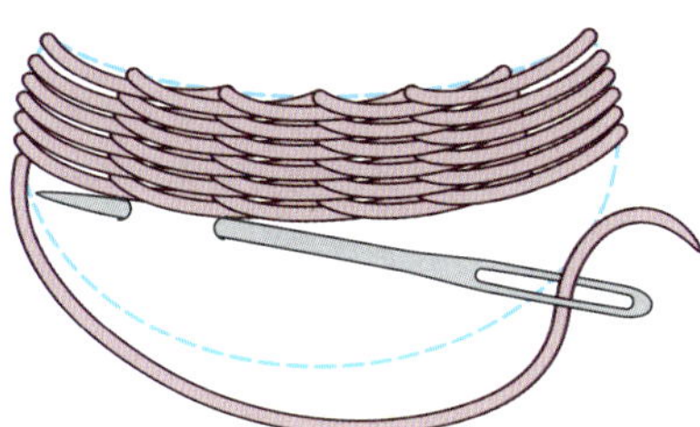

Outline stitch, when worked as a padding, is smoother than chain stitch. Make the stitches longer than you would normally do if you were working the stitch as an outline.

1 Start on the inside of the curve, so in other words, just inside the top line in the diagram.
2 Working in rows, bring the needle up at the beginning of the row on the left.
3 Go in a stitch length to the right without pulling through. Come up halfway between the beginning and the end of the stitch with the loop below the needle, which means that as you pull through, the working thread will hold the slightly curved stitch in place. Pull through.
4 Go into the fabric a stitch length to the right, coming up just beyond where you went in for the first stitch and pull through, keeping the working thread on the top, or inside of the curve.
5 Work rows forwards and backwards, keeping within the outlines, until you have filled the entire shape.
6 Once you have padded an area with this stitch, work over the top of and perpendicular to the padding, starting on the perimeter line of the shape and making sure that you cover all the padding stitches.

Portuguese knotted stem stitch

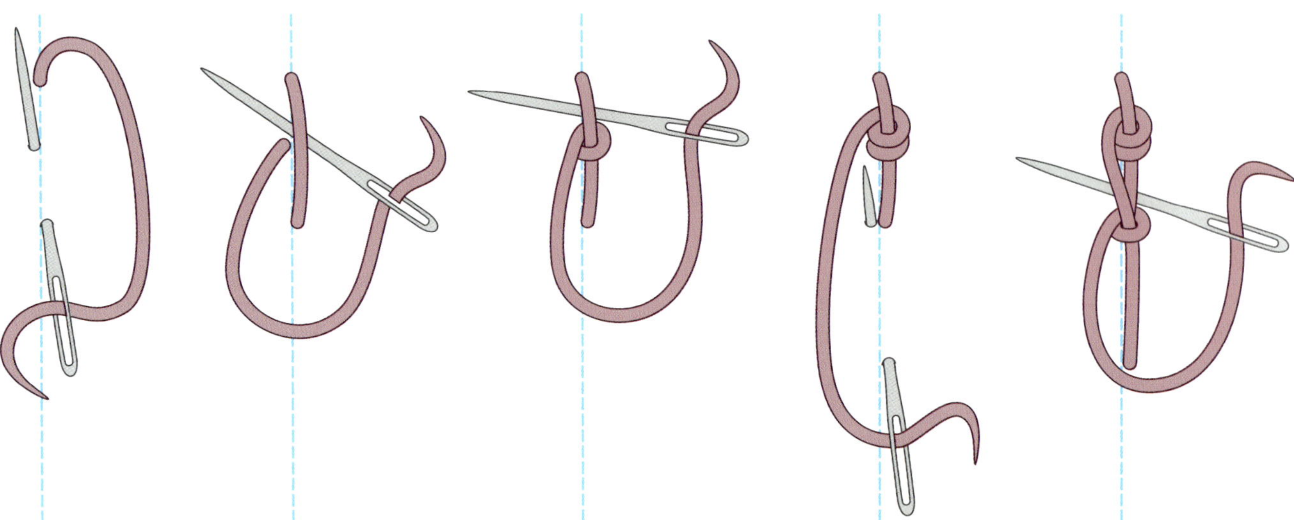

1 Starting at the beginning of the line working downwards, come up through the fabric. Leaving a stitch length, go in slightly to the right of the line a little way along and come up slightly to the left of the line halfway back. Pull through.
2 Go over and under that stitch, taking the needle from right to left above where the thread came out of the fabric on the left of the stitch.
3 Whip the stitch a second time, in the same direction from right to left.
4 Once again, make sure that the needle is above the thread on the left so that when you pull through the thread lies towards the top, as if you are working backwards.
5 Moving downwards (or forwards) again, and leaving a stitch length, go in slightly to the right of the line and come up either adjacent to or even out of the same hole as the end of the first stitch.
6 As you pull through, coax the working thread over so that it lies to the right of the needle.
7 As you did in steps 3 and 4, working upwards, whip twice one above the other, but this time making sure that you incorporate the bottom half of the first stitch and the top half of the second stitch, pulling them together as you whip.
8 Continue the line in this way and when you get to the end, having whipped upwards twice, take the needle into the same hole as you went into when you worked the final stitch.

Tip

Note that in the diagram above, the needle is brought up on the left which, if the line curved, would be the inside of the curve. If the line were to curve the other way, the needle would be brought up on the right.

Raised stem stitch

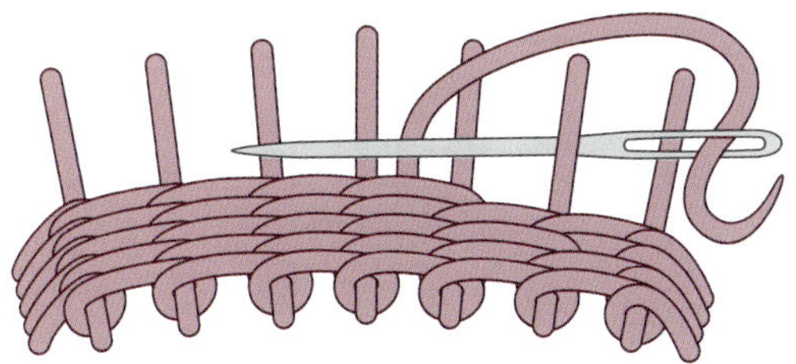

1 Raised stem stitch consists of horizontal rows that are whipped over vertical straight stitches. The starting point, therefore, is to work the straight stitches that form the basis of the stitch.
2 Work the stitches 2–3mm (1/16in) apart, fanning them around the shape as necessary.
3 Come up at the bottom left of the shape (or bottom right if you are left-handed).
4 Working to the right (or left if you are left-handed), take the needle over and then under each ladder stitch, going into the fabric a little way past the last ladder stitch when you reach the other side.
5 Return to the beginning and add rows in the same way, packing them close to one another, so that the space is well filled.

Rhodes stitch

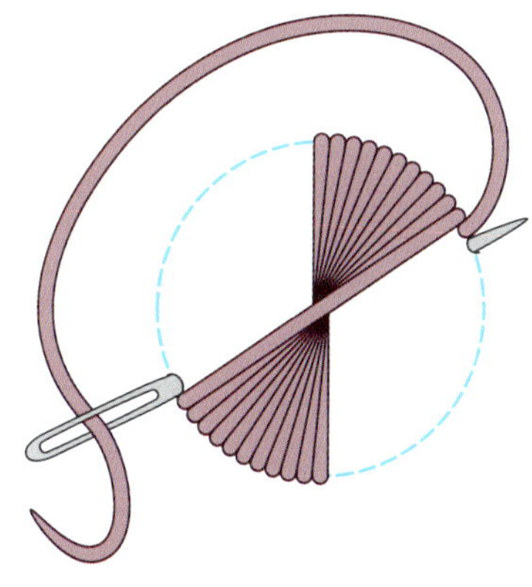

1 Divide the circle equally by bisecting it with a straight stitch worked from top to bottom.
2 Come up at the top, slightly to the right of the last stitch and go in the bottom, crossing over and going in slightly to the left of the previous stitch.
3 Repeat until you have filled the circle.

Satin stitch – small leaves

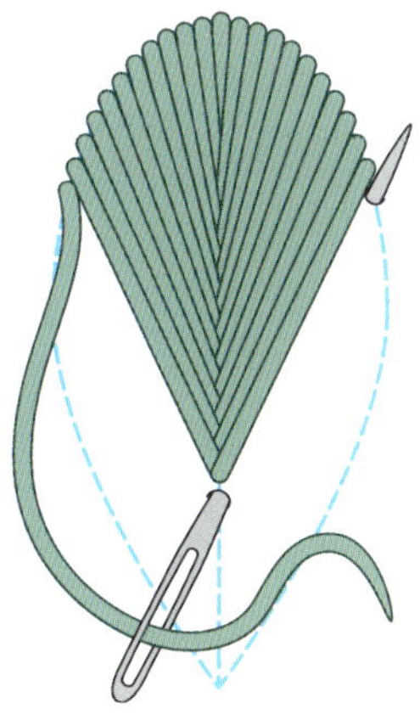

1 Come up at the tip on or just beyond the perimeter line. Work a straight stitch, going in on the midline around a quarter to a third of the way down the shape.
2 Leaving a small gap, come up on or just to the left of the perimeter line.
3 Go in below the end of the first vertical stitch leaving a space. Leave a slightly longer gap than you did at the top – this helps the angle of the stitches to stay fairly sharp.
4 Come up on the right, leaving a small space. Go into the same hole that you went into when you worked the stitch that came from the left.
5 Keep working pairs in this way until you get to the bottom of the shape, making sure that your angles remain sharp (leaving less space on the side and more space in the middle if they are beginning to flatten out) and always taking both stitches of each pair into the same hole to create the impression of a vein.

Satin stitch – padded

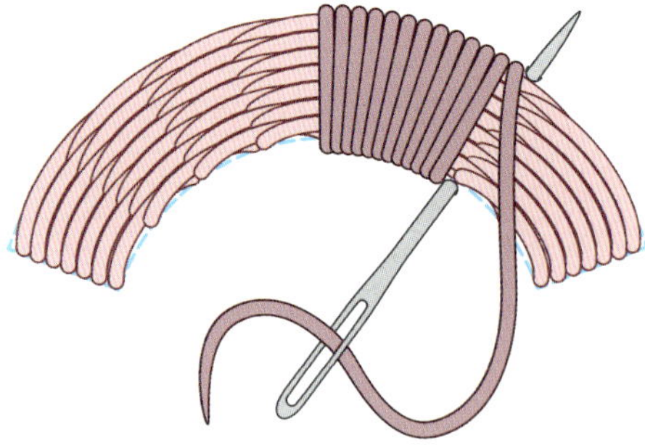

1 Following the guidelines for outline stitch padding (page 183), pad the area working the stitches in a direction that is at right angles to the direction that you will work the satin stitch.
2 When working satin stitch, use a single strand of thread and work perpendicular to the padding. Begin in the centre of the space you need to fill or, at the very least, away from the side. You will work to one side and then, return to where you started and work the other side.
3 Come up above the edge of the padding and working downwards towards yourself, go in at the bottom below the edge of the padding.
4 Come up at the top and continue working downward facing stitches that go in at the bottom. Fan the stitches if necessary, by coming up further apart at the top and going in closer at the bottom.
5 Continue working in this way until you have covered all the padding.

Tip

When working vertical satin stitch, the space between the stitches is the same at top and bottom.

Split backstitch

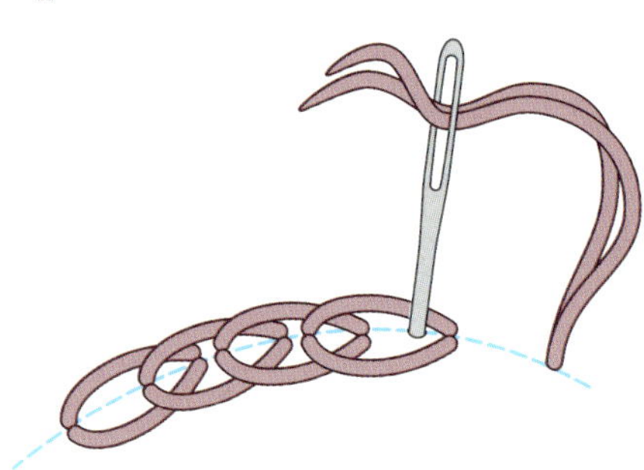

This is easier to work and gives a more pleasing result than traditional split stitch.

1 Work a backstitch. Come up further along the line and, instead of going back into the hole at the end of the first stitch as you would for normal backstitch, take the needle down between the two threads of the previous backstitch, making sure that the threads of that stitch lie side by side with no twists.
2 Continue working in this way.

Trellis couching – basic

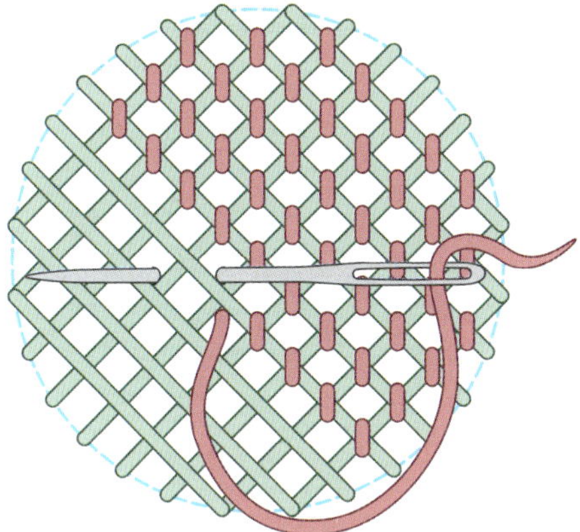

1 Using your first thread colour (green in the diagram), work a layer of long straight stitches across the area. These can be vertical or diagonal.
2 Work another layer of long straight stitches that are placed at right angles to the first layer.
3 Using your second thread colour (pink in the diagram), work small, straight couching stitches over the intersection of the stitches. In general, the couching stitches should be just long enough to cover the intersection but should not push the layers of long straight stitches out of place. You can choose, however, to make them longer. The direction of these stitches – whether vertical or horizontal – does not matter, provided they all go in the same direction.

Trellis with cross stitch couching

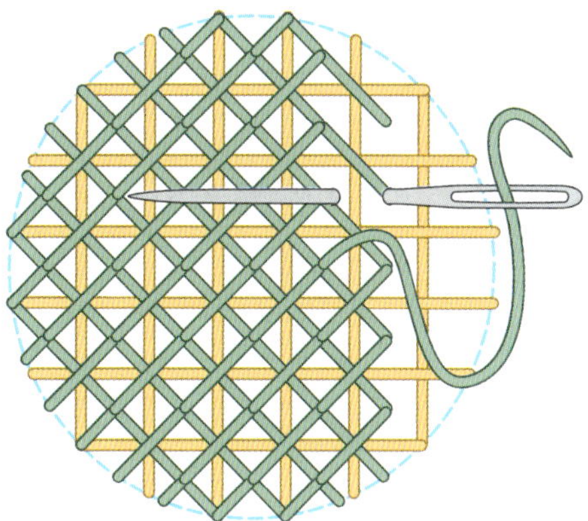

1 Work a layer of long straight stitches across the area. Work another layer of long straight stitches that are placed at right angles to the first layer.
2 Now work a pattern of cross stitches over this trellis background. Come up in the centre of a square, and go down in the centre of a diagonally adjacent square, as shown in the diagram above.
3 It is important to note that, like traditional cross stitch, all stitches should be worked in a consistent order, so that the threads underneath lie in one direction and the uppermost (crossing) threads in the other.
4 Also important to note is that where you can't complete a full-sized cross stitch at the perimeter of the circle or shape, make shorter stitches over the intersection. Don't leave it out just because you can't stitch to the full size as it would leave a noticeable gap. Alternatively, you can make the legs of close-by cross stitches a little longer.

Trellis couching – woven

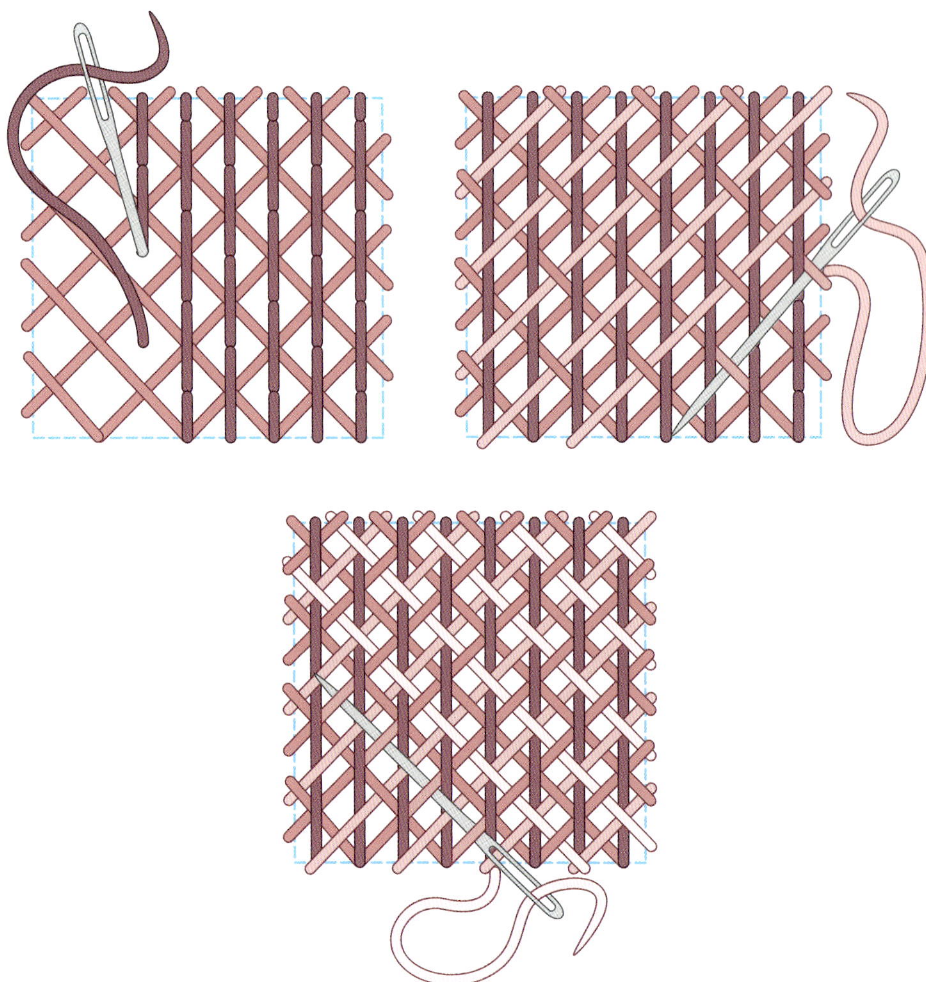

1 Choose three thread colours. Using your mid-colour thread shade (medium pink in the diagram), work a layer of long straight stitches across the area. These can be horizontal or diagonal. Work another layer of long straight stitches that are placed at right angles to the first layer.

2 Using the darker thread (dark pink in the diagram), work straight couching stitches over the intersection of the long stitches. These should start in the middle of an empty square between the long straight stitches, extending to the middle of the next empty square. It is usually easier to work them in lines of backstitch.

3 Using the lightest thread (light pink in the diagram), weave over and under the medium pink lines. Place the weaving exactly halfway between the medium pink stitches.

4 Using the light thread and working at right angles, weave under all the stitches of the first layer (medium pink) of trellis, and over all of the weaving (light pink).

Tufting – scruffy

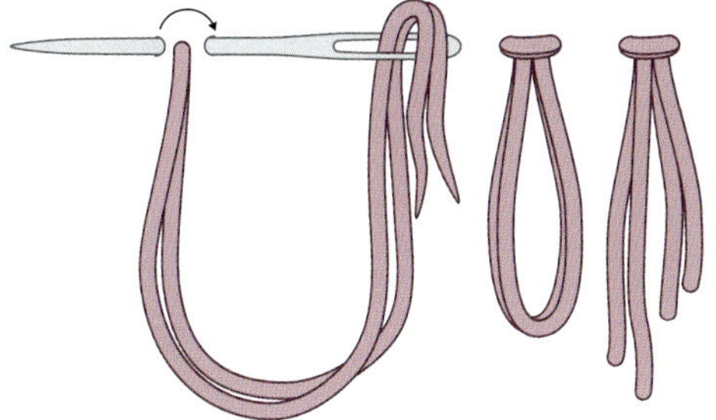

1 Using two strands of thread, come up through the fabric. Go back into the same hole, leaving a loop as you pull through.

2 Work a small backstitch over the base of the loop to secure the threads.

3 Continue working backstitched loops in this way until you have filled the area.

4 Stagger your stitches to create a slightly 'scruffy' effect so that they don't sit in a perfectly straight line. You might also leave small gaps, depending on your personal preference.

5 With a sharp pair of scissors, snip the loops to differing lengths so that the effect is not too neat or uniform.

Twisted thread

The easiest way to convert stranded cotton into cord is with a Kreinik custom corder. It is, however, possible to twist it between your index finger and thumb, or to place a pencil in the loop and turn that.

1 Cut a two-strand length of thread that measures approximately 2m (2¼yd).

2 Following the instructions in the project for the thickness that you require, either double the thread over for a heavy twist or, alternatively, put a knot at each end of the two strands to make a lightweight twist.

3 Whether you are using a corder, or just working with your fingers, loop one end over something that won't move, like a cup-hook or doorknob. Loop the other end over the hook on the corder and pull the yarn taut. If you are winding with your fingers, hold the far end between the thumb and index finger of one hand and pull the yarn taut. Stand away from where the loop of thread is attached so the thread forms a reasonably straight line, so that once you start twisting, it can't twist back on itself.

4 Now wind the threads until they are firmly twisted together. Test from time to time by relaxing the tension and allowing the threads to twist around one another. You do want them to twist tightly so that when you use the thread, it gives the impression of a cord.

5 When you are happy with the twist, double the twisted thread over by placing the two ends together. Hang something heavy where the threads fold at the bottom. The added weight will twist the cord together evenly.

7 Pull all the threads off the cup hook, or wherever you have attached them. Holding the ends together, allow the thread to hang from your fingers and twist freely. Once they stop twisting, make an overhand knot at the raw ends to keep them together, then snip off the raw ends after the knot.

8 Thread the folded end onto a large chenille needle and embroider with it as if it were normal thread.

Twisted thread couching

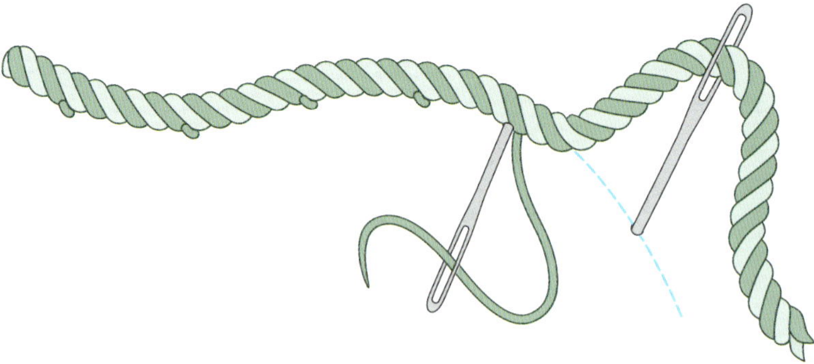

1 Following the guidelines for making twisted thread (see previous page), twist a length of thread.
2 With the twisted thread on a large chenille needle, come up at the beginning of the line at the top.
3 Working down the line with a single strand of thread on a separate needle, come up on the line about 5mm (¼in) below the top.
4 Holding the twist on the outside and working on the inside of the curve, take the needle and thread over just one of the threads that form part of the twist. By going over only one of the threads, it is easy to hide the couching stitch by rolling the twist towards the inside of the curve.
5 Take the couching thread back into the fabric, going in on the line where you came out.
6 Keep working down the line in the same way, placing your couching stitches at regular and even intervals.
7 As you get closer to the end of the curved line, take the twisted thread through the fabric at the bottom.

Twisted long and short stitch

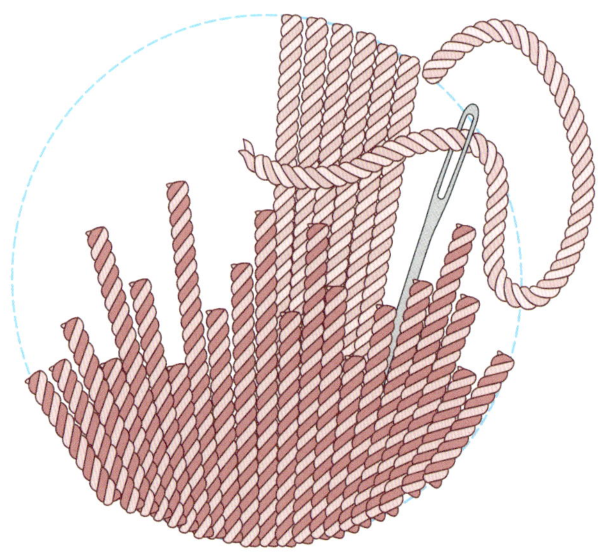

1 Following the guidelines for making twisted thread (see previous page), twist the length of thread.
2 With the twisted thread on a large chenille needle and following the guidelines for long and short stitch shading on page 182, fill the shape with shading using the thicker, more textured twisted thread.

Up and down buttonhole stitch

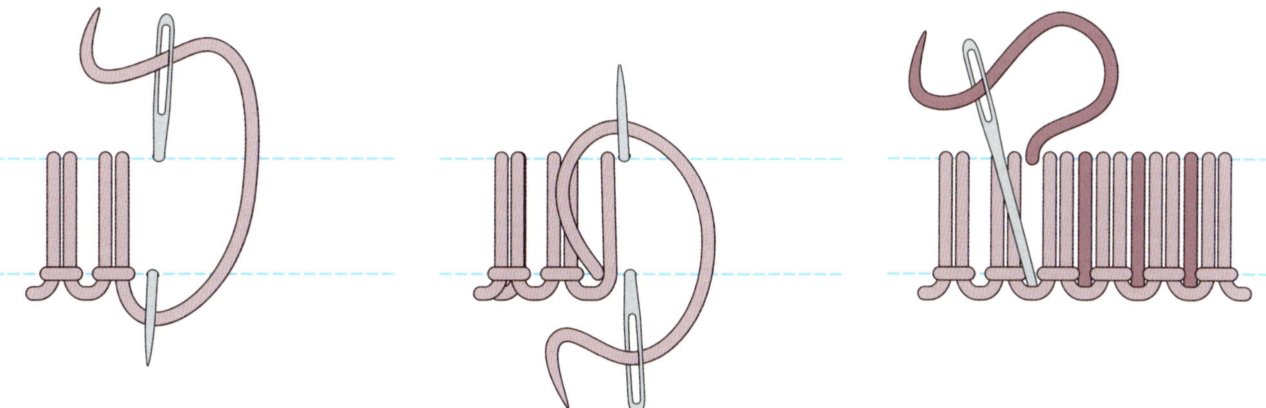

1 Working from left to right, bring the needle up on the bottom edge where you require the ridge.

2 Take the needle in at the top edge, and out again at the bottom edge, with the thread looped under the needle. Pull through.

3 Go over the thread as if you were doing a small couching stitch. Insert the needle on the line, scooping through the fabric and bringing it up again adjacent to the other end of the stitch.

4 Making sure that the thread is looped under the needle, pull upwards and then downwards to continue.

5 To add stripes to the up and down buttonhole stitch, use a darker or lighter shade of thread. Come up in the empty space between the stitches. Work a straight stitch, burying the end of the stitch under the ridge of the up and down buttonhole stitch.

Vermicelli couching

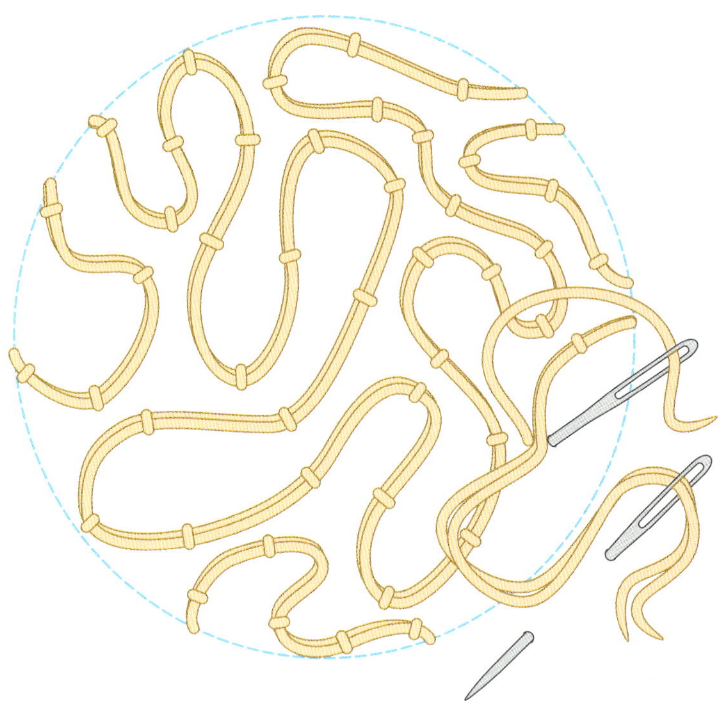

1 Thread a needle with two strands of thread and another with one strand of the same thread.
2 At the edges of the area, insert the needle thread with two strands of thread into the fabric, coming up again further along to continue the pattern.
3 Using the needle with one strand of thread, couch the three-strand thread into a series of rounded swirls that move all over the area that you wish to cover, but never cross over each other.
4 At the edges of the area, go into the fabric and come up again further along continuing the pattern.

Vermicelli couching – two tone

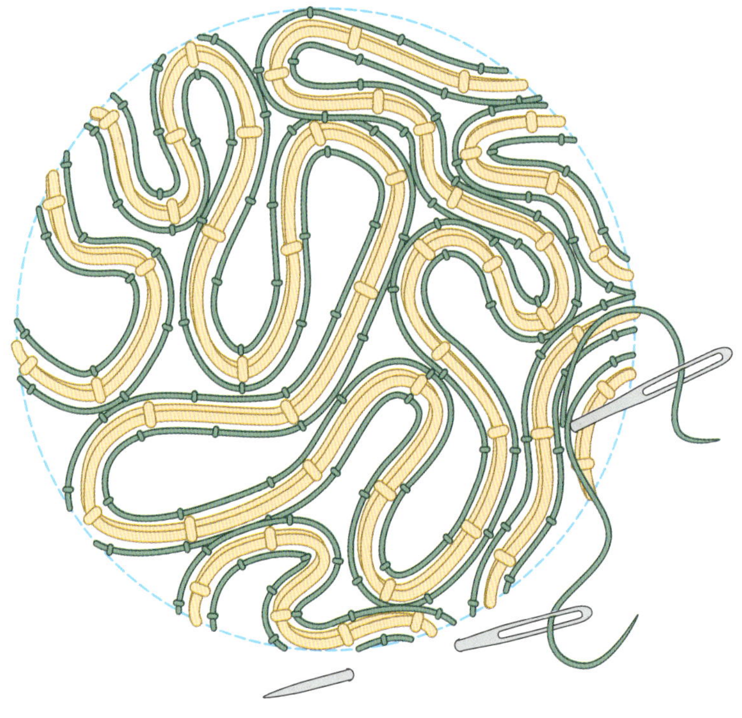

1 Follow the instructions for vermicelli couching (above), with two strands of cotton couched down with a single strand in the lighter shade. Make sure that the swirls are large enough to accommodate the second thread.
2 Thread two needles, each with a single strand of thread that is darker than the thread you used for step 1.
3 Come through the fabric with one needle and pin it to the side of the working area, keeping some slack in the thread.
4 Using the other needle with one strand of the darker thread, couch the single strand into a series of rounded swirls in between the two-strand couched swirls, leaving sufficient space for the darker couching to be visible.
5 You create single-strand swirls on both sides of the two-strand swirls, often coming together where the thicker swirls are close to one another.
6 At the edges of the area, go into the fabric and come up again further along continuing the pattern.

Wheatear stitch

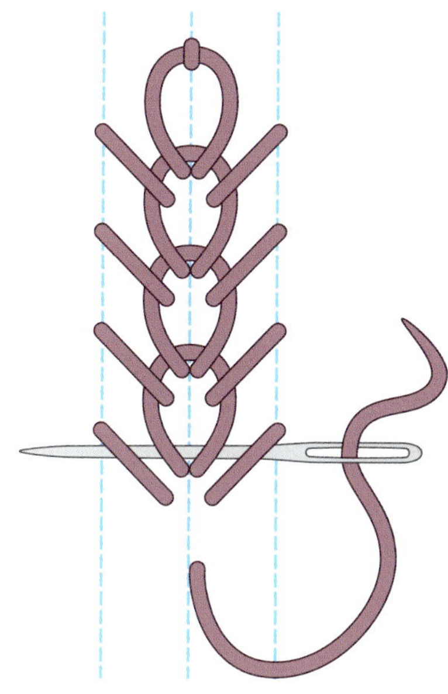

1 Starting at the beginning of the line and working downwards towards yourself, work a short straight stitch. Come up 2–3mm (1/16in) below that stitch on the line.

2 Take the needle under the straight stitch and go back into the hole you came out of, to create a looped stitch similar to a reverse detached chain stitch.

3 Referring to the illustration, come up on the right of and a little more than halfway up the side of the looped stitch.

4 Work a diagonal straight stitch, going in on the line close to the hole that you came out of when you created the looped stitch. Work an identical diagonal straight stitch on the left. Come up 2–3mm (1/16in) below these stitches on the line.

5 Take your needle under all of the stitches – the diagonal straight stitches and both threads of the looped stitch.

6 Go back into the hole you came out of to create a looped stitch.

7 As before, work diagonal straight stitches on both sides of the looped stitch. Continue adding stitches in this way.

8 When you reach the end of the line, work the two diagonal stitches.

Freestyle embroidery

Freestyle embroidery – random

Freestyle stitching uses a variety of stitches worked with a single strand of thread. This technique is used to fill the face of the cat in Tiny the Tabby (page 62). The threads used are listed in the instructions of the project and the stitches are described on the following pages. In general, your stitching will be worked freehand, without the drawing of any lines. However, for shapes such as a half-buttonhole stitch flower, which is difficult to work without lines to guide you, you will probably want to draw an outline. You can do this with a heat-erasable pen.

It is important to note that the shape of the areas filled with specific stitches should be irregular, no squares or circles. When you fill an area with a group of the same stitches, make sure that the edges of that group do not line up with the edges of any other group of stitches that has already been stitched.

Intersperse your stitching with single-wrap French knots (see page 179) to soften the effect and, also, to fill up spaces that can't be filled with the recommended stitches. You are aiming to create an overall texture.

3-petal lazy daisy bud

1 Referring to the instructions for detached chain stitch (page 175), work three stitches in a trefoil shape. Vary the length and angle of the stitches to accommodate the space you wish to fill.

2 Work a single-wrap French knot in the centre and at the base of the chain stitches.

9-petal lazy daisy flower

1 Referring to the instructions for detached chain stitch (page 175), work nine stitches in a circle. Vary the length and angle of the stitches to accommodate the space you wish to fill.

2 Work a single-wrap French knot in the centre, at the base of the detached chain stitches.

3 You can increase or decrease the number of detached chain stitches in the circle, sometimes working just a portion of a flower to fit in with the surrounding freestyle stitches.

Buttonhole bud

1 Work three single-wrap French knots in a group at the tip.

2 Starting with a straight stitch on the left, come out of the fabric at the bottom end and go into the fabric at the base of the bunch of French knots.

3 Coming out of the same hole that you came out of at the base of the straight stitch, work groups of four or five buttonhole stitches in a fan shape, all going into the fabric in the same hole at the base of the group of French knots.

4 Finish the group with a couching stitch on the right.

5 Work a detached chain stitch on each side of the buttonhole flower, starting close to the French knots at the top and working diagonally out to the side of the flower. You might work only a single detached chain stitch leaf, or leave them out altogether, depending on the space you want to fill.

Buttonhole stitch half flower

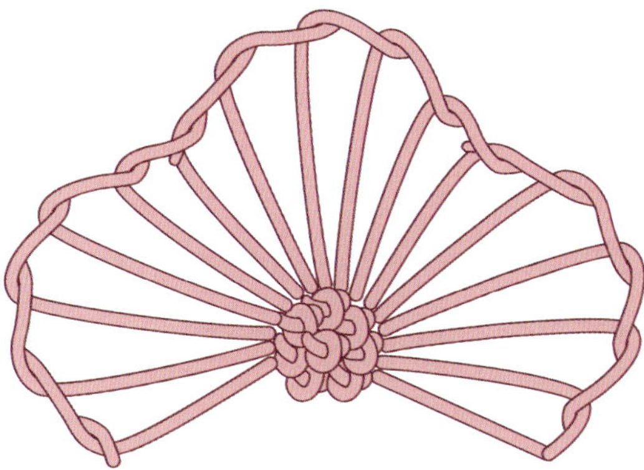

It is advisable to draw the half flower outline first with a heat-erasable pen.

1 Starting on the bottom right, come up on the line that depicts the outside of the flower. Go into the fabric on the line that depicts the centre circle, working a straight stitch.

2 Come out of the first hole that you made, going into the fabric on the centre circle, slightly to the right of the first (straight) stitch.

3 Without pulling through, and working up the first petal, come up a little further along the outside line, making sure that the working thread loops under the sharp end of the needle.

4 Pull through to create the first buttonhole stitch. Pull outwards, away from the flower, keeping a firm tension. Holding the thread outwards with your non-working hand, take the needle through the fabric on the line that depicts the outside of the centre circle to create the next stitch.

5 Once again, without pulling through and working up the petal, come up a little further along the outside line, leaving a similar space for each stitch. Make sure that the working thread is under the sharp end of the needle and pull through to form the second stitch.

6 Continue working buttonhole stitches in this way, working up towards the tip of the petal and then working down to the valley that is the end of the petal and start of the second petal. Keep the spaces between the stitches as even as possible. As you work downwards, make sure that the stitch which will catch the last loop of the petal will come out in the valley, the lowest point. When you have caught the loop, work a couching stitch over the thread, as if you were finishing off the line of buttonhole stitch.

7 Come up again in the space within the last stitch and continue working the second petal in the same way as the first. By working the couching stitch in the dip at the end of each petal, it helps to keep the stitches in place after their downward trend and it also creates a firm point between the petals.

8 Continue working the petals in this way, working the couching stitch in the valley at the end of each petal.

9 When you get to the end of the outside line, catch the last buttonhole stitch with a small couching stitch that comes out on the outside line of the circle, catches the loop, and goes back into the same hole.

Eye stitch variation

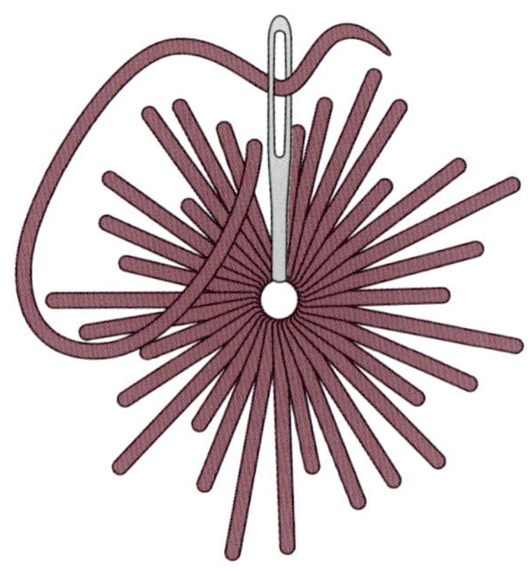

1 Come up on the outside and, working in a clockwise direction, make straight stitches of varying lengths into the same hole in the middle.
2 Pull reasonably tight so that the hole in the middle becomes a visible hole that creates the 'eye'.
3 Vary the length of the stitches to accommodate the space you wish to fill.

Sheaf stitch

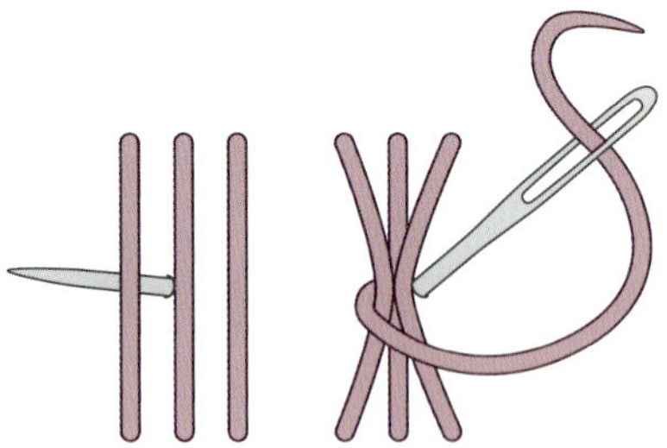

These small stitches are useful for filling in small spaces. They can be worked singly or in groups.

1 Start with a straight, vertical stitch. Place a straight stitch to the left of that stitch.
2 Make a stitch to the right of the middle stitch, but before you tighten it, bring your needle up adjacent to the centre of the middle stitch.
3 Pull through, tightening the right-hand straight stitch. Make a straight stitch over the middle of the three stitches, tucking it under the left-hand stitch, going in adjacent to the middle stitch to pull the three stitches together.

Single weaving filler stitch

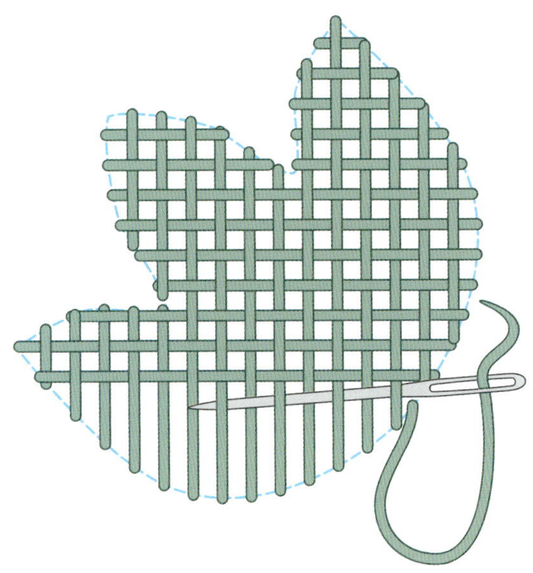

1 Working with a single strand of stranded cotton, create the warp, by working long straight stitches from top to bottom, making them 1–2mm (1/16in) apart. Vary the length of the stitches to accommodate the space you wish to fill.
2 Working horizontally, the weft stitches are spaced about the same distance apart. Work these long stitches going over one and then under one warp stitch, continuing this sequence until you have gone over and under all of the warp stitches in the space.
3 The next weft stitch is worked going under the weft stitches you went over, and over the stitches you went under, in the previous weft stitch.
4 Continue alternating the stitches in this way until you have woven all of the warp stitches that fill the space.

Freestyle flower embroidery

Work with two strands of thread, unless stated otherwise. When deciding which flowers to put in which areas, think about balancing the flower types and colours.

Refer to the colour images in the project instructions for the approximate placement and use of specific flowers. Below are some examples of suggested placement. Turn the page to find the instructions for the individual stitched flowers.

Freestyle flower embroidery *continued*

Worked with DMC stranded cotton, the threads listed below refer to the colours used in the Contemporary Eagle and Bluebird projects, see pages 102 and 126.

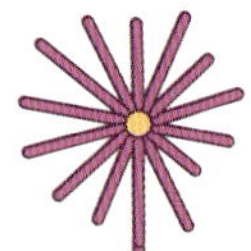

Chrysanthemum

Centre: French knot, 676 or 677

Petals: straight stitches, 1 strand 3834 or 3835

Daffodil

Trumpet: 4 to 5 buttonhole stitches into the same hole at the top, 676

Petals: detached chain stitches, 676 and 677

Daisy

Centre: French knots, 676 and 677

Petals: detached chain stitches, 3865

Delphinium

Flower: French knots, mixed but shading dark at the bottom to light at the top, 798 and 799

Bottom leaves: detached chain stitches, 561

Side leaves (if necessary): detached chain stitches, 563

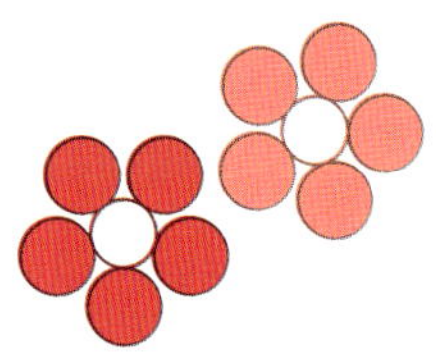

Dianthus filler

Flowers: centre French knot, 3865 with 5 surrounding French knots, 961 or 150

Dianthus stem

Flowers: centre French knot, 3865 with 5 surrounding French knots, 961 or 962

Stems: straight stitches, 561

Branch: couching, 561

Leaves: fly stitch, 561

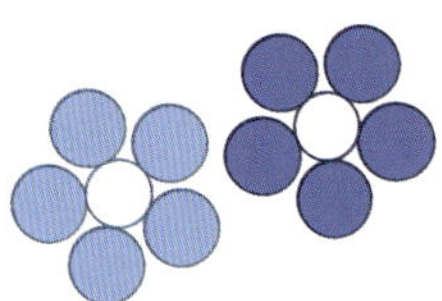

Forget-me-not filler

Flowers: centre French knot, 676 or 677 with 5 surrounding French knots, 798 or 799

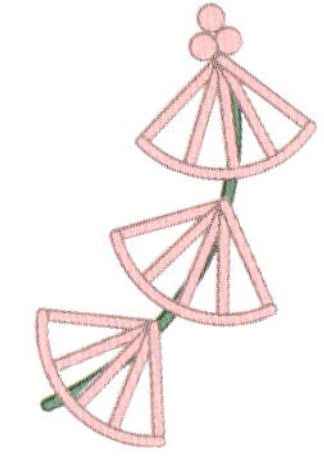

Hollyhocks

Branch: couching, 561

Flowers: 3 French knots at tip followed by buttonhole stitch flowers, 3716

Leaf and French knot fillers

Dark leaves: two strands detached chain stitch, 561

Light leaves: 1 strand detached chain stitch, 563

French knots: 1 strand, 563

Wisteria

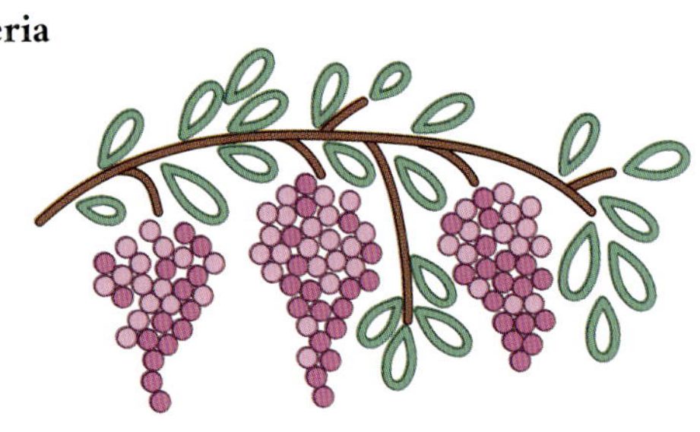

Branch: whipped backstitch, 610

Flowers: French knots, mixed but shading dark at the bottom to light at the top, 3834, 3835 and 3836

Bead embroidery stitches

Attaching a single bead

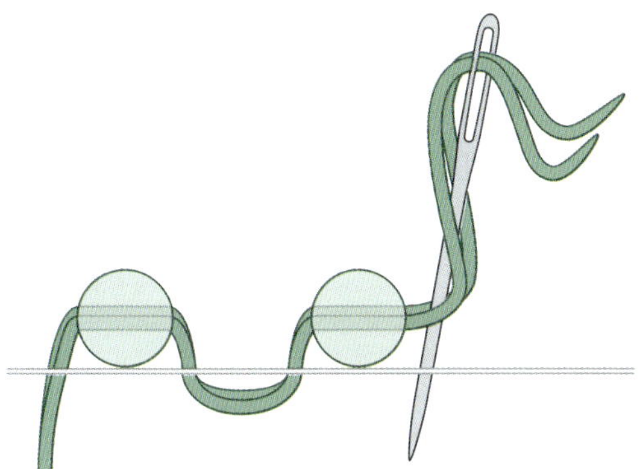

1 Bring your needle up through the fabric and pick up a bead.
2 Pull the bead down the thread until it touches the fabric.
3 Slide the needle down between the two threads until it touches the bead and go back into the fabric at that point. This will ensure that the length of the stitch holding the bead is the correct length and is a particularly useful way to attach bugle beads.

Attaching a smaller bead with a larger bead

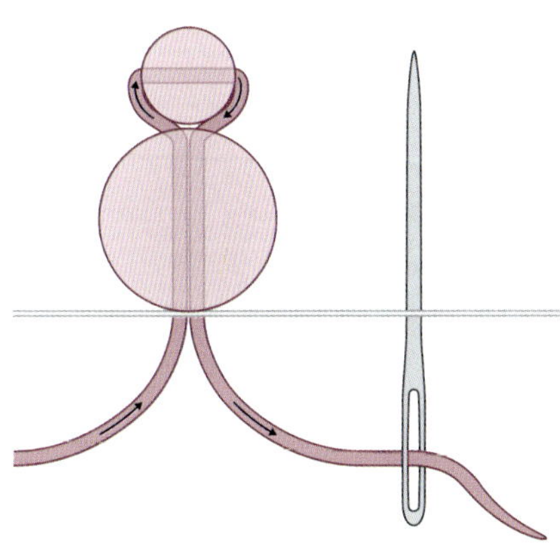

1 Bring your needle up through the fabric at the correct point.
2 Pick up the larger and then the smaller bead.
3 Return down through the larger bead and tighten the thread. The smaller bead holds the larger bead in place.

Beaded backstitch

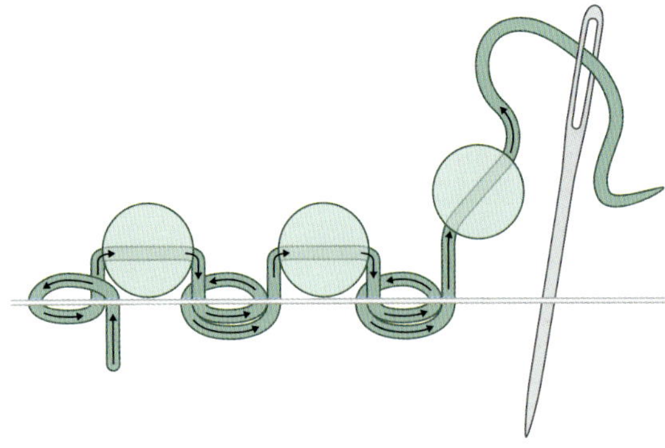

1 Thread your bead embroidery with a single strand of cotton. Double it over and tied the ends together with a knot.
2 Come up a backstitch length away from the beginning of the line. Go in on the end of the line and come up again through the same hole that you came through when you started the backstitch. Pick up a bead.
3 Moving to the right, push the bead back to where the thread comes out of the fabric, sliding the needle between the two strands of cotton, pushing the bead with the needle.
4 When you can't push it back any further, go into the fabric at that point, thereby making the stitch the exact size you need to hold the bead firmly in place.
5 Come up a backstitch length beyond the bead and finish the backstitch by going into the same hole that you went into when you attached the bead. Moving forward again, attach a bead and keep going in this way to complete the line.

Tip

In most instances you will start and end with a backstitch, particularly if you are making a tendril or a feather. To this end, as you get towards the end of the beaded backstitch line, try to space your stitches so that you will end the line with a backstitch.

Beaded backstitch picot line

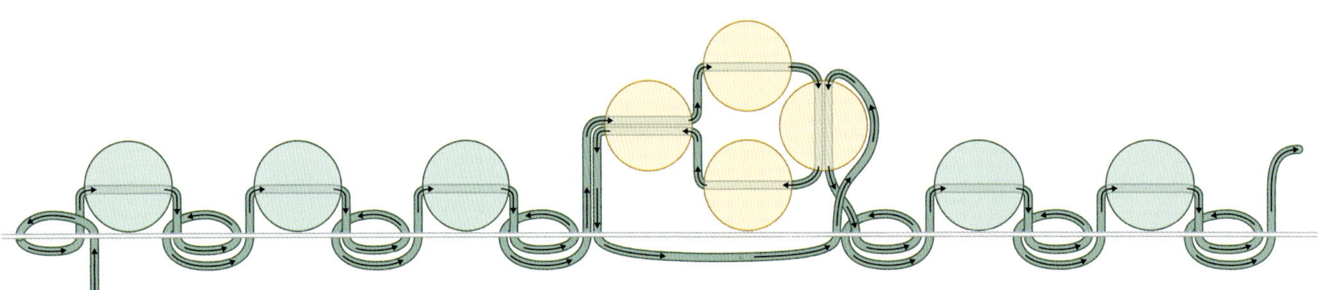

This stitch is a combination of beaded backstitch and attached bead picots (see above and page 202).

1 Following the directional arrows in the diagram, work beaded backstitch up to the point where you want to incorporate a picot. Thereafter, pick up four beads, return down the first bead, going back into the fabric at the same time.
2 Come up on the line slightly beyond the end of the picot. Go through the third bead in the picot and go back into the same hole in the fabric.
3 Come up a backstitch length beyond the picot, going back into the fabric at the tip of the picot and, having worked the first backstitch, continue with beaded backstitch until you need to add the next picot.

Beaded circles around a bead/crystal

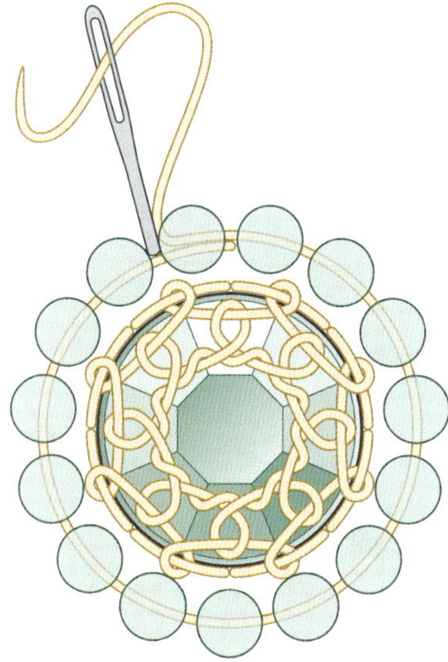

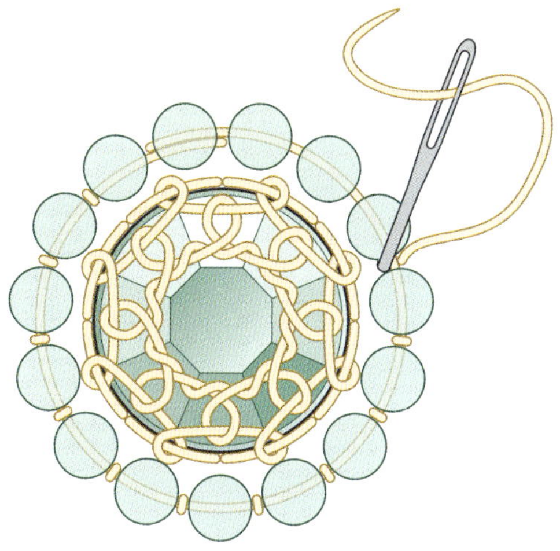

1 With a doubled over single strand of cotton on a bead embroidery needle, come up on the side of the bead or crystal, leaving sufficient space for the beads in the circle to sit comfortably.
2 Pick up the number of beads that you need to create the circle. This varies according to the size of the bead or crystal that has been attached.
3 Take the needle back through the first bead and pull the beads into a circle around the bead or crystal. Go into the fabric between the beads.
4 Come up between the next two beads in the circle and work a small couching stitch over the thread that runs between the beads.
5 Work a couching stitch between all the beads in the circle.
6 If your beads are not sitting in a perfect circle after you have worked the final couching stitch, come up between two of the beads and run a continuous thread through all the beads.
7 When you get back to where you started, tug the thread, and go back into the fabric to end off. This usually pulls them into a neat circle.

Beaded fly stitch

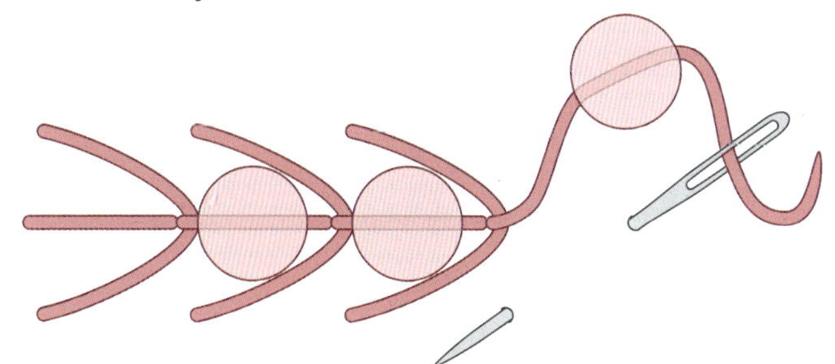

1 Come up at the start of the line and working downwards, work straight stitch.
2 Come up a few millimetres away from and at a level slightly lower than the start of the straight stitch. Pull through.
3 Go into the fabric on the other side of the straight stitch, leaving a similar space and going in at the same level, go into the fabric and come out at the base of the straight stitch. Make sure that you take the needle over the working thread so that when you pull through you will catch the loop, making a V-shaped stitch.
4 Pick up a bead and leaving sufficient space for the bead to lie comfortably, go in on the line.
5 Come up a few millimetres away from and at a level slightly lower than the start of the straight stitch. Pull through.

Beaded picot (attached)

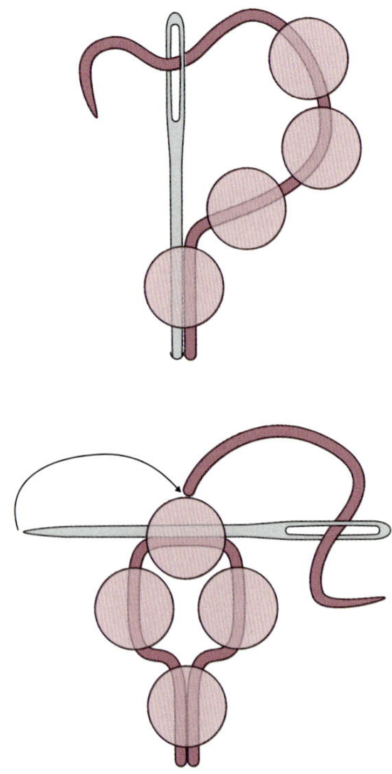

1 Come up through the fabric at the point where you want the base of the picot to lie. Pick up four beads.
2 Go down the first bead you picked up, going back into the fabric at the same place you came out of it.
3 Pull through, manipulating the beads to lie in a diamond-shaped formation.
4 Push the picot down towards the fabric in the desired direction.
5 Come up slightly beyond the bead at the tip of the picot.
6 Go through the bead at the tip, going back into the same hole in the fabric.

Beaded wheatear stitch

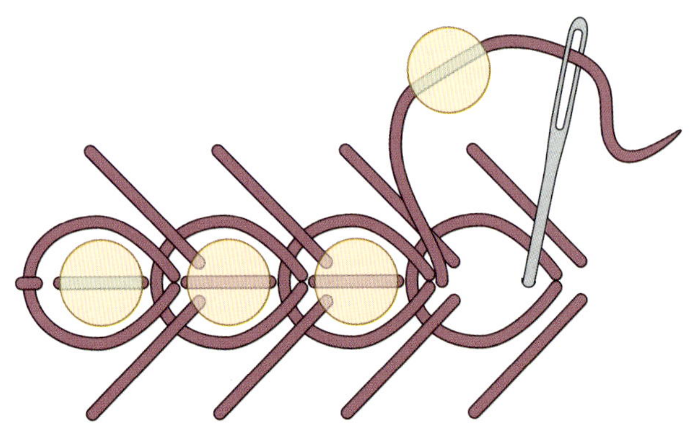

1 Work a line of wheatear stitch (see page 193). Make sure that the loops in the stitch are large enough to accommodate the bead.
2 Using a doubled-over length of stranded cotton on a bead embroidery needle, and starting within the loop of the first stitch, come up through the fabric immediately below the straight stitch that holds that loop in place.
3 Pick up the bead and, sliding the needle between the two strands of cotton, pushing the bead back towards the base of thread, go into the fabric when you can't push it back any further. This should be at the bottom of the loop.
4 Come up in the next loop immediately below the intersection of the stitches that formed the last wheatear stitch. Attach a bead in the same way in all the loops.

Caged crystals

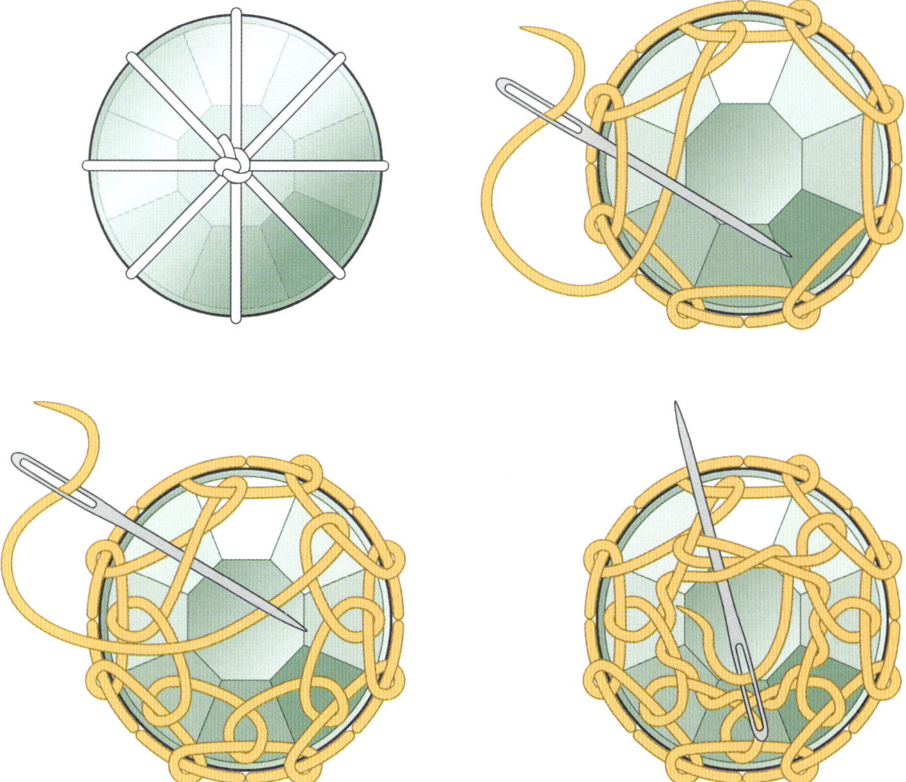

The instructions below are for caging a 20ss flat-back crystal.

1 The crystal needs to sit firmly in place on the fabric so that you can stitch around and over it.

2 Imagining a clock face, come up at the top of the crystal (12 o'clock) and, making a vertical stitch, go in at 6 o'clock.

3 Come up at 3 o'clock and, making a horizontal stitch, go in at 9 o'clock.

4 Come up midway between 1 and 2 o'clock, and take your needle under the intersection of the vertical and horizontal stitches. Go back and under the intersection to whip it and hold the stitches together.

5 Go in midway between 7 and 8 o'clock, and come up midway between 4 and 5 o'clock. Take your needle under the intersection of all the stitches, go back and under the intersection to whip again.

6 Go in midway between 10 and 11 o'clock. Come up between two of the stitches (it doesn't matter which ones) and go under all the stitches at the intersection.

7 Go back and under those stitches but, before you pull through, take the needle through the loop and pull, creating a knot. Snip off the thread next to the knot. Making the knot at the top will make it easier to snip and unpick.

8 Using a heat-erasable pen, divide the area into four, making small marks to mark each quarter.

9 Using a single strand of cotton, work two backstitches into each quarter.

10 When you work the last backstitch come up halfway between the beginning and end of the stitch before you pull through, so that your thread is ready to start the detached buttonhole stitch.

11 Going in a clockwise direction, work a detached buttonhole stitch into each backstitch.

12 When you get back to where you started, instead of going under the first backstitch, work the detached buttonhole stitch through the slanting loop that came out of the first backstitch, leading up to the first detached buttonhole stitch and pull through.

Continued overleaf

Caged crystals *continued*

13 Going in an anti-clockwise direction, work a detached buttonhole stitch into the loops between each stitch in the first row. As you tighten each stitch, pull inwards and upwards so that the stitches begin to hug the crystal.

14 When you get back to the beginning of the row, work the detached buttonhole stitch through the loop that formed when you worked the detached buttonhole stitch at the end of the first row, and pull through.

15 Whip through the loops between each stitch in the second row to complete the cage and to change direction so you are now working clockwise.

16 As you whip the loop between each stitch, pull tightly so that the stitches of the entire cage are pulled inwards.

17 When you get back to where you started, whip under the first loop again and, following the direction of the needle in the diagram, whip down the side of the cage – but change your tension. These whipping stitches shouldn't be tight because if they are, you'll get a kink in the circle at the top of the cage.

18 Go into the fabric between the backstitch and the crystal and end off at the back. Pull out the waste thread that secured the crystal to the fabric at the beginning of this process.

Chain stitch – interlaced and beaded

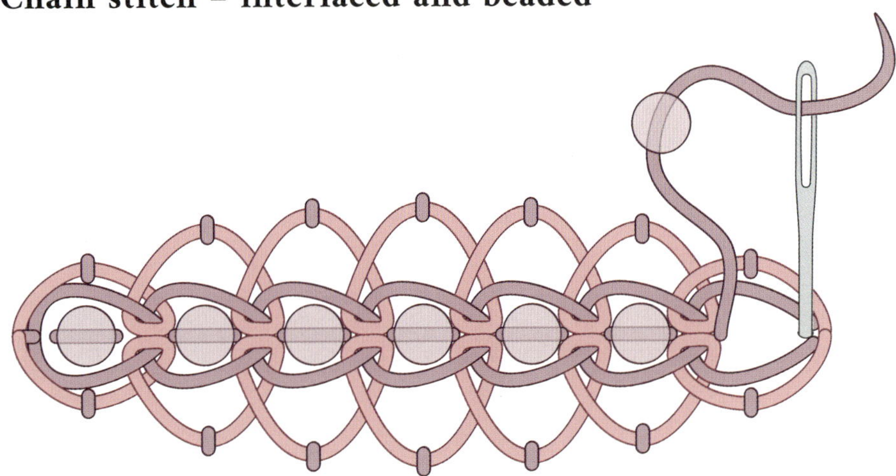

1 Following the directions for chain stitch – interlaced (page 176), fill the required area. Make sure that the loops in the chain stitch are large enough to accommodate the bead.

2 Using a doubled-over length of stranded cotton on a bead embroidery needle, and starting within the loop of the first chain stitch, come up through the fabric immediately below the straight stitch that holds that loop in place.

3 Pick up the bead and, sliding the needle between the two strands of cotton, pushing the bead back towards the base of thread, go into the fabric when you can't push it back any further. This should be at the bottom of the loop.

4 Come up in the next loop immediately below the intersection of the stitches that formed the last chain stitch. Attach a bead in the same way in all the chain stitch loops.

Covering a large bead

1 Bring your needle up through the fabric slightly off the centre of the area in which you want to place the bead, picking up a size 5° bead at the same time.
2 Holding the bead in place with your finger, take the thread over the bead, going back into the fabric at the side of the bead. Take the needle through at an angle so that it pierces the fabric slightly below the bead.
3 Make four stitches that divide the bead into quarters. Fill each quarter alternately with the others, stitching systematically so that the thread cover is neat. Keep going until the hole in the middle of the bead is almost full and the bead is tightly covered.
4 On the last stitch, come up through the middle, pick up a small bead, go back down through the middle of the large bead pulling tight so that the small bead sits in the dent in the middle of the large bead.

Needle lace stitches

Needle lace bars

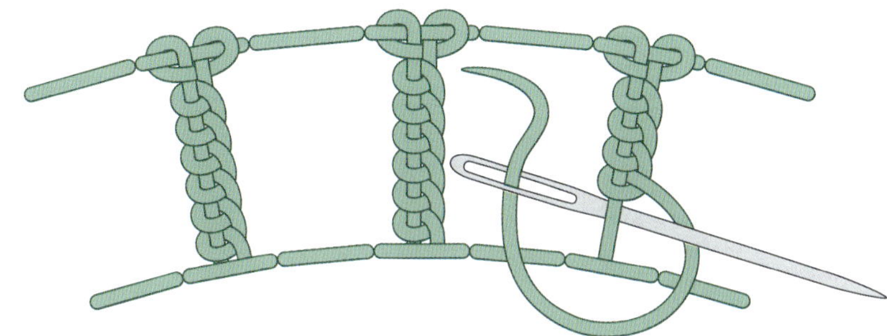

1 Work a line of backstitch along the top and the bottom of the area where you will work the bars. Make longer backstitches when working over the curve at the top. The stitches should be shorter at the bottom. These backstitches are used to anchor the bars at the top and will define the area at the bottom.
2 Starting on one side, miss the first backstitch, bringing your needle out from under the second backstitch.
3 Missing the first backstitch, work a group of two detached buttonhole stitches through the second backstitch at the top.
4 Turning your hoop or frame sideways, work horizontal detached buttonhole stitches into the loop that runs from the bottom up to the group of two. The number of stitches will vary, depending on the space that you are covering but will usually be in the region of three or four stitches. The stitches should fit comfortably into the space.
5 Go back into the fabric at the bottom, tucking your needle under the backstitch and, missing the next backstitch in the line, come up from under the following backstitch to work the next bar, in the same way.

Needle lace stitch no. 7

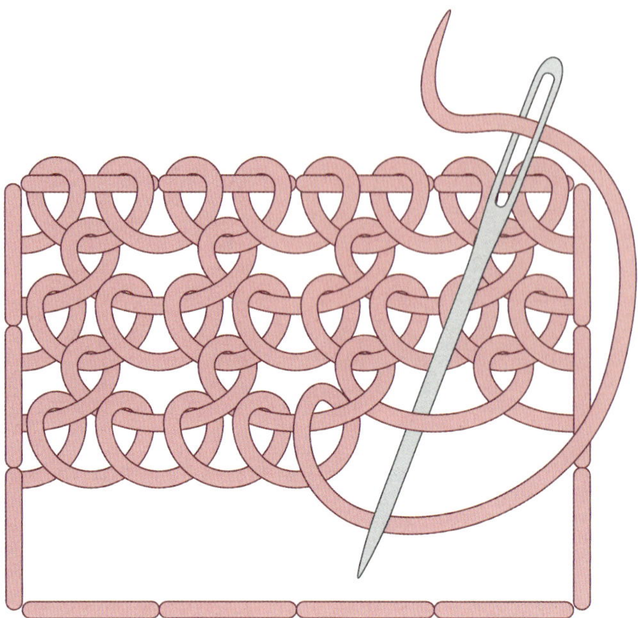

1 Work backstitch around the entire shape. Your stitches should be long enough to accommodate two detached buttonhole stitches with a little bit of 'wiggle' room.

2 Working from left to right (LR), work two detached buttonhole stitches (DBH) into each backstitch (BS) that makes up the first row.

3 When you reach the end of the row on the right, go into the fabric, tucking your needle under the BS that is level with where you started on the left. Leaving the space you need to accommodate the second row, come up from under the BS. This is called the step down.

4 #Working from right to left (RL), miss the first loop at the beginning of the row, [work one DBH into the next loop. Miss a loop]. Repeat [ ] to end. Step down.

5 Working LR, work two DBH into each of the large loops between the single stitches in the previous row. Step down.

6 Working RL, work a single DBH into the short loop between the two DBH stitches in the previous row. Step down.#

7 Repeat from # to # as many times as you need to, increasing and decreasing at the beginning and end of rows, if necessary, until you get to the bottom of the shape.

8 Join at the bottom by coming up from under the backstitch at the bottom, directly below the loops that you need to attach. Depending on which row of the pattern you are on, work either single DBH or a group of two stitches, and go back into the fabric, tucking the needle under the backstitch.

9 Come up below the next loop that needs to be attached, repeating until you have attached the entire row.

Note: the techniques on pages 206–215 are based on the stitches and patterns provided in the needle lace and needle weaving sections of the *DMC Encyclopedia of Needlework* by T.H. de Dillmont, published in 1890. These stitches have been modified for use as embroidery stitches, while retaining their original numbered names.

Needle lace stitch no. 8

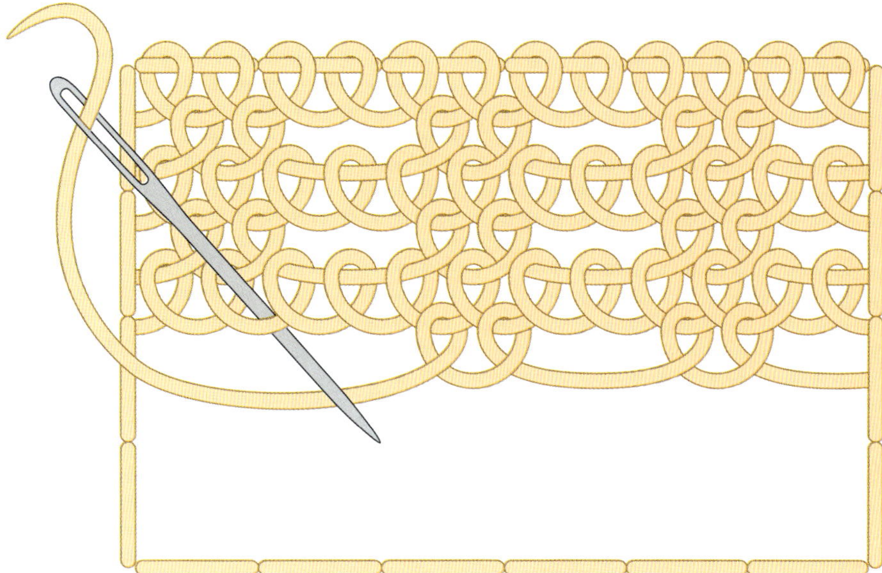

1. Work backstitch around the entire shape. Your stitches should be long enough to accommodate two detached buttonhole stitches with a little bit of 'wiggle' room.
2. Working from left to right (LR), work two detached buttonhole stitches (DBH) into each backstitch (BS) that makes up the first row.
3. When you reach the end of the row on the right, go into the fabric, tucking your needle under the BS that is level with where you started on the left. Leaving the space you need to accommodate the second row, come up from under the BS. This is called the step down.
4. Working from right to left (RL), [miss the first short loop, work 1 x DBH into next loop, one DBH into next loop. Miss 2 loops]. Repeat [ ] to end. Step down.
5. #Working LR, [work three DBH into each large loop and, 1 x DBH into each small loop that lies between the two DBH worked in the previous row]. Repeat [ ] to end. Depending on where you are in the pattern, you may have a shorter loop at the beginning or the end of the previous row. Fit in as many DBH as you can without squashing them. Step down.
6. Working RL, [work one DBH each into the two short loops that are in the middle of the group of three in the previous row]. Repeat [ ] to end. Step down.#
7. Keep working the rows from # to # until you have filled the required space, trying to make sure that your last but one row is a left to right row, the row that is a solid row of DBH with no longer loops in between.
8. Working RL, attach the needle lace to the bottom of the circle by coming up from under the backstitch immediately below the short loop that runs between stitches two and three of the group of three in the previous row.
9. Work one DBH through this short loop and go back into the fabric, tucking the needle under the backstitch.
10. Come up again immediately below the short loop that runs between stitches one and two of that same group of three in the previous row. Work one DBH into that loop and go back into the fabric, coming up again below the next group of three to attach it in the same way.
11. Repeat as many times as necessary to fill the space.

Needle lace stitch no. 9

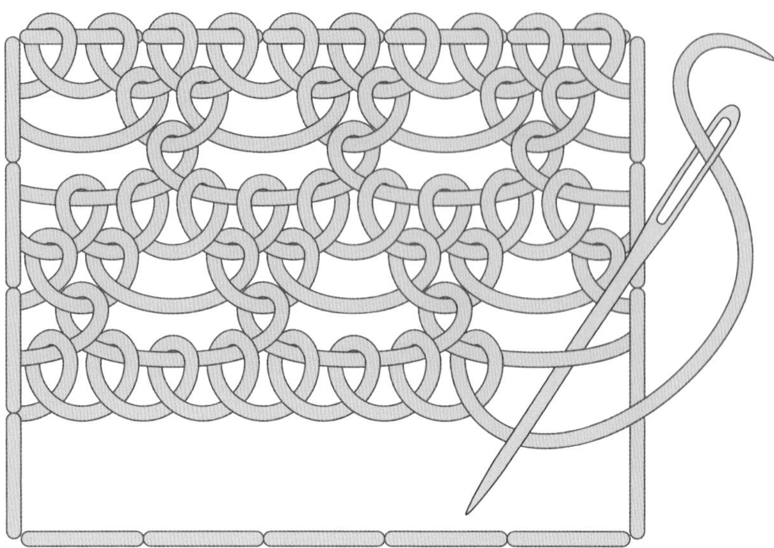

1 Work backstitch around the entire shape. Your stitches should be long enough to accommodate two detached buttonhole stitches with a little bit of 'wiggle' room.

2 Working from left to right (LR), work two detached buttonhole (DBH) into each backstitch (BS) that makes up the first row. When you reach the end of the row on the right, go into the fabric, tucking your needle under the BS that is level with where you started on the left. Leaving the space you need to accommodate the second row, come up from under the BS. This is called the step down.

3 Working from right to left (RL), [work one DBH into first loop, one DBH into next loop. Miss a loop]. Repeat [ ] to end. Step down.

4 #Working LR, work a single detached buttonhole between the stitches of each of the pairs of DBH in the previous row. Step down.

5 Working RL, work three DBH into each long loop between the single DBH stitches in the previous row. You may find that the loops at the beginning and end of the row are not long enough to fit a group of three DBH. Fit in as many as will sit comfortably in those loops and adjust the pattern as necessary in the subsequent rows.

6 Working LR, [work one DBH between stitches one and two, work one DBH between stitches two and three of the groups of three in the previous row.] Repeat [ ] to end. Step down.#

7 Repeat from # to # as many times as you need to until you get to the bottom of the shape.

8 Join at the bottom by coming up from under the backstitch at the bottom, directly below the loops that you need to attach. Work single detached buttonhole stitch/es in the loop/s for that particular area, and go back into the fabric, tucking the needle under the backstitch. Come up below the next part that needs to be attached, repeating until you have attached the entire row.

Needle lace stitch no. 10

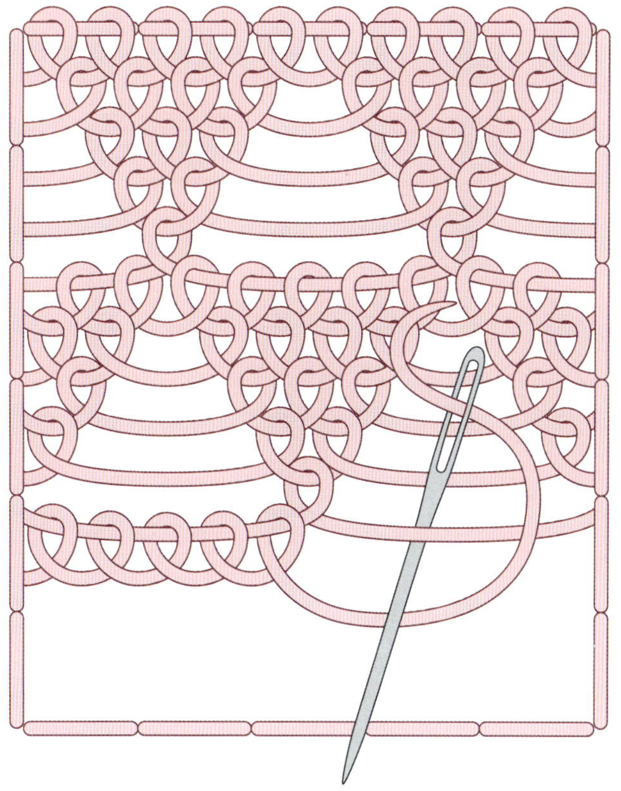

If you examine the diagram on the left, you will note that this pattern forms downward facing triangles. While the top row of these triangles is essentially a solid row of detached buttonhole stitches (DBH), you should imagine these as divided into groups of five, which means that the top row of each triangle consists of five DBH.

The second row consists of four DBH plus one gap, the third row consists of three DBH plus a wider gap, the fourth row consists of two DBH plus an even wider gap and the fifth row consists of a single DBH between the two in the previous row, with a long thread (or gap) between each stitch.

The pattern then repeats, and the first row of that pattern repeat consists of five DBH in the long loops between the single DBH stitches in the previous row. From that point, the triangle reduces, once again, by leaving out one DBH per triangle in every row.

1 Work backstitch around the entire shape. Your stitches should be long enough to accommodate two detached buttonhole stitches with a little bit of 'wiggle' room.
2 Working from left to right (LR), work two detached buttonhole (DBH) into each backstitch (BS) that makes up the first row. When you reach the end of the row on the right, go into the fabric, tucking your needle under the BS that is level with where you started on the left. Leaving the space you need to accommodate the second row, come up from under the BS. This is called the step down.
3 #Working from right to left (RL), [work single DBH stitches into four loops in the previous row, miss a loop]. Repeat [ ] to the end of the row. Step down.
4 Working LR, [work single DBH stitches into the three loops between the four stitches in the previous row, miss the longer loop]. Repeat [ ] to the end of the row. Step down.
5 Working RL, [work single DBH stitches into the two loops between the three stitches in the previous row, miss the longer loop]. Repeat [ ] to the end of the row. Step down.
6 Working LR, [work single DBH stitches into the short loop between the two stitches in the previous row, miss the longer loop]. Repeat from [ ] to the end of the row. Step down. This completes the triangle pattern.
7 Start the next set of triangles by working five DBH in each long loop between the single DBH in the previous row.#
8 Repeat from # to # as many times as you need to until you get to the bottom of the shape.
9 Join at the bottom by coming up from under the backstitch at the bottom, directly below the loops that you need to attach. Work single detached buttonhole stitch/es in the loop/s for that particular area, and go back into the fabric, tucking the needle under the backstitch. Come up below the next part that needs to be attached, repeating until you have attached the entire row.

Needle weaving patterns

Note: in the patterns O = over, U = under.

Instructions in brackets are only worked once at the beginning of a row. Thereafter, continue with the pattern, repeating as many times as needed until the row is complete.

Basic: double weaving

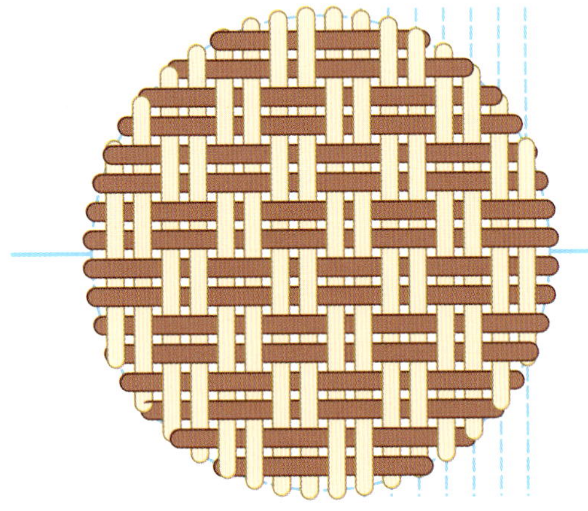

1 Starting on the centre vertical line and using colour 1, work vertical warp stitches to fill both sides of the shape.
2 Weave the horizontal weft stitches, starting at the widest part of the shape on the centre horizontal line, working downwards.
3 The pattern repeat is four rows. When you have worked rows 1–4, repeat the sequence as often as necessary to fill the bottom half of the circle.

Colour 2

Row 1: (U2) O2, U2

Row 2: (U2) O2, U2

Row 3: O2, U2

Row 4: O2, U2

4 When you have completed the bottom half of the circle, return to the centre and work to the top, working the pattern sequence in reverse:

Colour 2

Row 4: O2, U2

Row 3: O2, U2

Row 2: (U2) O2, U2

Row 1: (U2) O2, U2

Basic: triple weaving

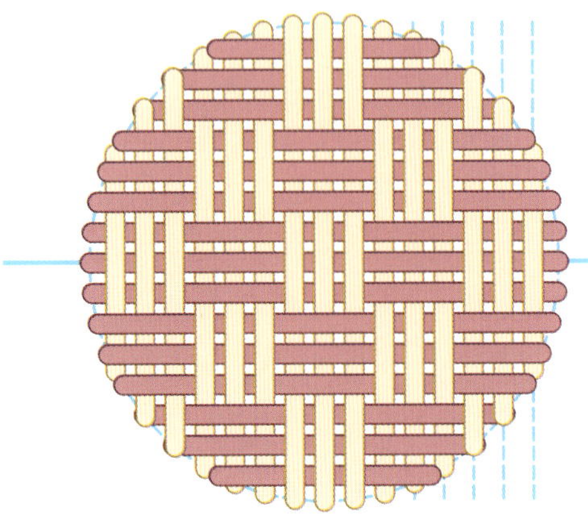

1 Starting on the centre vertical line and using colour 1, work vertical warp stitches to fill both sides of the shape.
2 Weave the horizontal weft stitches, starting at the widest part of the shape on the centre horizontal line, working downwards.
3 The pattern repeat is six rows. When you have worked rows 1–6, repeat the sequence as often as necessary to fill the bottom half of the circle.

Colour 2

Row 1: (U3) O3, U3

Row 2: (U3) O3, U3

Row 3: (U3) O3, U3

Row 4: O3, U3

Row 5: O3, U3

Row 6: O3, U3

4 When you have completed the bottom half of the circle, return to the centre and work to the top, working the pattern sequence in reverse:

Colour 2

Row 6: O3, U3

Row 5: O3, U3

Row 4: O3, U3

Row 3: (U3) O3, U3

Row 2: (U3) O3, U3

Row 1: (U3) O3, U3

Needle weaving texture no. 2

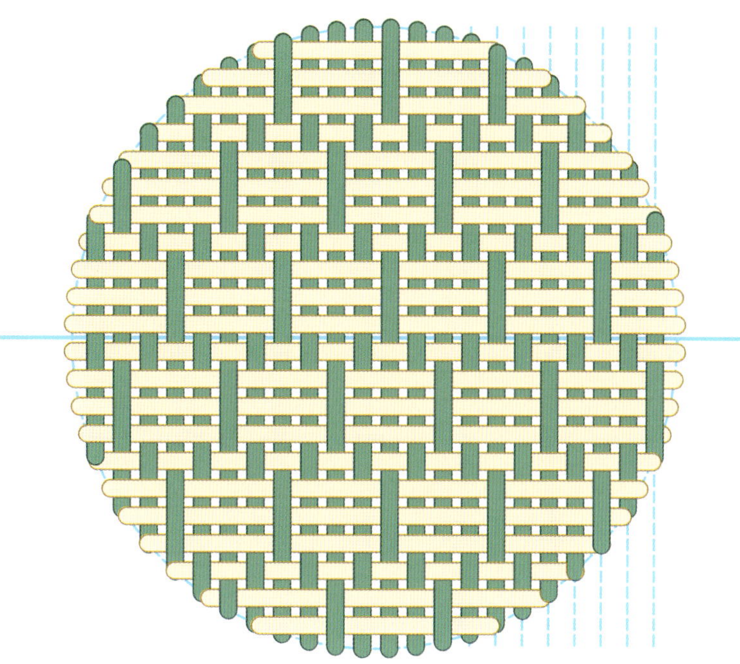

1 Starting on the centre vertical line and using colour 1, work vertical warp stitches to fill both sides of the circle.

2 Starting on the centre horizontal line, work the horizontal weft stitches.

3 The pattern repeat is eight rows. When you have worked rows 1–8, repeat the sequence as often as necessary to fill the bottom half of the circle.

Colour 2

Row 1: O1, U1

Row 2: *(U1) O3, U1*

Row 3: Repeat from * to *

Row 4: Repeat from * to *

Row 5: O1, U1

Row 6: #(O2, U1) O3, U1#

Row 7: Repeat # to #

Row 8: Repeat # to #

4 When you have completed the bottom half of the circle, return to the centre and work to the top, working the pattern sequence in reverse:

Colour 2

Row 8: #(O2, U1) O3, U1#

Row 7: Repeat # to #

Row 6: Repeat # to #

Row 5: O1, U1

Row 4: *(U1) O3, U1*

Row 3: Repeat from * to *

Row 2: Repeat from * to *

Row 1: O1, U1

Needle weaving texture no. 3

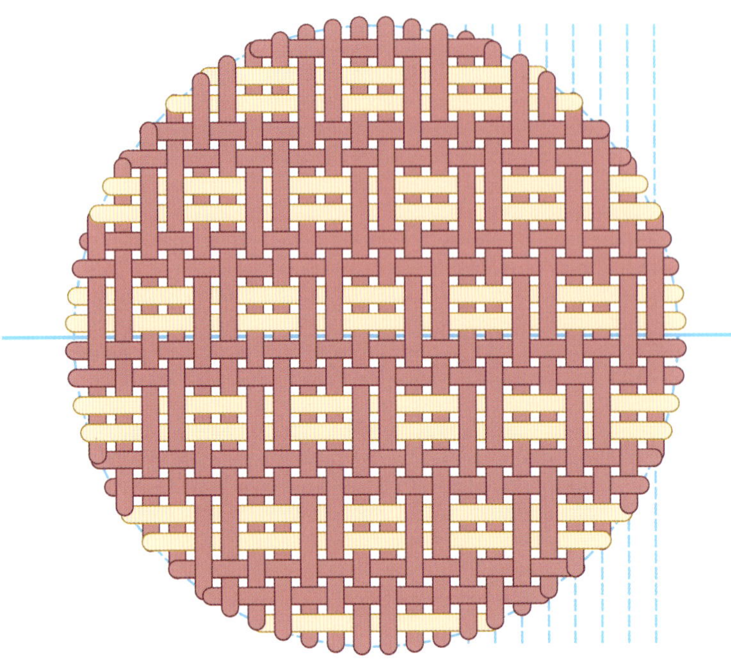

1 Starting on the centre vertical line and using colour 1, work vertical warp stitches to fill both sides of the circle.

2 Starting on the centre horizontal line, work the horizontal weft stitches.

3 The pattern repeat is eight rows. When you have worked rows 1–8, repeat as often as necessary to fill the bottom half of the circle.

Colour 1

Row 1: O1, U1

Row 2: (U1) O1, U1

Colour 2

Row 3: O2, U2

Row 4: O2, U2

Colour 1

Row 5: O1, U1

Row 6: (U1) O1, U1

Colour 2

Row 7: (U2) O2, U2

Row 8: (U2) O2, U2

4 When you have completed the bottom half of the circle, return to the centre and work to the top, working the pattern sequence in reverse:

Colour 2

Row 8: (U2) O2, U2

Row 7: (U2) O2, U2

Colour 1

Row 6: (U1) O1, U1

Row 5: O1, U1

Colour 2

Row 4: O2, U2

Row 3: O2, U2

Colour 1

Row 2: (U1) O1, U1

Row 1: O1, U1

Needle weaving texture no. 5

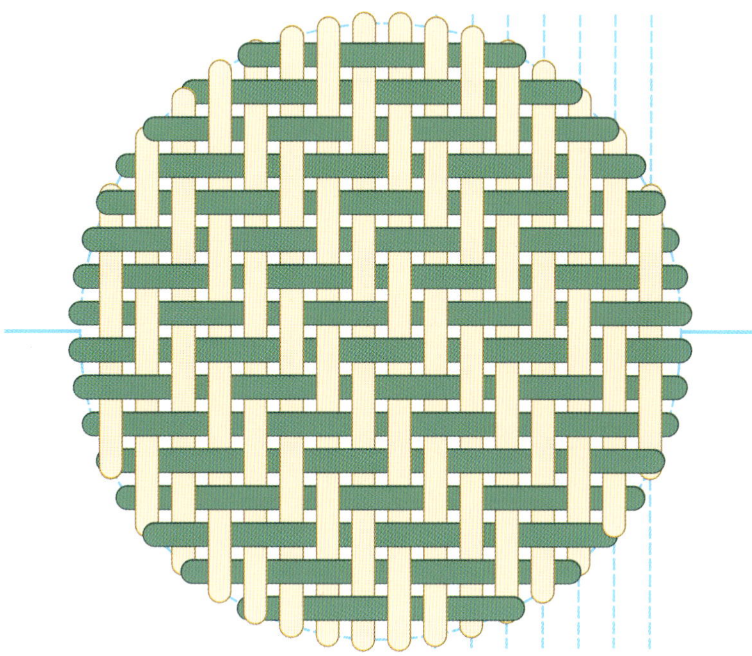

1 Starting on the centre vertical line and using colour 1, work vertical warp stitches to fill both sides of the shape.

2 Starting at the widest part of the shape as shown above, on the centre horizontal line, working downwards, weave the horizontal weft stitches.

3 The pattern repeat is four rows. When you have worked rows 1–4, repeat the sequence as often as necessary to fill the bottom half of the circle.

Colour 2

Row 1: (O1, U2) O2, U2

Row 2: (U2) O2, U2

Row 3: (U1) O2, U2

Row 4: O2, U2

4 When you have completed the bottom half of the shape, return to the widest part of the shape and work upwards to the top, working the pattern sequence in reverse:

Colour 2

Row 4: O2, U2

Row 3: (U1) O2, U2

Row 2: (U2) O2, U2

Row 1: (O1, U2) O2, U2

Needle weaving checks and stripes no. 1

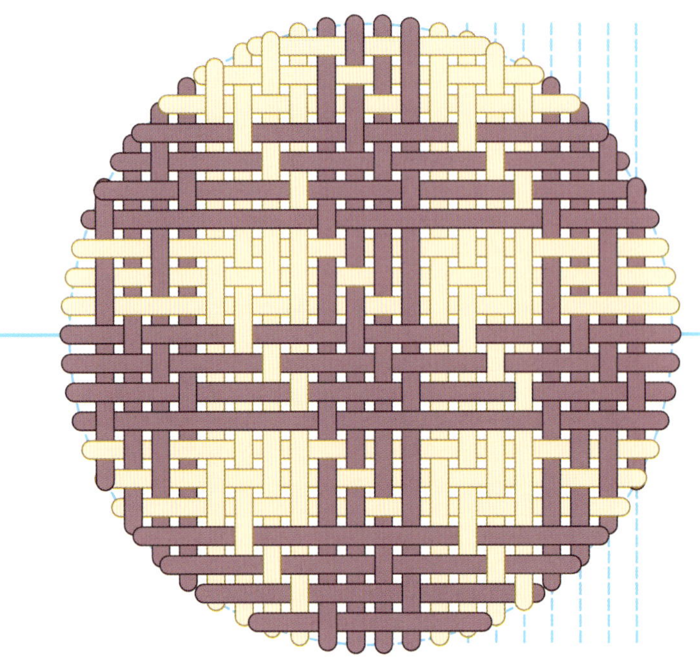

1 Starting on the centre vertical line, work vertical warp stitches to fill both sides of the circle:

4 x colour 1 (purple)

4 x colour 2 (ecru)

(repeat as necessary to fill the circle)

2 Starting on the centre horizontal line, work the horizontal weft stitches.

3 The pattern repeat is seven rows. When you have worked rows 1–7, repeat the sequence as often as necessary to fill the bottom half of the circle.

Colour 1

Row 1: (O2, U1) O3, U1

Row 2: (O1, U1) O3, U1

Row 3: (U1) O3, U1

Row 4: O3, U1

Colour 2

Row 5: (U3) O1, U3

Row 6: (U2) O1, U3

Row 7: (U1) O1, U3

4 When you have completed the bottom half of the circle, return to the centre and work to the top, working the pattern sequence in reverse:

Colour 2

Row 7: (U1) O1, U3

Row 6: (U2) O1, U3

Row 5: (U3) O1, U3

Colour 1

Row 4: O3, U1

Row 3: (U1) O3, U1

Row 2: (O1, U1) O3, U1

Row 1: (O2, U1) O3, U1

Needle weaving checks and stripes no. 9

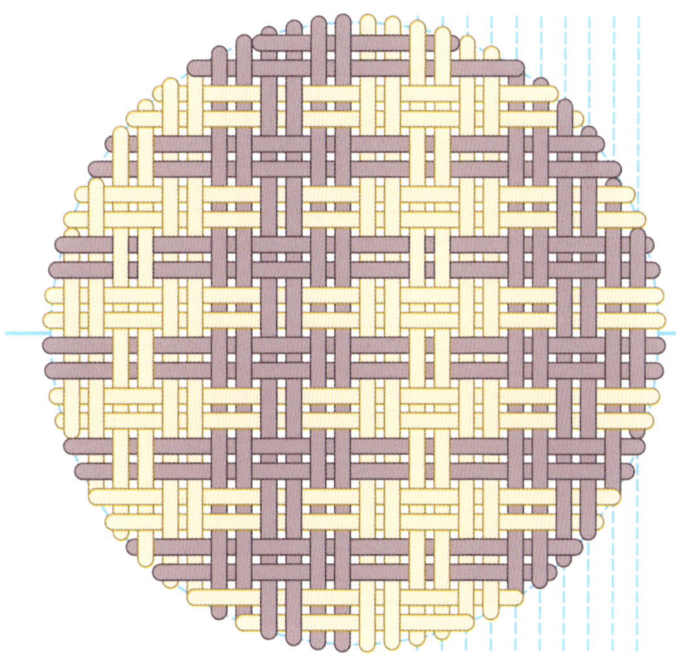

1 Starting on the centre vertical line, work vertical warp stitches to fill both sides of the circle:

   6 x colour 1

   6 x colour 2

   (Repeating as necessary to fill the circle)

2 Starting on the centre horizontal line, work the horizontal weft stitches.

3 The pattern repeat is four rows. When you have worked rows 1–4, repeat the sequence as often as necessary to fill the bottom half of the circle.

   Colour 1

   Row 1: (U2) O2, U2

   Row 2: (U2) O2, U2

   Colour 2

   Row 3: O2, U2

   Row 4: O2, U2

4 When you have completed the bottom half of the circle, return to the centre and work to the top, working the pattern sequence in reverse:

   Colour 2

   Row 4: O2, U2

   Row 3: O2, U2

   Colour 1

   Row 2: (U2) O2, U2

   Row 1: (U2) O2, U2

INDEX

For a list of all stitches used in the book, see also pages 145–146.

backstitch 147, 170
  split 186
  whipped 170
Bayeux stitch 147
bead embroidery 199–205
beads 140
beeswax 143
blanket stitch 171
  padded and striped 170
block shading 147
blocking 14
bullion knots 171
burden stitch 172
buttonhole stitch 148, 171, 173, 174
  up and down 191

chain stitch 175–177
  and backstitch combination 175
  detached 175
  heavy 180
  interlaced 176, 177
  reverse 177
charts 15, 43
  abbreviations 18, 28, 90, 116
  transferring from 143
  using 15, 43
closed fly stitch 148, 149
contemporary 44, 62, 100, 124
coral stitch 150
crewel stem stitch 151
crewelwork
  comparison of 83, 144
  contemporary 39, 40–81
  eighteenth century 12
  evolution of 40–41
  origins of 10–13, 144
  seventeenth century 12
  traditional 9, 17–37
  twenty-first century 144
crystals 46, 64, 140, 203, 204

embroidery frame 142
  seated 142
embroidery hoop 142
eye stitch 178

fabric 138, 141
  backing 138
  project base 138
    cotton/linen mix 138, 140
    cotton twill 138, 140
    Jacobean linen twill 138
    seeded cotton 138, 140
  transferring designs to 143

fan stitch 152
fern stitch 152
fly stitch 178
  whipped 179
freestyle embroidery 193–196
French knot 153
  loose 179
  single wrap 179

herringbone stitch
  interlaced 181
  raised 181

Jacobean 10, 12, 13

laid and couched work 154–159
leaf stitch 160
long and short stitch 160–165, 182
  shading 182
  twisted 190

Morris, May 10
Morris, William 10

needle lace stitches 205–209
needle weaving 210–215

needles 139
  replacing 139
  stabbing 144

outline stitch 183
  with padding 183

pistil stitch 166
Portuguese knotted stem stitch 184
projects
  contemporary 42
    Blue Bird 124
    Eagle 100
    Summer Jewels 44
    Tiny the Tabby 62
  traditional 14
    Blue Bird 114
    Eagle 88
    Greedy Squirrel 16
    Phoebe's Vineyard 26

raised stem stitch 185
Rhodes stitch 185

satin stitch 167, 185
  padded 186
  raised 167
seeding stitch 168
slate frame 142
split stitch 168
stem stitch 169
  whipped 169
stitch directory 144
stretcher bars 46, 64, 102, 126, 142, 143

The Progress of the Soul 12, 27
thread conditioner 140, 143
threads 140
  crewel wool 140
  fine cordonette 140
  perle 140
  stranded cotton 140
Traquair, Phoebe Anne 12
traditional 16, 26, 88, 114,
trellis couching 187
  woven 188
trellis stitch 157
tufting, scruffy 66, 67, 189
twisted thread 48, 68, 69, 81, 140, 189
  couching 190

vermicelli couching 69, 72, 75, 80, 107, 130, 192

wadding (batting) 102, 113, 126, 138
wheatear stitch 193
  beaded 202
whipped spider's web 168